A complete guide to:

THE MACCLESFIELD CANAL

Written and Illustrated by:
H. J. Gilman

First published 1992
Copyright © M.G. Publications 1992

British Library Cataloguing In Publication Data.
Gilman- Harold John
The Macclesfield Canal.
1. Title
No. 914.2716

ISBN   0 9518608 0 1

Body text Goudy 10pt on 12.
Printed by St. Edward's Press Ltd, Macclesfield,
Tel: 0265 619358
Published By M.G. Publications, 1/7 Cole Hill Bank,
Congleton, Cheshire. CW12 3AD
Tel. 0260 278972

ACKNOWLEDGMENTS

When a project takes as long as this one to reach fruition, numerous people invariably become involved to a greater or lesser extent along the way and leave their mark on the finished product.

The contribution that some make is blatantly obvious; people like Wendy Brookes, Anne Potts and Debbie Ball who, with powers almost beyond my comprehension transformed a massive typed manuscript into a disc of plastic about the size of a beer bottle label!

Countless friends readily volunteered valuable imformation about specific topics or places ie. Dave Roberts, Stephen Ball, Derek Murray, Albert Williams and Henry Preece. Contributions which are less specific but no less valuable must be credited to William Dean, Valerie Griffiths, Alan Painter and to William Ball of Old Vicarage Publications.

Iain Thornhill has been extremely supportive and helpful throughout, in many diverse ways, principally by being a close and valued friend but his specific contribution has been to open my eyes to the humble hedgerow, following my introduction to the delights of making country wines!

Special acknowledgment is due to my partner in the project Nino Manci. He has been responsible for the type setting and overall layout of the book. His experience in the field of artistic and graphic design has been invaluable both inside the book and in the cover design, but his expertise can be felt throughout the whole book.

Luckily acknowledgements such as these are never arranged in order of merit or importance, so, with that in mind, final mention goes to my wife Diane, daughter Rosemary, and son Christopher who have tolerated many, many hours and miles of 'towpath trudging'. To them this work is dedicated.

CONTENTS

Chapter One	Marple to High Lane	1
Chapter Two	High Lane to Lyme View Marina	15
Chapter Three	Adlington to Bollington	42
Chapter Four	Bollington to Macclesfield Marina	68
Chapter Five	Macclesfield to Oakgrove	89
Chapter Six	Oakgrove to Bosley	116
Chapter Seven	Bosley Locks	128
Chapter Eight	The Dane to Dane-in-Shaw	147
Chapter Nine	Hightown to Astbury	177
Chapter Ten	Astbury to Hall Green	199
Chapter Eleven	Hall Green to Kidsgrove.	230
Place Name Index		240
Bridge Index		241
Pub Index		244
Bibliography		249

INTRODUCTION

Thousands of people live within a few minutes walk of the Macclesfield Canal if not actually within sight of it. A percentage of this multitude occasionally, if not regularly join the waterway at a given point which is convenient to them and walk a length of its towpath (often accompanied by the dog) only to turn around and retrace their steps or to leave the canal to return home by some circular route. Surprisingly few of the canal's 'regulars' ever extend their range beyond that familiar stretch which is close to home. During the last two decades, the local canal user has been joined by a new breed - the holiday maker or tourist. Since Britain's formerly neglected inland waterways have been brought back to life as major tourist attractions, the family who hire a narrow boat for a week or maybe a fortnight have an understandable desire to see as much as possible and to travel as far as the time allows.

The following account will hopefully be of use and a source of information to all of the different types of canal user. Its highly detailed, step by step, almost inch by inch progression along the entire waterway from its beginning at Marple through to its end at Kidsgrove, is intended to make it the ultimate walking or boating guide. Of far greater importance, is that it represents an almost photographic record, in a world of rapid and drastic change, of how the waterway and, its surroundings, appear in the closing stages of the twentieth century.

The account could, therefore, be looked upon as a detailed guide to a North - South 'slice' through the county of Cheshire, using the canal as a basis or even a justification for the hypothetical journey. The studies and observation of plant life and of mammal, bird, fish and insect species are intended to be representative of the canal's flora and fauna and not an attempt at a detailed biological survey. The very fact that on several occasions I have been asked by the occupants of a passing boat or by a fellow towpath traveller what the wild flower is called which a member of my family has plucked from among the pathside grasses indicates that we are beginning to experience a new awareness of the simpler things in life. The account attempts to attach as much importance to an agricultural hamlet, consisting of no more than six or eight buildings such as Ciss Green or Mitchell Fold, as it would to a major town such as Macclesfield or Congleton, for each plays its own vital part in the rich tapestry of the journey.

I make no excuse therefore in presenting an unashamed celebration of the passage of this memorable waterway through this splendid county, and if it inspires the short distance walker to extend his or her range, and the boating tourist to enjoy the journey more fully, then all the better.

Harold John Gilman
Great Moreton Hall

Chapter I
MARPLE TO HIGH LANE

The Macclesfield Canals 27 3/4 mile journey through the most tranquil and also the most panoramic scenery that Cheshire can produce, begins in an idyllic spot where the Peak Forest Canal cuts its way through Marple, a suburb of Greater Manchester. The Peak Forest Canal commences by a junction with the Ashton Canal at Dukinfield and proceeds through Hyde, Woodley, Romiley and on to Marple, where it gives birth to the Macclesfield Canal.

It continues from Marple to Disley and New Mills to Bugsworth. On its way through Marple, the Peak Forest Canal is lifted by a series of 16 locks. Several hundred yards above the top lock is Macclesfield Canal junction marked by Bridge No.1. The Macclesfield Canal is renowned for the superb architecture of its bridges, its "graceful stone arches", and Bridge No.1 is no exception. Many of the canals 98 bridges are constructed of millstone grit, as are many other canal features, lock chambers, bank linings etc. During its industrial heyday, the canal transported colossal quantities of Gritstone throughout the region from the numerous quarries which predominate the eastern side of the canal's progress through Cheshire.

Bridge No.1 is a classic roving bridge, standing amid a haphazard cluster of stone houses and cottages with picture book cottage gardens and manicured grass. Standing at the foot of Bridge No. 1, amid this haven of dressed stone, still water and relentlessly cackling mallards, it is hard to imagine that Marple, dormitory base for Stockport and Greater Manchester is home to a population in excess of 25,000. The roving bridges were sometimes known as 'turnover' bridges as their function was to transfer the towpath to the opposite side of the canal so that the horses which towed the narrow boats could cross sides without having to be unhitched.

Beneath Bridge No. 1 is the first of many milestones to be seen along the canal's length, some are original, some restored and some are new, but all are of millstone grit. The vast majority of the canal's original milestones were reinstated in the mid 1980's by the Macclesfield Canal Society as they had been removed or buried in 1939 amid the national effort to confuse Hitler's forces should they ever need to find their way round Cheshire, or any other county of the British Isles for that matter. The original stones were cut from quarries on Kerridge Ridge and engraved with the distances from Marple and Hall Green, (the opposite ends of the canal). The small percentage of original stones which defied re-discovery have been replaced with new stones again cut from Kerridge stone and the first one is one of these. It reads on one side "Marple" and on the opposite side, "Hall Green 26 1/4 miles"

MILESTONE

(It must be explained at this point that from Hall Green, the Macclesfield Canal joins the Trent and Mersey Canal via a short branch of 1 1/2 miles which, in the interests of continuity, the author will class as a continuance of the main canal, thus making up the total distance of 27.3/4 miles.) The official end of the waterway at Hall Green is marked by a stop lock. The lock was constructed by the Macclesfield Canal Company because the 1 1/2 miles (approx) 'extra' length up to the Trent and Mersey junction was built by the Trent and Mersey Canal Company who felt that they should have some influence over the boat traffic entering the Trent and Mersey via the newly completed Macclesfield Canal.

Immediately below Bridge No.1 the canal narrows and runs through the stone lined chamber of a former stop lock. Stop locks such as these were normally constructed at junctions literally to prevent one canal companies water escaping into another's canal. Bridge No.1 was built as a roving bridge to enable the towing horses to be led directly from the towpath of the Peak Forest Canal to the Macclesfield towpath without having to remove the tow line while the boat negotiated the stop lock (now removed). Leaving Bridge No.1 behind, the journey to Kidsgrove begins with the towpath on the left hand or eastern bank. As the canal widens out from its passage through the stop lock chamber, there is a stone building on the opposite bank which is currently owned and used by British Waterways Board. Its original function throughout the canal's working life was as a warehouse for perishable cargoes. The boats were steered right inside the building via a specially constructed waterway and could thus be loaded or unloaded completely undercover.

From Bridge No.1, Bridge No 2 is but a short distance ahead. The towpath between the two bridges is wide and level and between the path and the foot of a high wall, a well kept verge of grass sports several wooden benches. Such luxuries as well maintained towpaths and seats for the weary rambler are very much in evidence along the 15 or so miles of towpath which is maintained by Macclesfield Borough Council. The canal in their area has, with agreement from British Waterways Board, been designated a conservation area.

Leaving Bridge No. 1, the canal is moving from its most northerly point and travelling south,.Bridge No.2, is like No.1, a roving bridge. The two bridges are strikingly similar in design but no two along the whole canal are exactly alike. Bridge No. 2 carries 'Church Lane' a busy highway over the canal and promptly transfers the towpath to the right hand or western bank. Virtually on top of the bridge the first of the numerous canal side pubs is encountered namely the "Ring of Bells". The bridge, as with No, 1 is a timeless tribute to the stonemasons art, perfection in dressed stone.

From Bridge No 2, the canal sweeps into a left hand bend, its first deviation from a straight course and the bridge is soon lost from sight behind. The view to left and right is now totally dominated by housing. Suburbia spreads a far as the eye can see. Back at Bridge No. 1 it was difficult to imagine Marple town centre was just four minutes walk from the waterside. Now, beyond bridge No. 2 with the sounds of traffic and surrounding houses, the contrast is total. Once round the canal's bend the suburban scene is completed by allotments stretching away from the towpaths side down to a maze of houses. Beyond the bend, the canal begins to narrow as it passes through the sturdy millstone foundations of a long lost swing bridge.

Numerous swing bridges were originally employed along the Macclesfield Canal's course but, at the time of writing, only two remain in working order. In some instances the bridges have been left 'swung open' for decades until their largely wooden structures have rotted but the majority have been removed. By comparison, the sturdy mill grit foundations and, in some instances, the heavy metal swing mechanism, will forever remain to mark the position of the lost bridges. The swing bridge was so inexpensive to build, compared to the ornate stone bridge, that many were used in rural stretches for livestock to cross the canal from field to field.

The canal resumes its normal width beyond the old swing bridge and, looking ahead, the view in the distance is totally dominated by a towering building of red brick. The building is so vast that, from this distance, it appears to rear out of the water of the canal itself. The dense housing to left and right continues as the canal widens out into a bay some 30 or 40 feet wide. Beyond the bay a line of moored boats along the canal's eastern bank begins and continues, unbroken as far as the eye can see.

Ducks are very much a feature of these busy,built up urbanized lengths of canal, far more so than in the quiet peaceful rural lengths as one would expect. This strongly indicates that the teeming hoards of birds encountered are actually feral ducks as opposed to wild birds, and they are very largely opportunist feeders. Any countryman will be familiar with the true wild duck which explodes into the air from stream or brook at the lightest foot fall.The dedicated angler, arriving at the remote farm pool, pit or lakeside as dawn breaks will have witnessed the total chaos as the entire duck population vacates noisily. Canal ducks are an entirely different matter, the faintest rustle of a bread wrapper will bring them winging in from all directions. Closer inspection will reveal that, although basically Mallard stock, the hordes of birds contain some weird and wonderful 'mongrels'. One of the most frequently encountered hybrids is the Mallard/Aylesbury cross. A slender light bodied flying duck; characteristics acquired from its Mallard parent, but pure white in colour like the Aylesbury. It is a far cry from the fat, waddling farmyard Aylesbury which is also seen in considerable numbers on the Macclesfield Canal due to the increaseing number of householders who 'keep a few ducks' at the bottom of their waterside gardens. Khaki Campbells and Welsh Harlequins when integrated with the basic Mallard population produce a staggering range of variations and varieties on the Mallard theme.

The moored boats on the far side of the canal stretch on, towards the towering form of Goyt Mill. To the right of the towpath, a council housing estate sprawls away into the distance beyond a tall and unruly Hawthorn hedge. Goyt Mill owes its very existence to the Macclesfield Canal. It was built in 1905 by the Goyt Spinning Company and its very heart, an enormous steam engine, was fueled by coal constantly ferried from collieries in Staffordshire along the Macclesfield Canal. Its raw material, cotton, was brought in by the canal from the docks in Manchester by the Rochdale, Ashton and Peak Forest Canals and in turn its spun cotton, in part, probably left by canal .Amid the maze of houses and quietly moored boats, the canal bends quite sharply to the right.

Once round the bend, bridge No.3 is just beyond with Goyt Mill immediately behind it. The Mill is an integral part of Marple's industrial past and, in turn, part of Marple's very existence in its present form. The township of Marple was in existence long before the Norman Conquest but, like many of the other towns on the edge of the Pennines, it blossomed into a thriving industrial community in the late 1700's. In Marple's case the boom' was in textiles and the key figure in the formation of Marple's industrail revolution was Samuel Oldknow, who was also one of the main promoters of the Peak Forest Canal. Authorised by an Act of Parliament in 1794, the Peak Forest Canal was completed in 1800, many years before the conception of the Macclesfield Canal. On the approach, bridge No. 3 appears to be the first 'standard' canal bridge to be encountered, i.e. not a roving bridge but, on passing beneath, it is found to have been doubled in width in recent years to carry the busy two lane carriageway above. 'The extension' is in concrete and, when compared to its original stone north face, its concrete south face looks inferior, ugly and out of place. On top of the bridge, a side the buzzing highway, 'Upper Hibbert Lane', a road sign advises the passing motorist that he is entering the Borough of Stockport at Hawk Green. Technically, Marple is now behind us.

Once past bridge No. 3, Goyt Mill towers above the canal; six stories high plus a two storey tower at its northern end. To the right of the towpath, behind a neat Hawthorn hedge, the Stockport and Marple Golf Course now stretches away to distant housing beyond. The Mill stands above a stone loading stage which runs the whole length of the building, forming the canals left bank. Beyond the mill, Bridge No. 4 is clearly visible in the near distance. Standing below the mill today with the water gently lapping against the stone wall and the loading winch arm stretching out uselessly across and above the canal, it is difficult to picture the scene of hustle and bustle which must have been played out, day and night from 1905, through to the mills's closure in 1960. A fire escape snakes up the side of the mill in nine dizzy flights. The only sounds to be heard at the mill today, replacing the chaotic noise of industry, is the almost imperceptible cooing of numerous feral or 'town' pigeons, who make use of the mills lofty window sills and ledges as a roost. To them, Goyt Mill is a cliff face, the ancestral home of their predecessor, the Rock Dove. Since 1960, the mill has housed small industrial units and much of the roomy interior is used for warehousing. Beyond the mill, the outbuildings in the mill yard also support light industry.

Bridge No. 4 is a typical 'narrow canal' bridge not spectacular but, as ever beautifully built in mill grit. A short ramp goes from the tow path up to the top of the bridge where a track leads either to the golf course or to a lane which serves the small industrial units. Once past Bridge No. 4 , to the right of the tow path, the high grassy bank has been replaced by a tall Hawthorn hedge beyond which, the golf course rolls away into the distance. Beyond that, the metropolis which is Stockport and the fringes of Greater Manchester, stretch away to the sky line. The distant outlines of tower blocks rear up from the sprawling maze which is a modern city. Across the canal, industrial units and garages still dominate the eastern bank.

Beside the towpath, tall, mature Lombardy Poplars are dotted along the line of the Hawthorn hedge which borders the golf course. Looking across the rolling fairway, it is rewarding to see an occasional ancient Oak tree standing here and there, the remnants of long lost farm land which the undulating golf course now occupies. In turn, the fairways have been planted with numerous spinneys of mixed broad leaf trees which are now semi mature. Despite their some what hazardous position, they must represent a welcome haven for wildlife; a classic example of an artificially created wildlife habitat amid the urban jungle. The canal enters a sweeping left hand bend and the golf course is left behind.

For the first time since leaving Bridge No. 1 at Marple junction the canal is surrounded by farmland. The contrast between this and the previously encountered housing and suburban gardens and the industrial heritage of textile mill town is striking and yet soothing. In the field to the right, a flooded pit, surrounded by Willow and Hawthorn trees provides a sheltered drinking hole for livestock; fat continental cattle wallow in the mud around its edges. The canal here is straight in its course but deviates again to the left ahead. The land to the east is more chequered in its nature and resembles small holding land with hen sheds dotted here and there, some in use, others without roofs and leaning at crazy angles. From behind a cluster of small farm buildings, an orchard stretches down to the canals edge.

Once around the left hand sweep, Bridge No. 5 comes into view. On the higher ground to the east of the bridge stands a small farm house with a variety of quaint and slightly ramshackle outbuildings crowded around it. From behind the cluster of barns and sheds, Gorse bushes clothe the steep bank down to the waters edge at the foot of the bridge. A riot of bright yellow flowers even in the depths of the greyest winter, the Gorse stands out against the mellow old stone of Bridge No. 5. On the tow path side of the canal, a narrow lane snakes up to the bridge from the pasture land to the west to link the isolated farmstead with civilisation. Like many of the Macclesfield canal bridges, Bridge No. 5 bares the scars of its working past. Deep grooves cut into the angles of its stones below the arch by wet and gritty tow ropes, dragged against the stonework between laden narrowboats and straining horse.

At the waters narrowest point, beneath the bridge, stop plank grooves can been seen in the stone lined banks either side of the water. These grooves go right down to the bed of the canal. At this narrowest point stop planks can be slotted into the groves, one on top of another until the canal is effectively sealed off or damned off. Somewhere up ahead, probably at another bridge, (as this is always the narrowest point) will be another set of plank grooves so that the section of canal in between can be drained for repairs. Leaving Bridge No.5 behind, the towpath is once again a tribute to Macclesfield Councils towpath improvements policy. It is a mixture of crazy paving and concreting which complements so well the old stone work of the bridge and the original canal bank lining of millgrit blocks.

By comparison, across the water, there is no bank lining and the fields begin at the waters edge. It is rough hard grazed paddock land with shaggy coated ponies working hard at gaining a living from the heavily cropped turf. Beside the towpath, the rough bank which extends up to the Hawthorn hedge obscuring the view beyond, is glorious hedgerow habitat for wildlife. From the tow paths edge, right up to the hedge is an impenetrable mass of thorns, brambles, nettles, Willow herb and Wild Dog Rose's. The abundance of small mammals, bird and insect inhabitants are largely safe from outside predation due to the sheer denseness of the thorny tangle and feed avidly on the abundance of autumn berries rich scarlet hips of the Dog Roses and the autumn ripening haws . Beyond Bridge No.5, the canal runs straight for a while leaving a cluster of farm buildings behind to the eastern bank.

To the right of the tow path, the high bank falls away to , once again provide a view to the west of lush pasture fields dotted with dairy cattle. It is at this point that the first milestone since Marple junction is encountered. This is an original stone which reads "from Marple one mile " and "from Hall Green 26 1/4 miles". This stone was defaced in 1939 to obliterate the 26 1/4 and one mile distances. These are now readable again, having been restored. It is ironic that in more recent times, this particular stone has been further defaced, this time with an aerosol paint can.

DOG ROSE & HAWS

The original 1939 damage can well be forgiven, coming as it did in those dark war time days in a desperate effort to disorientate a would be invader but the logic behind the later addition of "Liverpool F.C" is not so clear.

One mile from our journeys start we are still in the metropolitan borough of Stockport at Hawk Green and, as yet, a considerable distance from the Cheshire border. A low well kept hedge runs beside the towpath and beyond, the lush pasture land gently drops away towards distant housing. For the first time, a stream is culverted under the canal. Its deep valley stretches away to the east and west. On the eastern bank, the first of many overflow points along the Macclesfield canals course is encountered.

The overflow points are all positioned where the excess water can be directed into a stream. Constructed, as ever, from dressed stone, they take the form of an artificial stream course, which starts at the canals normal water level and channels the canal water into the stream below. As an artificial waterway, the canal is not prone to sudden and dangerous increases in water level like a river. It does, however, collect a certain quantity of extra water from rain directly entering it, and to a lesser extent, it collects water from the surrounding ground. Consequently, unlike a river, the canal can never be 'in flood' as the strategically positioned overflows are designed to divert away any quantity of extra water. The stream valley is deep and crowded with Oak and Ash, Sycamore and Holly trees.

At the point where the stream passes below, the canal sweeps to the right and just around the bend, on the towpath side, the first drain off paddle is encountered. The canal drain off paddles are free standing iron winches which are manually operated by a windlass. A series of interlocking cogs lift a shutter far below in the bed of the canal which drains dry a length of canal which has been sectioned off by the previously described stop planks. As with the overflow point, the drain off water is directed into the stream below.

DRAIN OFF PADDLE

The stream which started life just below Marple Ridge (the high ground just visible in the distant east) runs into Torkington Brook between Marple and Offerton Green and eventually joins the River Goyt at Offerton. Once round the right hand bend Doodfield Primary School is visible on the eastern bank, its playing field separated from the canal by a chain link fence. On the tow path side beyond the hedge, lie the immaculately manicured lawns and well stocked gardens of a most desirable residence. On the eastern bank, a strip of rough ground separates the canal from the school playing field, dotted with clumps of Holly trees and short scrubby Oaks.

Bridge No. 6 stands ahead with a tree lined tarmac drive leading down to the house beside the canal. The busy road over the bridge carries traffic from High Lane, back through Hawk Green to Marple. The Bridge is stone built, small and unspectacular but more than adequate for carrying the busy thoroughfare above, which it was never designed to carry. Once past Bridge No. 6 the next one is visible some 6 or 7 hundred yards ahead. Between the two bridges, the canal curves quite sharply to the left. The banks to left and right are both high so the view to east and west is totally obscured. The tall right hand bank, beside the towpath is again a tangled mass of brambles, nettles and Briar Roses. The grass bank opposite leads up to a pasture field and is dotted with Willow and Hawthorn trees. The stone lined towpath stands high above the water level but beyond this, huge clumps of flowering rushes grow out from the waters edge; their delicate flowers flushed pink purple in July and August. Mixed Hawthorn, Holly and Oak trees crowd up to Bridge No. 7 on the eastern bank. A gravel track leads over the bridge linking isolated farms. Bridge No.7 like No. 5 bares deep rope cuts in its stone work. Beneath the bridge, stop planks grooves denote the opposite end of the drainable length of the canal or, in fact the start of the next length.

Onward from Bridge No. 7 Hawthorn trees and Elderberry bushes overhang the eastern bank. Between the towpath and the waters edge, a dense belt of aquatic vegetation has invaded the narrow marshy zone which is neither dry land nor canal. Here you will find thick clumps of Common Reed with their soft feathery flowerheads of brown violet, tall thickets of Willow herb and clumps of Soft Rush. On the approach to a sharp right hand bend, the view to the east opens out to reveal a deep green valley, dropping away from the canal and soaring up in the far distance to form a ridge of high ground at the horizon. Once round the bend, the view to the west also opens out to a valley. For the first time, the canal is carried, via an artificially constructed embankment, across a deep valley. Like most waterways built late in the canal era, the Macclesfield was built on the 'cut and fill' principal which literally meant creating embankments (some truly enormous and staggering in scale) out of spoil from cuttings.

The canals progress across the valley is marked by a long, dead straight length which stretches out ahead. The beautiful lush valley to the east is grazed by a sizeable herd of Red Deer. The deer are farmed commercially so, at any time of the year, sixty to seventy head can be seen. The upper edge of the valley forms the high ground known as Marpleridge, Ridge Fold and Ridge End.

Immediately beyond Marple Ridge, less than half a mile from the Macclesfield, the Peak Forest Canal makes its way through Strines on its way to Disley. It is unlikely that, in ancient times, the Red Deer was ever native to this valley. Cheshire in the far distant past was the stronghold of the Roe Deer. Prior to the Roman occupation, Cheshire was densely forested so the Roe Deer, which was primarily a woodland inhabitant, proliferated. In our area, the larger Red Deer was probably confined to the Peak District.

RED DEER

To the left of the canal, for the duration of its passage across the valley, tall deer fences tower nine to twelve feet above the water. A second stream is culverted under the canal which drains the steeply sloping valley land. The whole of the canals length across the span of the valley has its banks lined with metal sheet piling. There are many miles of sheet piling in use today along the Macclesfield course. Modern engine powered narrowboats tend to travel faster then the heavily laden horse drawn narrowboats of old so consequently, create a turbulent wash behind the boat which leads to serious bank erosion. Silting up of the canal is the direct result of erosion of its banks as the loosened material is not carried away by the flow as in a river or stream. To prevent further damaging erosion British Waterways Board have clad the majority of the vulnerable soft banks. The sections of bank which were lined with stone when the canal was completed in 1831 will probably never require maintenance of any kind. The canal sweeps to the right and beyond the bend, the view is dominated by a large ruined building which stands above the canal on the eastern bank.

Bridge No.8 , Windlehurst or Back Lane Bridge is completely over shadowed by the derelict shell of Windlehurst Hall. Just short of the bridge, a strategically positioned bench allows the resting rambler a few moments relaxation while enjoying the final view of the Red Deer grazing the high fields towards the Ridge. Below the bridge more stop plank grooves are to be seen. Bridge No. 8 was built as an accommodation bridge. These bridges were necessary where the canal cut through a landowner's property, for the owner to reach his home or his land unhindered. Attached to the stone work of the bridge are the remnants of iron brackets which formerly held cast iron rollers in place. These rollers were designed to protect the leading edge of the arch from the grinding and rasping action of the wet and gritty tow ropes. Conversely, the provision of rollers would greatly increase the working life of the tow lines. The pronounced rope cuts and grooves which appear on Bridge No. 8 suggest that the protective roller was a short lived feature.

BRIDGE No 8, WINDLEHURST

Beyond the bridge, Windlehurst Hall stands above the canal on the eastern bank amid the jungle which was once a well kept garden. Fully mature specimen trees such as huge Beeches and Scots Pine, Austrian Pines and Yews have become choked and strangled by the 'weeds of the wood', Sycamore and thickets of Elderberry. The remnants of Windlehurst Hall stand partly barricaded in the interests of public safety but the boldly lettered notice of warning which has been prominently fixed high on the gable which faces the canal is more then necessary to stimulate the curiosity of even the more disinterested passer by. Statements such as "Dangerous Structure Keep Away!" are guaranteed to attract the curious in droves. The once fine gardens of this sad Victorian pile actually form part of an unofficial footpath which is phenomenally popular with local residents as it passes within inches of the front door. The dangerous shell of Windlehurst Hall, complete with gaping holes through floors into a particularly deep cellar space, must be one of the most frequented of potential death traps. The chequered recent history endured by this once proud 'Gentleman's Residence' has reduced it to the gaunt skeleton of bricks and rubble seen today. Once the home of opulent jewellers from Manchester, death and dereliction, fire, vandalism, and neglect have all taken their toll.

Leaving the bridge behind, a set of steps lead up from the tow path to the track above the bridge . To the right of the towpath, a sheep netting and barbed wire fence separates the walk way from a pasture field which rolls away into the distance. A spinney of tall well spaced Sycamore and Ash trees form a shelter for livestock in the field corner in the lee of the bridge. The canal sweeps to the left and, beside the towpath, the bank rises to obscure the pasture land. Tall Silver Birch trees overhang the towpath as the sweeping bend continues, Bridge No. 9 can be seen in the distance . The whole length of canal bank between the bridges 8 and 9 is stone lined.

The overgrown grounds of Windlehurst Hall on the eastern bank degenerate into a woodland wilderness of Birches and scrubby Oak trees, marking the original position of Windlehurst mill, a cotton spinning mill which was gutted by fire in the 1890's but was totally destroyed on 22nd February 1908 by a whirlwind! To the right of the towpath, the pasture land slopes down to a busy lane which leads from High Lane, back to Hawk Green, through Doodfield. In the far west, the city stretches to the horizon; here and there pylons, tower blocks and church steeples rear up out of the maze of buildings. Incredibly the view behind, even at this distance is still completely dominated by Goyt Mill, towering up out of surrounding countryside.

Up to Bridge No.9 a tall orderly line of Lombardy Poplars tower above the waters edge on the eastern bank, interspersed with Silver Birches and tall Willows. Just before the bridge, another stream is culverted beneath the canal and beside the towpath, a drain off paddle diverts its excess water into the stream below. The valley of the stream is crowded with tall Willows and Birch trees. Stop plank grooves are again, to be found in the stonework beneath the bridge.. The roadway over the bridge buzzes with traffic. A modern iron footbridge has been suspended across the canal alongside the original stone one to take the pedestrians away from the motor traffic which monopolizes the old bridge.

The Macclesfield canal is famous for striking contrasts. This is one of the factors which makes it a national favourite with the pleasure cruising fraternity and so beloved by walkers who throng its towpath every day of the year. The contrasts between the views to the east, to the foothills of the Pennines and the views to the west, across the sweeping panorama of the Cheshire Plain. The contrast of the canals passage through deep sheltered cuttings and in the next breath, its passage across deep valleys atop high windswept embankments. Yet. another striking contrast is evident on passing under Bridge No. 9, the view ahead is now totally of housing, reminiscent of the journey through Marple's outskirts. Prior to the bridge, the woodland touches the waterside to the left and pasture land to the right, now houses crowd in from both sides. The canal bank on the towpath side has no bank linings of any kind, consequently, a thick belt of dense reeds, Yellow Flag Iris and Willow Herb clothe the waters edge far into the distance.

To both right and left, the houses and gardens slope down to the canal from above. An ever changing display of conifers, Weeping Willows, neat Privet hedges and rockeries. Some householders have made use of the embankment down to the towpath and created terraced gardens in miniature. An occasional garden boasts its personal canal mooring, upturned rowing boats or canoes await the week-end. Here and there the 'home moored' vessel is a sizeable cruiser and in an occasional instance, an immaculately pampered narrowboat with gleaming paintwork and pretty lace curtains and always, the obligatory plant trough on the cabin roof. Where moored boats are absent the 'canal end' of the garden is often the Bar-Be-Que area or simply the patio.

The housing which we are passing through comprises the outskirts of High Lane. High Lane is the last of the Greater Manchester County or Borough of Stockport towns to be negotiated. Beyond the boundaries of High Lane lies Cheshire with its mills and market towns and its beautiful villages. As with the urbanized sections of canal in Marple, High Lane is notable for its ducks. The large showy Muscovy duck is to be seen in large number through out High Lane. Like the previously described Mallard, the Muscovy, which is normally smartly turned out in black and white, displays some hybridization when free to mix with other stock. By far the largest domestic duck, it is comparable in body weight to a small goose and makes a fine display when in flight for it flies strongly, if only for short distances, low to the water and is particularly impressive swooping along the canal. The drake can be an awesome creature when, during the breeding season, it displays a swollen and bloated fleshy protuberance above the bill which, like the bare skin around the eyes, is bright blood red. The black on the plumage stands out against the white as it glows with an iridescent green sheen. Through out the breeding season the male Muscovy greets all passers by (human, dog or boat) with threatening hissing and aggressive head gestures. Through the thronging suburbian scene, crowding the canal, the greenhouses and garden swings, the washing lines and conservatories, the yapping dogs and the goldfish ponds and beyond a slight curve to the right, bridge No.10 comes into view.

The bridge looks small and squat from a distance dwarfed as it is on the towpath side by a towering Hawthorn hedge and hemmed in on all sides by yet more and more gardens. To the right of the towpath, partially concealed by tall grass nettles and brambles is the next milestone. It is an original stone. It reads "Marple 2 mile " "Hall Green 25 1/4 miles". Beyond Bridge No, 10 the houses are slightly larger in scale with long gardens and lawns sweeping down to the waters side, each with their Weeping Willows, flowering cherries, Forsythias and Laurels. To the right, a tarmac footpath from the bridge runs parallel to the towpath. A drain off paddle stands beside the towpath and the excess water which is released is culverted beneath the footpath and into a drainage brook. A wooden post and rail fence separates the towpath from the pedestrian way beyond. The pathway abruptly opens out into extensive municipal playing fields to the west The green open space is a busy place indeed; dogs by the hundred are exercised on the marked out football pitches which on week end days host 'The Big Match'. Joggers, lunch time office escapees, the pram and pushchair pushing fraternity all seem to be attracted here. The air reverberates with sound of traffic.

The housing across the canal on the eastern bank moves away from the waterside to make way for one lone triangular field of maybe three quarters of an acre. Every imaginable variety of livestock is to be found grazing this much abused island of green turf. Sheep nibble it down to the soil, ducks and geese paddle the residue into sloppy mud in wintertime. From the jumble of ramshackle farmyard buildings come tell tale sounds of pigs and horses. The ducks and geese are among the fattest, most overfed examples to be found in the kingdom, for at High Lane bridge, the duck feeding is almost a ritual. A word of congratulation must go, at this point, to the small holder who reaps the reward from these over-nourished water fowl. Their prolific egg yield and their unquestionable body weight is surely the end product of High Lanes obsession with 'feeding the ducks'. Anyone (even innocently) walking the towpath is instantly accosted by wildly honking Ebden geese or hissing and spitting Muscovy ducks and the ever present Mallard.

Come rain or shine, winter or summer, someone can be guaranteed to be feeding the ducks at High Lane Bridge. At any hour of the day (there may even be a night shift) some grubby toddler or office gent in pin stripe suit will be unloading copious quantities of medium sliced white or wholemeal brown into the ever attentive hoards of feathered recipients. High Lane, in truth, is hardly a tourist destination, consequently, this phenomenon is very much a local custom and the canal bank must unconsciously fill the gap which is created by the lack of the public park with its boating lake or duck pond. Four wooden benches are provided below the bridge to make the duck feeding ritual even more pleasant. The other feathered resident of the High Lane playing field area, much in evidence in winter, is the large resident flock of land locked gulls. They are often to be seen, when not feeding, roosted in a line, side by side on the cross bars of the goal posts.

On the approach to Bridge No.11, the bank on the towpath side is stone lined and the path is wide and concreted. To the right of the towpath, the corner of the playing field is occupied by a childrens playground with swings, slides, round abouts and climbing frames. Frequent mooring rings in the wide towpath hark back to the mid 1800's when this area was actually a wharf from which an enterprising Ashton businessman ran a passenger boat service, serving Macclesfield, Marple and Duckinfield. These fast boats carrying upwards of a hundred passengers, travelling at eight to ten miles per hour were towed by two horses each. The A6 trunk road which transports a huge volume of traffic between Hazel Grove and Buxton, passes over Bridge No. 11, on its way through High Lane to Disley.

Above the bridge, the brilliantly white painted Bulls Head Hotel attracts water borne business while on the actual stone wall of the bridge a painted sign board advertises the warm welcome to be found at The Dog and Partridge, two hundred yards up the busy A6. To the left of the bridge, the ramshackle outbuildings of smallholding crowd up to the waters edge. To the right, a flight of steps lead from the towpath up to the roadway above.

Bridge No. 11 is reminiscent of a tunnel as it carries a sixty five feet length of canal beneath it, indicating that the highway above was broad and carried a high volume of traffic at the time of the canal's completion in 1831.

CHAPTER 2
HIGH LANE TO LYME VIEW MARINA.

Beyond Bridge No. 11, buildings loom above the canal to left and right. The Bulls Head overshadows the right bank as it stands above a high stone wall which stems from the bridge itself. Due to the proximity of the canal, the Bulls Head public house was extremely popular with navvies and bargees and also with High Lane native colliery workers. Friction would often develop between the various factions leading to unruly behaviour and brawls. As a direct result of this unsavoury behaviour, the landlord of the Bulls Head organised controlled boxing matches in the field behind the pub as a release for pent up aggression.

On emerging from the mini tunnel beneath the bridge, the canals banks are stone lined and, as beneath many bridges, stop plank grooves are to be seen. For the first time, however, at the foot of the high stone wall, the actual stop planks are to be found. They are stored in a wooden clamp which is made vandal or thief proof by the planks being strapped down and bolted in place with a metal band. The planks are eleven feet long to coincide with the width of the canal beneath the bridge. Ahead, the canal sweeps sharply to the left. The towpath is wide and, as ever, beautifully maintained and sports another wooden bench which stands near to a flight of steps leading up to the "The Bulls Head".

On the way round the left hand curve, housing once again tops the high bank beside the towpath. Likewise, on the eastern bank, houses with long gardens and lawns back down to the canal bank. One after another, mooring rings are set in the gravel of the towpath. The canal begins to widen out quite drastically, eventually becoming a bay or lagoon some eighty to one hundred feet wide. Up ahead, alongside the wide bay, the towpath is carried over a spectacularly architectural humpbacked stone bridge. The towpath is transported steeply over the arch of the bridge in beautifully even stone cobble setts. Beneath the humpbacked bridge, the High Lane canal arm leaves the main Macclesfield canal.

The short High Lane arm was originally constructed for the easy transfer of cargoes from canal to road vehicles (as the arm reaches back to the modern day A6). The main cargo to be loaded in the arm was coal. The narrowboats loaded up with coal from pits at the nearby Norbury Colliery. Coal also arrived at the wharf on High Lane arm from more distant shafts via a private railway. The mining of this most valuable commodity actually reached right up to the pathway beside the canal arm itself, for, to the immediate left of the path, the sealed up entrance of a shallow drift mine which was worked during the last war can be seen.

HIGH LANE CANAL ARM

From leaving the main canal, the arm runs straight for approximately four or five hundred yards then turns sharply to the right at forty five degrees and runs for another five or six hundred yards to the site of the original coal companies crane warehouse and wharf. The total length, as recorded at the arms completion was 1 1/2 furlongs. At the point where the arms turns at forty five degrees, a second arm used to branch off to the left, namely Messrs Clayton and Brookes canal arm now long filled inland almost totally overgrown and obliterated by nature. In addition to the coal interest, at the bend in the canal arm, the original site of a sizeable lime kiln can just be detected.

After the closure of the Norbury Colliery in 1892 the waterway arm gradually began to silt up. In 1943, the North Cheshire Cruising Club, which is one of the oldest canal cruising clubs in the United Kingdom was formed. They lease the High Lane Canal Arm. The boats and their boat-houses totally dominate the arm. The boat-houses themselves are another of the Macclesfield Canal's unique features, as very few of their age and design exist elsewhere.

The humpback bridge, which is actually Bridge No. 12, bares a blue painted wooden sign at the entrance to the canal arm bearing the letters "N.C.C.C." and the associations insignia. The boat houses, are mostly of corrugated tin sheet, with some of wooden plank and they totally occupy both banks of the arm right round to the wharf at the end where the club house now is. The wide bay in the main canal beside the humpbacked bridge is used as a turning or manoeuvring area for boats negotiating the turn into the High Lane arm. This wide, deep bay like similar areas along the canals course, provides a valuable sanctuary for the canal's fish population; a place to escape from the often frantic and incessant boat traffic. Fish are of course, to be found throughout the whole of the canal length, but they certainly favour the wider bays.

Normally, the water is at its shallowest at either edge of the canal, deepening into the centre which is the boat channel. When a powered boat passes through the water, logically, it must displace the resident fish from the deeper water and the only place that they can escape is in to the shallower margins where they must be buffeted by the turbulent wash from the boat. Consequently, it is little wonder that they are to be found in the quiet and deep bays, out of the way of the cruiser traffic. The most common fish of the Macclesfield Canal is, by far, the humble Roach, arguably the most prolific coarse fish in the British Isles. It is to be found in colossal numbers along the canals length, particularly during May, June and July when vast shoals of Roach fry drift in the cloudy water, flashing in the sunlight as they turn, like thousands of iron filings.

The Roach is as adaptable as it is numerous. It is to be found in chalk streams, in the lower trout reaches of most rivers, farm ponds, reservoirs, mountain lakes, middle reaches of rivers, estuaries and canals. The Roach of the clean fast river is a princely fish, silver scales like so many silver coins, bright reddish or coppery eyes, creamy white bellies and often orange fins. By comparison, the Roach from the often turbid canal water is an entirely paler, duller fish, grey fins, dull eye and quite often, the body is clothed in a coating of sticky, protective mucus.

ROACH

The Macclesfield Canal provides an easily accessible stretch of water to many thousands of anglers each year. The fisherman's main quarry will be the Roach. The average size of fish, which he will catch will be very small but, on a good day, quite numerous. A couple of ounces in weight is the norm. A 'good' canal Roach is half a pound in weight. Three quarters of a pound is exceptional. A respected local history book mentions a Roach of three and a half pounds being caught from the Macclesfield Canal in 1894! Just beyond the humpbacked bridge, two wooden benches are positioned beside the towpath where the passer by with a little time to spare can sit and look out across this often busy area. In summer, narrowboats jostle for position, awaiting their turn to negotiate the narrow aperture below the bridge into the High Lane arm. This is a favourite temporary mooring area at any time of the year because of the space offered by the extreme width of the waterway and the close proximity of High Lane town centre with its numerous shops, stores, takeaway food bars, telephone kiosks and hostelries.

Heading onward towards Cheshire, a long straight length of canal stretches away with a stone lined bank on the towpath side. Beside the towpath, a high bank with a wooden fence along the top clothed with dense brambles and thickets of Dog Rose obscures the view beyond. What actually lies beyond the wooden fence is High Lane cricket field. A peaceful setting for this most English of summer sports, well away from the main road, and surrounded by Silver Birch woodland. Below, it is totally undermined and honeycombed by the frenzied tunneling of High Lane's coal hungry past. Local legend tells of a superb heavy roller loaned to the club to improve the surface of the wicket which was left out overnight. First light the following morning revealed a large crater in the field and some distance below, the prized roller was lying prone at the bottom of a pit shaft. A lush green patch on the pitch marks forever the position where the yawning hole was filled in.

Across the water, an occasional garden still reaches down the steep terrace. The towpath is superbly smooth, rivaling many roadside pavements. Looking along the canal ahead is reminiscent of looking into a tunnel of trees as the waterway is dead straight as far as can be seen and the banks either side climb ever higher. Mature tall Oak trees and full grown Hawthorn trees soar up from each bank, towering Alders and Ashes rise out of an undergrowth of Cornus (Dogwood) and ground smothering Ivy.

From the commencement of the journey at Marple, the canal now passes through its deepest cutting as the banks and trees loom skyward on each side. Flitting to and fro across the canal, flocks of Long Tailed Tits are frequently to be seen. The steep wooden

LONG TAILED TIT

banks are, to the birds, belts of woodland, their natural habitat. Particularly in winter, the flocks are constantly on the move, in search of spiders, insects, seeds and buds. These tiny birds measure just five and a half inches overall and the long tail is more than half of the birds total length. A severe winter will account for eighty per cent of the bird population. Some of the taller Ash or Alder trees, on the far side have dense, strangling Ivy growing up their trunks to a height of thirty to forty feet from the ground. The unseen field which lies beyond the high bank to the right of the towpath suffers a similar handicap to the cricket field. During the last decade, the local pony club has sought to secure a lease on the field to practice and to stage its events but has completely failed to acquire third party insurance to cover liability at gymkhanas etc. due to the ever present danger of the ground opening up and swallowing competitor, pony or spectator alike.

Up ahead, the trees on both banks can be seen to be coming to an end and the view in the far distance is of hills, topped by bleak windswept moorland. Across the canal, the tall eastern bank levels out into a picturesque spinney or glade of stunted Oak trees, Silver Birches and Hollies. Beside the towpath, a post and rail fence separates the walkway from a vehicle track, but up ahead the fence suddenly turns across the towpath reaching the waters edge. A kissing gate set in the fence allows the towpath walker to pass through. Beyond the kissing gate the towpath no longer exists. The walker now walks along the trackway. On the opposite bank, the spinney suddenly and dramatically drops away into the deep valley. The contrast here is due to absolute masterpiece of canal engineering.

Upon emerging from the deepest of cuttings the canal is carried across a soaring embankment. Seventy to eighty feet below at the bottom of its steep wooded valley, via an aqueduct, the Stockport Disley & Whaley Bridge Railway passes under the canal. The line opened in 1857 and since then, locomotives have struggled and strained up this gradient, one of the steepest on the national railway system. The line now goes to Buxton in Derbyshire, directly from Manchester. The woodland which reaches the canal while on its way through the deep cutting and which crowds into the railway valley is the eastern edge of the remains of an ancient forest called Middle Wood. Middle Wood probably covered vast tracts of land between Hazel Grove, High Lane and Poynton and gave its name to the settlement of Middlewood to the west of the canal, which sprang up around a large brick works. The works, up to its closure in the nineteen fifties, produced vast quantities of bricks and clay products for colliery buildings, mine shaft linings and land drains.

The settlement of Middlewood, in turn, gives its name to The Middlewood Way. The Middlewood Way is the modern day name for the dismantled Macclesfield to Marple Railway. The Middlewood Way runs roughly parallel to the Macclesfield Canal for its first 11 miles although, up to this point, the one has not been visible from the other. As our canal journey began at Marple Junction the

Middlewood Way also began in Marple at Rose Hill Station. It too ran through Hawk Green and High Lane. Today, it is a phenomenally popular walkway, cycle way and bridleway. The line originally opened in 1869, linking the Poynton coalfield and the textile towns of the Pennine Edge with the main lines to the cities of Manchester and the Stoke on Trent Potteries. As a goods line, the Macclesfield, Bollington and Marple carried coal, gritstone, raw cotton, finished yarn and agricultural produce. Strong competition from road transport eventually forced its closure in 1970.

The combined Borough Councils of Macclesfield and Stockport rescued it from 15 years of dereliction in 1985, having landscaped and softened its embankments and cuttings. As it once competed with Macclesfield canal as a means of transportation for industry, The Middlewood Way now competes once again for its share of the recreation market. On the Middlewood Way the iron horse has been replaced by the trekking pony and the bicycle. It is ironic that after the decline of the narrowboat as a means of haulage during the late nineteen forties and nineteen fifties, on the canal, the narrow boat once again reigns supreme.

Once the Macclesfield canal has passed over the Manchester to Buxton Railway Aqueduct, - it enters the county of Cheshire. Beyond the aqueduct, the canal is stone lined on either bank for the duration of its passage across the embankment. The views to the east are of banky green pasture fields climbing gradually up to a belt of woodland and, above that, high bleak moorland. The distant belt of woodland separating grass from moor is regimental conifer plantation, so totally different from the relic of ancient forest now disappearing behind to the west of the canal. The moorland above the treeline is clothed in heather. Beyond the tall Hawthorn hedge which runs beside the trackway, the deep valley drops sharply away. The magnitude of this embankment is quite breathtaking. The Macclesfield canal as a whole, is a technical masterpiece of engineering and a fitting tribute to the original surveyor, Thomas Telford.

It was Telford who specified where embankments were needed and where cuttings and bridges were required. The great skill with which the canal is transported over or through the undulations in the landscape, cuts out the necessity for countless locks. In fact, the Macclesfield is so well designed that all of its locks are to be found together (12 in number), lifting the canal 118 feet in one mile at Bosley which is almost exactly half way along the canals length. Consequently, Marple to Macclesfield and almost to Congleton can be negotiated by boat without the hindrance of locks and by the same token, Congleton to the Trent and Mersey Canal at Kidsgrove is also lock free, so, the Macclesfield Canal could almost be described as being on two levels. Telford also had to plan where each stream, river, culvert and even land drain had to be laid beneath the intended canal. It is said that Telford's biggest problem was not an engineering difficulty but the seeking of permission of landowners for the right to take the canal through their land. He described Cheshire's property owners as being of "an unaccommodating disposition". Having planned the Macclesfield canals route, Telford moved on to the Birmingham and Liverpool junction canal. The supervision of construction of the Macclesfield canal was carried out by William Crosley Junior. Crosley was also involved with the Lancaster, Rochdale, Worcester and Birmingham Canals.

The Bollinghurst Brook passes beneath the canal several hundred yards further along the embankment. It snakes along the bottom of its deep grass valley between tall mature trees and squat Hollies. The brook, is as wide and broad as many upland streams and, in winter time when swollen with flood water or snow melt, it roars beneath the canal in a torrent. Bollinghurst Brook is created by four or five springs and rain fed cavities among the hills near and above Lyme Hall, specifically Whaley Moor near Dissop Head and Bow Stones at an elevation of 1300 feet above sea level. It flows through Horse Coppice reservoir which is linked by a dam to Bollinghurst Reservoir, on the Lyme Park Estate. It flows down through the southern fringes of High Lane, beneath the canal, through Middlewood, Norbury Hollow and, south of Norbury Wood, it becomes Norbury Brook. It flows to Bramhall where it becomes Lady Brook and on to Cheadle where it becomes Micker Brook, before eventually joining the River Mersey near to Northenden.

At the top end of the valley, to the right of the canal, a tall brick chimney is visible, peeping out of dense woodland. This is the previously mentioned Cheshire Brick Works which has stood idle since the nineteen fifties. Along this, the highest section of the embankment, a wooden post and rail fence runs along either edge of the canal affording some protection from the steep incline beyond. Looking down the grassy valley side to the west, a low ridge can just be see. This marks the line of a long dismantled tramway which used to carry coal from a mine in the same field to the canal side. The laden colliery trucks would be hauled by teams of horses. Today, horses graze the lush valley grass, their role is not as arduous as that of their predecessors; a round of fence jumps at a gymkhana will be the nearest that they are likely to come to earning their keep.

Beyond the valley, the canal begins to curve to the west. The private driveway to Hill Top Farm leaves the waterside trackway to the right. Hill Top Farm lies away to the right of the canal, at the top of the valley. Its only vehicle access and link with the outside world is this length of canal bank. Mixed woodland across the water on the left bank drops away and large pasture fields rise up to the distant conifer plantations and the wild moorland above. Quite suddenly the next Bridge, No. 13 comes into view around a seemingly endless curve. The wooden fence which has run beside the trackway since its passage across the embankment continues up to the bridge ramp art and a second kissing gate with an optional stile beside it gives access from the trackway to a standard towpath which begins again, just short of the bridge. The fence, gates and stile are further example of Macclesfield Council towpath improvements. The area before the bridge is occupied by two wooden benches and two information boards. One, quite justifiably draws attention to Macclesfield Borough Council's commendable groundwork to be seen all around. The second is in diagram form and shows the route of the Macclesfield Canal from Marple Junction through to Bosley Locks. The Middlewood way is shown running roughly parallel from Rosehill Station in Marple to Macclesfield and also pinpoints all bus stops, pubs, marinas, pic-nic areas, car parks, bus stations. and railway stations along the route. All footpaths linking the canal with the Middlewood Way are detailed as are the footpaths linking the canal to the more distant gritstone trail to the east.

Glancing up to the eastern horizon before arriving at Bridge No. 13, the first of several landmarks to be seen along the canals route, comes into view on the hillside. The high moor in the distant east has for many centuries formed part of the Lyme Estate and has, since Elizabethan times been known as Cage Hill. Just above the dark conifer plantations which are Ryles Wood and Elmerhurst Wood, a tall stone tower, square with corner turrets, looms dark and mysterious against the dramatic backcloth of the wild moor. The tower is Lyme Cage. The mystery surrounding this enigmatic building extends to the uncertainty about its exact date. It is accepted that it is Elizabethan and was built as a vantage point from which to follow the stag hunt. Red deer are still a feature of Lyme Park today the famous herd numbering at least two hundred and fifty head.

From the very earliest times, the deer herds were contained both for ornament and for the hunt. Today there is also a herd of the smaller. more delicate Fallow deer which, together with the flocks of hardy gritstone sheep, roam the park. The Cage was built by the Legh family of Lyme Hall who have held the estate since the late thirteen hundreds. The land at Lyme was awarded to Thomas Danyers by King Edward 11 for his bravery in the battle of Caen in 1346. In 1388 Margaret Danyers married Piers Legh, thus the Legh name began an association with Lyme which would carry through to 1946 when Richard Legh gave Lyme Park over to the National Trust.

The present Lyme Hall is as majestic as The Cage is mysterious. The largest house in Cheshire, parts of Lyme Hall date from the late 16th century. Major alterations in the first part of the eighteenth century are responsible for the house as it is seen today. The early sections, dating from 1570, are to be found in the more modest north front with its Elizabethan frontage displaying interesting use of columns and pediments. The sensational south front is Lyme Hall's monumental facade. Often admired, frequently photographed, its perfect reflection in the quiet lake with lawns rolling up to the very stonework is exquisite. The fifteen bays in three stories, centred by a portico of four enormous columns supporting a huge pediment, is the masterpiece of Italian architect Gacomo Leoni. The building is, throughout, constructed of gritstone from the estate quarries. Further alterations between 1816 and 1822 were undertaken by Lewis Wyatt and involved the addition of an oblong tower to the south front and alterations to the east. Setting aside, for a moment, the fabulous house at Lyme, it is to the Cage that the attention of the canal user is drawn. Its position on the desolate hillside and its brooding appearance set it apart from the surrounding landscape.

By comparison, to the Cage, Bridge No.13 is positively diminutive and even humble but, non the less, unique and of great interest in its own right. The bridge is the first to be encountered, so far, that is not a complete stone arch. It consists of a stone rampart on either bank but a bridge of concrete, girders and timber is slung between the stone parapets. This was not a cost cutting operation like the opportune use of swing bridges, neither is it a shoddy repair. It is, in fact, ingeneous design. Willliam Crosley, the engineer, designed this type of bridge specifically for use in areas where subsidence, due to intensive mining was likely to be encountered. The gentle sinking or buckling of the ground would wreck havoc with a full stone bridge but here, the central section could easily be removed and the stonework on which its sits, either raised or altered to bring it back to dead level before being quickly reassembled. Another feature of Bridge No. 13 is the concrete pill-box which is tucked up to the stonework of the bridge on the eastern bank, across from the tow-path. Built during the second world war, the pill-box was protection against canal borne invasion. Its weathered concrete is green with algae and moss growth so it almost blends with its surroundings.

BRIDGE No 13

Against the stonework of the bridge beside the wooden benches, a large, unruly Snowberry shrub grows. Its spongy, white berries which decorate the tangle of branches stand out against the mellow stone of the bridge, particularly in winter. Introduced from the American Continent in the 19th century, the Snowberry rapidly became a popular specimen and hedging shrub. It soon made good its escape into woodland where it forms dense thickets.

Beyond Bridge No. 13, the canal instantly widens out into a large bay. The bay is permanent mooring for twenty to twenty five boats; a mix of cruiser craft and narrowboats. Beyond the bay with its cluster of boats, the eastern bank of the canal is over shadowed by a large raised mound. The hillock, over an acre in extent is densely covered with tall scots pine trees. Interesting and hard to explain mounds like this are occasionally to be seen in the countryside; some, are covered in densely planted trees in otherwise level, open land, such as here, are actually mass cattle graves dating from the cattle plague in the nineteen century. Others far more ancient, are barrows or human burial chambers, but this, artificially planted mound is actually cleverly a disguised colliery spoil heap.

The whole area here to the east of the canal was, during the last century, occupied by Middle Cale Pit. The boat mooring bay was once a busy coal loading wharf. Beside the mound, the small holding cottages with stables and outbuildings to be seen today were originally colliery engineer's cottages. Between the yard(with its stables and steaming loose box muck heap,)and the canal's edge, the rough uneven ground shows signs of a capped off mine shaft. Slabs of concrete and piles of bricks now overgrown and matted with grass conceal the point where the miners were dropped in a flimsy cage basket to hack at seams of coal. Other workers brought up the waste, dirt and coal dust, tipped it behind, eventually forming the mound which is now perfectly grassed over and was long ago planted with the Scots Pine.

Across the canal, the towpath is narrower than usual and is bordered by a low neat Hawthorn hedge. The pasture fields beyond the hedge slope away to distant woodland in which stands the brickworks at Middlewood. A long, straight length of canal stretches ahead The boat mooring continues along the eastern bank beyond the old Middlecale wharf. Beyond the Hawthorn hedge beside the towpath, a pond or flooded pit shimmers and twinkles in the field beside the canal. At the approaching foot fall of a passer by, Moorhens ,probing the turf of the pasture field for worms and other invertebrates make a headlong dash for either the safety of the pond or for the far bank of the canal. This is usually a half running, half flying escape which ends in a splashing stop.

The Moorhen is numerous along the Macclesfield Canal but is more secretive and retiring than the semi tame duck population. Its take off from the water is a drawn out dramatic affair. It takes a long pattering run along the surface before take off is achieved. The only time that the towpath walker has a chance to study the moorhen closely is during the spring when the adult female swims, guarding the young which strongly resemble tiny black blobs of soot frenziedly following her every move. On the eastern bank, Middlecale Farm nestles among the patchwork of fields, beyond which the Cage is now clearly visible on the hillside. The intense feeling of great antiquity which surrounds the distant but clear view of this strange building is overwhelming. During the 1750's a written account tells that the old approach to Lyme Hall went right over Cage Hill and the gradient was so steep that no conveyance would attempt the route without a team of four or even six horses.

In addition to the Red and Fallow deer herds, the pastures below The Cage and the moorland above it were, up until the beginning of this century, also grazed by a herd of wild cattle. White cattle had grazed the Lyme Estate since the beginning of recorded history, enclosed and protected but left alone to remain pure in form and uncontaminated by interbreeding. As a breed, the Wild White or White Park Cattle achieved renewed popularity during the Victorian period as it became popular to have a herd 'running in the park'. It is sad that today, despite increased protection of traditional breeds of livestock, only a handful of herds of these beautiful animals now exist in the British Isles. With Middlecale Farm lying to the east of the canal, another farm can be seen down to the west, among pasture fields, this is Pool House Farm.

The next milestone stands between the towpath and a neat but now taller Hawthorn hedge, it reads "Hall Green 23 1/4", "Marple 3 miles". Well grazed pasture slopes quite steeply away to the west to Pool House Farm, and beyond, to Middlewood. A tiny brook, culverted under the canal, snakes away towards Middlewood. On the eastern bank, between Middlecale Farm and the canal's edge lies a strip of very rough uneven ground, baring all of the grassed over scars of colliery spoil, dotted with low, bushy Willow trees. The canal is now lined at both banks by sheet metal. A mini embankment takes the canal across a shallow grassy valley which slopes gently down to Middlewood where orange roofs peer out here and there among the distant trees.

On the eastern bank, much evidence of past mining activity can be seen all around. The ground here has never recovered to become reclaimed pasture instead it is almost like a lunar landscape with hummocks and crators. The hollows are filled with water and gorse bushes grow on the poor soil of the hummocks. In some places, the soil and turf are so thin that it has broken through to reveal coal dust and waste. As ever, the view to the distant east is of The Cage and the brooding moorland beyond.

The canal is very wide and enters a sharp curve to the left. A public footpath which links the Macclesfield canal to the Middlewood Way via Prince's incline leaves the towpath to the right over a neat wooden stile. The footpath follows the bottom edge of a mound which rises quite steeply to the right of the canal. The mound is covered by tall Silver Birches and Oak trees and is scattered with the ramshackle remnants of colliery buildings. This is the site of yet another shaft; the aptly named Canal Pit shaft. In fact, both banks of the canal, at this point, boasted a colliery, namely Higher and Lower Canal Pits. These colleries were a bustle of activity throughout the last century, the coal having the benefit of not having to be transported before entering the mainline haulage route which was the nineteenth century canal system.

The walker taking the footpath around the edge of the wooded mound today will almost immediately encounter a large concrete bed, not quite visible from the canal towpath, which was once the mounting for "Red Legs". This was the nickname for the steam engine which provided the power, not only to pump water out of the pit shafts, but to winch coal up and men down. The engines drive was geared by a pair of red painted rods which moved up and down alternatively like the legs of some huge cricket, hence the nickname. Flooding was a constant problem throughout the Poynton coalfield so "Redlegs" drew water from neighbouring mines to assist in keeping them dry.

Boats are moored solidly along the curve of the canal's left hand bank as Bridge No.14 comes into view in the distance. A feeling of openness is accentuated by the customary path side Hawthorn hedge being replaced by a fence of concrete posts carrying four strands of tensioned smooth wire which continues to the distant bridge. The canal is now passing over yet another small scale embankment and beyond the wire fence, a gentle grassy gradient slopes down to a large pasture field which lies some thirty feet below the canals level. On the far side of the field, housing stretches away across the Cheshire plain. The housing is on the fringes of Higher Poynton. The more distant view is of Poynton, Bramhall and across to the vast area occupied by Manchester International Airport and beyond even that, the horizon is dotted by the faint outlines of cooling towers and factory chimneys.

Poynton is best described as a commuter village despite being comparable in size to many a small town. Poynton is still technically a village with a parish council and its own agricultural and horticultural shows. Poynton park and pool are the beauty spots at the centre of the community, being the place in which 'The Towers', the manor house of the Vernon family was situated. When the estate was eventually split up 'The Towers', a robust stone building, was pulled down and the Vernons took up residence at Sudbury Hall, now a National Trust Property.

On the approach to Bridge No 14 Barlow House Farm comes into view on slightly raised ground to the east of the bridge. A large expanse of deciduous woodland forms a backcloth to the neat buildings of Barlow House Farm, stretching away to the moor land beyond. Down to the west, what, at first glance looks like a black volcano rears above the tree tops, apparently right out of the housing of Higher Poynton. The apparition is the enormous spoil heap which marks the site of Anson pit, the largest and most productive pit on the Poynton coalfield. Throughout the eighteen hundreds, the collieries one thousand tons per week output was maintained by a workforce of one hundred and fifty men. The weekly coal output was the equivalent of forty narrowboat loads, considerable contributing to the canals industrial traffic prior to the pits closure in 1926.

Bridge No.14 is almost identical to No.13, a fully adjustable girder and timber construction slung between two stone supports. Another wooden seat gives the footsore traveller chance to sit and admire the tranquil scene which, less than a century ago would have been a hive of industrial activity. A tiny lane goes over the almost fragile looking bridge to provide Barlow House Farm with vehicle access to Higher Poynton.

Just through the bridge, a second seat is set in a neatly cobbled area, sheltered by a towering Hawthorn hedge. As is so often the case during our journey along the canal, stepping through Bridge No.14 is almost like moving from one theatrical set to a totally new and different one. A tall unruly Hawthorn hedge overhangs the towpath as far as can be seen ahead, across the water, a rough pasture dotted with clumps of rushes rises away from the canals edge but, beyond this, some fifty yards from the bridge, the waterway opens up into a crowded marina.

The canal widens out to become a sheet of water two to three hundred feet wide with boats moored solidly beside the towpath along the west bank, all along the far bank and also, either side of a jetty which runs up the centre of the waterway. The moored craft are mostly narrowboats but a staggering variety of smaller cruisers of all shapes, sizes and types are also represented. Among the numerous narrowboats, every imaginable colour and shade of paintwork vies for attention, presenting a kaleidoscope of rainbow colours. As with any area benefiting from dense human population, the marina is patrolled by flocks of ducks, ever watchful for the carelessly discarded food scraps or for the arrival of the duck feeding fraternity. The far bank of the canal has its own vehicle access and beyond that, arable fields climb away to the distant moorland.

Beside the towpath, a black and white painted British Waterways sign board explains that permits must be obtained before using 'Poynton Long Term Moorings'. The lettering on most of the narrowboats indicates that the majority are residents of Poynton. During the winter season, when most of the mooring are occupied, the marina will house between one hundred and thirty and one hundred and fifty boats.

Up ahead, the towpath is, once again carried over a humpbacked bridge. The bridge like the one which carried the towpath over the junction of the canal at High Lane, also, transports the towpath steeply over a second branch arm. Across the wide canal, the far bank proudly sports tall specimen conifer trees, ornamental shrubs and manicured grass.

The waterway widens out into a huge bay opposite to the junction of the Lord Vernon canal arm. From the beautiful stone bridge, this delightful spot can be viewed to advantage. The short canal arm was built by Lord Vernon of Poynton to enable boats to be loaded with coal quickly and efficiently two at a time. The coal arrived in enormous quantities from the nearby Anson, Nelson and Park pits. Boats waiting to take up their position in the loading bay arm, assembled in the wide bay opposite. The canal arm is still in private ownership although today, it is not coal but pleasure boating which occupies the arm and its moorings. The owners, Constellation Cruises, have a small shop, housed in one of the waterside buildings in addition to their own fuel pumps and other facilities.

Lord Vernon was the owner, not only of the canal arm, but also of the collieries so it is little wonder that this whole area, which must have represented the hub of Lord Vernon's industrial wheel, became known as 'Mount Vernon'. The hey day of Mount Vernons industrial life was the period between 1830 and 1880 although the wharf remained in use until 1930 when the last of the pits closed. From the junction of the canal arm, looking along the canal from the wide bay, Bridge No.15 is just ahead.

MOUNT VERNON

Lyme Road is carried over the bridge which gives vehicle access to the eastern bank of the canal for the benefit of the marinas Just prior to Lyme Road's passage over the bridge, a row of terraced cottages overlook the canal. The cottages bear the inscription "Mount Vernon 1835". These modest dwellings once housed miners or Lord Vernons boat loaders. On the stonework of the bridge, a sign board describes in detail the working of Mount Vernon at its height and an artists impression of the scene graphically portrays the bustle of activity during the 1830's and 40's.

The scene depicts boats being towed in and out of the canal arm, others jostling for position in the bay where stands the boat builders shop, boat-house and stables. The bridge itself is almost identical in design to the previous two, fully adjustable in the event of subsidence. The scene portrayed beyond bridge No. 15 is the only actual evidence of subsidence to be seen along the length of the

Macclesfield Canal. The canal, here opens out into a sheet of water, 3 - 4 hundred feet wide, more reminiscent of a park lake than a canal.. The 'lake' caused by underground subsidence is known as "The Wide Hole". The result of running a waterway through the heart of a coalfield; the underground workings of Nelson pit have attempted to swallow the canal. The bed of the canal has sunk into the labyrinth of pit shafts, creating a deep lagoon which, in turn, offers a unique opportunity to the canal's fishermen.

At any hour of the day on almost every day of the year, somewhere along the canal's twenty seven and three quarter mile course, an angler will be found pursuing his sport. During the summer months, the fair weather pleasure fisherman flocks in thousands to the canal bank. Pleasure boats fairly bristle with children's rods and crude tackle. Early morning and late evening, year round will find the serious angler with his sophisticated equipment and specimen baits in search of the larger, more elusive specimen fish. The'Wide Hole at Higher Poynton will rarely be without its dedicated angler. It is here that the Bream will be found in numbers and will attain a good average size. In the natural course of things, the Bream, is found in deep lakes and pools which have a soft muddy bottom, and the slow moving rivers of fenland and the Broads. Man has been responsible for introducing the Bream to waters which it would never colonize naturally and a good many which are totally unsuitable. The artificial introduction into the canal system quite often provides the Bream with the necessary depth of water, but rarely the protection from the incessant boat traffic ,which it requires for the intensive feeding needed for it to attain any size. As a species, the Bream, another member of the Carp family, can reach 15 pounds in weight but, in a canal, will rarely reach 1 pound. It hybridizes very freely with the prolific Roach, a smaller member of the same family.

BREAM

The angling interests on the Macclesfield canal have long been dominated by organised angling societies who have, over the years been responsible for stocking the waters with many hundreds of thousands of stock fish. The Wide Hole has many features which are characteristic of a lowland lake. The distant east bank is reed fringed and over shadowed by tall Alders and Willows. The Moorhen which probably has a nesting site along every hundred yard length of the entire canal is joined here by the Coot. The Coot is a bird of roomy expanses of water. In Cheshire, it nests in the reedy margins of the numerous meres, lakes and reservoirs whereas the Moorhen exploits the smaller ponds, pools and the countless thousands of Marl-Pits which are so much a special feature of Cheshire. The Coot is a considerable larger bird than the Moorhen but to the layman, the overriding difference, even from a distance is the brilliant snowy white blaze on the Coots head and face.

Bridge No.15, bares a commemorative plaque celebrating the towpath improvements by Macclesfield Borough Council dated 1985 and opened by the chairman of British Waterways Board. The towpath edge is sheet metal lined as far as the eye can see. The whole length of canal and towpath which runs through the Wide Hole is shored up by a study stone wall. Beyond the fence is a drop of 12-14 feet down to an extensive playing field. The perfectly level, rectangular playing field sports a full sized football pitch plus a five a side pitch and a children's playground. The playing field lies sandwiched between two highways. On its one side, the canal towers above, separated by the stone wall. On the other side, a dense belt of Birch trees mark the route of the Middlewood Way, running in a deep cutting, parallel to the canal. This is the first time that the old railway has been clearly visible from the canal since both left Marple almost simultaneously, and never more than a quarter of a mile apart and frequently much closer together than that.

Actually in the water, along the length of the Wide Hole, British Water Board signs denote where the boat channel runs and serve to exclude boats from the majority of the sheet of water and also warn of dangerous underwater obstructions. A flight of wooden stairs leaves the towpath to link it with the children's adventure playground end of the playing field below. As the canal begins to return to its normal width, the eastern bank is increasingly densely wooded, tall Birch and Willow, thickly underplanted with Rhododendron reach the water edge. For centuries, this area of woodland has been known as Elm Wood; it is unlikely that a single Elm tree will be seen today as a result of the devastating Dutch Elm disease which ravaged the nations Elm trees to virtual exstinction during the 1970's. To

RHODODENDRON

the west of the canal, at the end of the playing field Elm Beds Road reaches up towards the canal, having crossed the Middlewood Way. The canal, which is still somewhat wider than usual, begins to curve gently to the left. On the eastern bank, cottages crowd up to the towpath.

The canal briefly resumes its normal width before opening out once more into a small bay which provides a turning area for boats. Beyond the bay, the canal stretches away, lined at each bank by metal sheeting. The field which occupies the eastern bank is dotted with dips and irregularities which quite often hold water and for most of the year, it plays host to a small group of Canada Geese.

The birds crop the grass and swim, bathe and wallow in the small pools. They frequently take to the canal and honk loud warnings to passing boats and walkers. The colony of geese usually number about ten individuals and are yet another example of a species which certainly is not tame or domesticated but neither is it truly wild. The canal seems to be the perfect habitat for these misfit species. The semi tame ducks, largely dependent on man for food, the scavenging land gulls and the Canada Geese, anxious to abandon their natural caution at the offer of a scrap of bread, all seem to fit so well into this unnatural waterway so exploited by mankind. The handsome Canada Goose was originally introduced from Canada in the seventeenth century to decorate parkland lakes and yet its gradual escape into the wild has not significantly altered this role. Attempts to mass rear it as a game bird failed as it is naturally too tame and flies much too low to be a sporting target. So large and showy, the goose still fulfils its original purpose to decorate the waterside.

CANADA GOOSE

A trim neat Hawthorn hedge runs alongside the towpath. At intervals, wild Honeysuckle rambles through the Hawthorn, its reddish stems twining spirally clockwise through the hedge. The flowers of the Honeysuckle and their heady perfume attract pollinating moths in large numbers on sultry summer evenings. The flower heads, peach coloured when in bud, open

*HONEY-
SUCKLE*

into as many as a dozen trumpet shaped flowers of delicate cream in each head. The canal begins to narrow slightly and curve to the right and, as it does, the next milestone is encountered. Again, this is an original stone which reads 'Hall Green 22 1/4 miles', 'Marple 4 miles'. On this stone, it is the words Marple and Hall Green which were removed by chisel in defence of the country.

The Hawthorn hedge beside the towpath borders a large garden of mature shrubbery and neat lawns. In places, garden shrubs grow through the Hawthorn, Laurels, Privets and Rhododendrons all reacing towards the towpath. The pasture land on the east bank begins to drop into a wooded valley. Once again the canal begins a journey across a valley via an embankment. Across the water the valley plunges steeply away from the waters edge. Only occasional glimpses through the impenetrable towpath side Hawthorn reveal the valley below. A white painted small holding briefly comes into view then is lost. Hagg Farm which nestles out of sight, in the valley gives its name to this area which is separated from High Poynton by the Middlewood Way and by Poynton Coppice.

JAY

To the east of the canal, the valley is densely wooded with Oaks, Birches and Hawthorns predominating and representing the western tip of Bens Wood. Winter and summer alike, the shrieks and cries of Jays and Magpies reverberate throughout the valley. The Jay is heavily dependent upon trees, Oaks in particular, and is more often heard than seen. Any intruder encroaching upon its territory is accosted by a raucous scolding barrage of verbal abuse. An intruder may be an innocent bird, its close cousin the Magpie or, another Jay. The hideous screeching voice seems strangely out of place when the handsome bird is actually seen. The pinkish buff plumage, the black and white streaked crown, white rump and the vivid blue wing patches combine to make the Jay one of the most exotic of native birds.

MAGPIE

By comparison, the Jays close relation, the Magpie is almost an exhibitionist. It is to be seen in every conceivable habitat including suburban areas but it is still, most at home in its native woodland and in the open field. The Magpies hoarse laughing chatter along with its distinctive plumage make it instantly recognizable. Beyond the valley, the land to the east of the canal slopes steeply upwards. Firstly 'Throstlenest Farm' then 'Green Farm' nestle among green hills and beyond, high moorland, totally barren and featureless, bare of trees or buildings meets the sky.

Bridge No. 16 comes into view a short distant ahead. Down in the valley, a stream, which passes beneath the canal via a culvert through the embankment, can be heard, faintly babbling but, it is totally lost from sight amid the dense foliage. Further down its course, the steam will become Poynton Brook after flowing through Poynton Coppice and picking up more feeders on its way. Poynton Brook makes its way through Poynton before joining Norbury Brook near to Hazel Grove on its long journey to the River Mersey. Once the valley has been crossed, the field to the east is unnaturally 'hummocky' and where the thin turf has broken through, the hillocks are revealed as piles of coal dust and waste. The unexpected mounds and dips in the field are often accentuated by a lone, stunted Hawthorn bushes.

The eerie cries of Lapwings ring out above the open, exposed meadows which rise towards the moorland. From the canal, the Lapwing will often be seen circling above these high meadows, in small flocks; their aerobatic twisting rolling and diving is breathtaking to watch. It is their plaintive cry which, gives the bird its alternative name, of Peewit, and this distinctive sound will frequently be heard above the incessant twittering of hedgerow birds and the summer drone of insects.

Like the Jay, the Lapwing is a strikingly handsome bird which is rarely if ever seen at close quarters. Like the Magpie, the Lapwing is outwardly a black and white bird which is actually a vivid iridescent green. In flight, the broad rounded wings are black with white tips and the breast is white with a black band. The orange under tail patch and the long black crest on the handsome head often go unnoticed, but it is the shining green of the supposedly black back which provides another of the birds pseudonyms 'The Green Plover'.

Up ahead Bridge No. 16 is quite unlike any so far encountered. A footbridge constructed from metal supports and represents a superb piece of engineering. The bridge is kept beautifully painted in green and red and, in every way is a delight to the eye. Immediately beneath the bridge, the canal banks are, in actual fact, the gritstone remnants of a swing bridge. Set in the stonework at water level on the far bank is a large metal plate which once formed part of the swing bridge mechanism. The appearance of the fine footbridge, so stoutly constructed, in this apparently remote spot, with no habitation of any kind in sight may seem mysterious. It is a mystery which deepens further considering that the long removed Hag foot swing bridge spanned the canal almost directly below the pedestrian foot-bridge. This curious arrangement is yet another remnant of the coal industries domination of the Higher Poynton area throughout the last century.

The higher ground to the east of the canal was once pitted by mines. The footbridge gave access across the canal to numerous colliers making their way from Higher Poynton and surrounding areas. Hag Foot Swing Bridge carried heavier horses and wagons and equipment. Ironically today, the footbridge carries, at times, almost as great a volume of traffic as it did in its heyday, particularly at the weekends when leisure time is at its peak. Todays traffic comprises the relentless hoards of ramblers as, the footbridge is part of a footpath route which is almost a motorway among footpaths, leading as it does from Higher Poynton, up to Lyme Park.

Despite the fact that The Cage disappeared from view some distance behind, the canal here is at its closest to Lyme Hall which is just out of sight, a little over one mile due east. The path climbs up past Throstle Nest Farm and Green Farm up to and over the hill tops then splits to lead either south to West Park Gate, which is the pedestrian entrance to Lyme or north to Disley and Lyme Halls main entrance. The footpath also forms a direct link with the Gritstone trail. Once under the bridge, a stile gives the towpath walker access to the footpath leading gently down towards Higher Poynton. Another Macclesfield Borough Council information board stands beside the bridge at this intersection of pathways, with its map showing the route taken by canal, in relation to the Middlewood Way and the linking footpaths.

Beyond the bridge, the canal widens out into a long straight length. The view south from Bridge No. 16 even a half a century ago would have looked very different from the view to be seen today. Thirty to forty yards ahead the towpath was originally transported over another humpbacked bridge which spanned the entrance to yet another canal arm. This long filled in canal arm was owned by the Legh family of Lyme. A dense belt of waterside vegetation stretches along this canal margin beside the towpath due to the fact that the bank is unlined. Rushes and Flag Iris have colonized the shallow margin.

The yellow Flag Iris is indeed a handsome flower, particularly when seen in large groups such as in this instance where they stretch away into the distance. It forms a swaying sea of canary yellow flowers through May, June and July. The Iris, Rushes, Willow Herb and other herbage, form a dense colony reaching 4 to 5 feet in height which creates a separate habitat for wildlife between the canal and towpathThis forms a perfect nesting site for the ever present Moorhen, and a home for the frequently encountered Water Vole, the canal's, the canals commonest mammal, it also makes a strategic perch from which the Mayfly the Caddisfly and the Giant Lacewing can pupate and hatch after their lengthy aquatic juvenile stage into their brief adult life as a flying insect. The huge green seed capsules of the Flag Iris are almost as conspicuous as the flowers and they survive well into the autumn.

Across the canal, on the far bank, the fields slope away directly from the waters edge which is dotted with Alder and Willow trees. The pastures which gradually climb away towards the horizon show signs of under nourishment and poor drainage, dotted as they are by clumps of Gorse and Rushes. Above the Lapwings wheel and circle. The dense Hawthorn hedge beside the towpath, entwined with Ivy comes to an abrupt end and is replaced by a barbed wire fence. The ground beyond the fence shows the barely covered over signs of past upheaval. The turf just manages to clothe strange mounds and depressions. Sizeable slabs of dressed stone lie haphazardly as if abandoned and, just off the towpath, a section of the long demolished bridge wall can be seen. At this point, the towpath becomes suddenly uneven, raising and dropping again where the Legh canal arm once lay beneath the humpbacked bridge.

MAY FLY

The east bank is increasingly more wooded, mature Alders and Hollies dominate. Beside the towpath, a bank rises up to form a sheltered passage along the canal. In sheltered cuttings like this, woodland birds live out their lives, seemingly oblivious to the fact that the canal runs through their woodland habitat. The tall Alders on the eastern bank provide a perfect hunting ground for the small and relatively insignificant Treecreeper.

Only fractional larger than the Blue Tit, the Treecreeper is dressed in a uniform of dull browns, grey and a white eye stripe. Very large claws on long toes and a fairly long stiff tail enable the Tree creeper to progress jerkily up tree trunks in a spiral manner. The bird is incapable of working downwards like the larger and infinitely more colourful Nuthatch so it has to fly to the base of another tree and begin again its lifelong upward journey. The canal side Alders and Oaks make an ideal habitat as the Tree Creeper feeds on insects in deep fissures in the bark probing with its long curved bill.

Once again, the canal begins to narrow as it approaches the site of another long removed swing bridge. What remains of the bridge, the stone foundations, are virtually lost from sight in the undergrowth. Matted grass has crept across the stone, forming a thin turf and saplings of Willow grow from between the huge blocks of Mill Grit. Across the canal, on the eastern bank, the remnants of a cart track drops down through the trees from the field above to the point where it used to cross the swing bridge. Tall Sycamore trees tower up out of the Hawthorn hedge beside the towpath which further add to the illusion of being surrounded by woods on either side. Immediately beyond the swing bridge foundations, the canal widens right out to its normal width. To the left of the towpath, the canal bank is once more lined with stone blocks and the waterway begins to curve very abruptly to the right. Beyond the pathside hedge, the ground drops sharply away to a group of whitewashed cottages below. In places, the Hawthorn hedge has been replaced altogether by the row of Sycamore trees, interspersed by an occasional solitary thorn bush, invariably entwined and strangled by either Honeysuckle or Ivy.

Right on the canal curve on the far bank an overflow is situated, only the second so far encountered. Designed to help maintain the canals water level to an exact degree, the excess water is taken down a wooded course into a tiny stream which is culverted beneath the canal and runs away to the west, behind the row of cottages.

Ahead another of the Macclesfield canals 'instant contrasts' is executed masterfully. Emerging from the wooded cutting, the canal now flows to on an open, airy embankment, crossing a narrow but deep valley, and continues to curve sharply to the right. Mid way across the embankment the lane beside which the row of cottages stand, passes below the canal via Red Acre aqueduct. Since leaving Marple, this is the first roadway to have passed under engineer Crossley's waterway though several have passed above. Shrigly road runs alongside the Middlewood Way from Higher Poynton before branching away near to Hag Farm, passing beneath the canal, leading eventually to West Park Gate, giving access to Lyme Park before moving on to Pott Shrigley.

Immediately prior to the passage over the aqueduct, a dizzy flight of almost forty steep stone steps, much dished and hollowed by the tread of innumerable feet, descend steeply to the lane below. Once over the Red Acre Aqueduct, and round the curve in the canal, Bridge No. 17 comes into sight, immediately ahead. Across the canal the spinney which occupiesd the eastern bank prior to Shrigley Road, has now been replaced by a small pasturefield which slopes up from the waters edge to a cluster of smallholding cottages. Known as Mitchell Fold, the tiny hamlet must once have formed a small farming community, indeed, with the area around the cottages occupied by hen sheds looseboxes, tractors and implements standing all around and the land to the west of the canal, is occupied by a livestock yard and barns, Mitchell Fold is still deeply involved with matters agricultural.

On the immediate approach to Bridge No.17, beside the towpath, a tangled bank of Dog Roses and Brambles present a dense impenetrable barrier between the towpath and the stock yard above. The bridge itself is almost identical to Numbers 13, 14 and 15 and is the last of the flat topped adjustable bridges. A stone cobbled ramp leads up from the towpath to the top of the bridge where a tiny wooden gate gives access to the narrow, unsurfaced track which passes over the bridge linking the cottages to the yard with its cattle sheds and barns. The stonework of the bridge itself bares deep rope cuts. The footbridge which spans between two stone supports is made entirely of wooden planking supported by stout bulks of timber. Relentlessly yapping farm dogs, the crowing cockerel, the deep lowing of cattle complete this scene of rural tranquillity; today, as in years gone by, Mitchell Fold is synonymous with small scale agriculture. Beyond Bridge 17, the canal quickly resumes its normal width and enters a sharp curve to the left. Across the canal, a pasture field slopes up from the waters edge where clumps of Common Rush crowd the waters margin.

The view down to the west, now available over the towpath hedge is of a pasture field. The field bares the remains of the embankment of a tramway which brought coal to the canal for loading from the nearby Red Acre Colliery. The grassy ridge of the tramway is marked by a fence. In the centre of the pasture is a flooded pit, probably a result of subsidence, which is surrounded by Alder trees. The pit or pool is distinguishable from the many others which are to be encountered in fields to right and left of the Macclesfield Canal by the fact that this one has the rusting remains of what appears to be a vintage car half in and half out of the water. From the towpath, the vehicle resembles a 1930's or 1940's Austin or Morris. Accurately identifying wild fowl from several hundred yards distant is infinitely simpler than identifying the crumbling remains of a vintage vehicle from fifty or sixty yards!!

Across the canal, the view to the east is now of green fields rising up to Red Acre Hall Farm, a large, well appointed farm which nestles among the hills . Beyond is the vast expanse of Park Moor, a huge tract of bleak moorland which again forms part of the Lyme Estate. A dense belt of marsh vegetation now stretches away parallel to the towpath. In places, a five or six feet width of vegetation separates the towpath from the actual water. Reeds, Iris, Willow Herb, Water Plantain with its broad leaves and long stalked flowers in whorles of palest pink reach out into the water.

To the west, a thin belt of mixed woodland stretches away down to the far edge of the pasture field from the canal bank. The woodland of Oak, Holly and Alder marks the position of another stream valley. This stream is not a natural one but begins its life at the canal side where a drain off paddle is situated at the head of the stream valley. The tiny stream which comprises solely of excess water from the canal and its deep valley with its mature trees, form another 'woodland' habitat within the rolling pastureland. Longtailed Tits, Blue Tits and Great Tits all inhabit the valley and flit among the trees which also conceal cooing Wood Pigeons. During the months of March and April, the canal population of Canada Geese (which spread out during their breeding season) split up into smaller groups and occupy territories while incubating their eggs. The eastern bank here is one such area which three or four geese have choosen as 'their patch'.

The land to the immediate right of the canal comprises an uneven little paddock which is separated from the towpath by, not only the customary Hawthorn hedge, but also an additional wooden post and rail fence with the extra security of sheep netting at the bottom of it A handful of goats browse in the little croft, which explains the necessity for the 'high security' fencing as goats are the natural escapologists of the livestock world. Adjacent to the grassy croft with the incessantly browsing goats, fenced off enclosures teem with scores of bantam hens. Each enclosure contains a hen shed, from the roofs of which the multicoloured bantam cockerels frantically crow their defiance to one another. The bantam stock present a staggering kaleidoscope of colour, shape and form. Brilliant iridescent colours, crests, flamboyant tails and bristling spurs set the cocks apart from the drab and dowdy hens.

The cottage to which this veritable menagerie belongs comes into view at the canal side, right on the curve in the waterway. The cottage is the classic picture postcard dwelling with tiny windows hardly big enough to admit sufficient light and petit gardens hugging the whitewashed walls. The most noticeable feature, however, is the total lack of vehicle or, for that matter, pedestrian access to the property. There is an upturned boat in the garden and the tiny wooden garden gate leads via a stone cobbled path across the towpath to an intimate stone boat jetty This small, private mooring is the sole link with the outside world other than the footway along the towpath. The backcloth to the cottage and its teeming livestock is yet another stream valley.

Immediately beyond the cottage the canal is briefly carried across the narrow but very deep valley of Rams Clough, via an embankment. Not only does the picture book cottage stand right against the canal bank, it is precariously positioned on the brink of the cascading valley side. Rams Clough stretches away from the canal to the east and west as far as the eye can see. The stream which runs through Rams Clough valley begins its journey just below Lockgate Farm on the eastern hillside. After passing through the canal embankment, the stream picks up the streamlet from the drain off paddle and Rams Clough continues westward to merge with Poynton Coppice where the stream joins Poynton Brook. The valley is wooded throughout its length, densely clothed with Hollies, Ash, Oak, Birch and Hawthorns. Down the sweeping valley sides Honeysuckle and Ivy ramble among the bushes and trees.

With Rams Clough disappearing behind, the endless crowing of the proud Bantam cockerels rings in the air. An odd pair of Canada Geese glide silently on the water and pluck at the aquatic vegetation. Pasture land slopes away from the waterside Alders on the far bank while the high bank beside the towpath is, once again a mass of tangled brambles, Ivy and Honeysuckle with, here and there, the tall stately spires of Foxgloves, growing through the thorny undergrowth. With as many as eighty separate bell flowers on a single stem, the Foxglove is one of our most conspicuous and instantly identifiable wild flowers. The beautiful pale pink-purple bells with spotted 'throats' mask its deadly toxic quality. Every part of the plant is poisonous from the roots to the exotic blooms

The high bank totally obscures the views to the west. Strong shafts of sunlight penetrating the shallow water at the canal's edge, illuminating the canal bed, reveals groups of large bivalve mollusc shells which appear quite out of place in a canal or, in fact, in a British freshwater. Shells as large as these would grace a tropical coral reef. The freshwater or Swan Mussel, sometimes reaching a shell length of nine inches, is however, a comparatively common native of muddy bottomed still waters.

The canal enters a curve to the left and the view to the east opens up as the Alders come to an end. The high bank beside the towpath also drops away to open up the view to the west. From the onset of the curve, boats are now moored in an unbroken line against the left bank. Almost as an early warning to the fact that human habitation lies directly ahead, groups of Mallards patrol the waterside. Beyond the neat Hawthorn hedge beside the towpath, a neat pasture field sweeps away from the canal. Within it lies a sizeable reed fringed pool, a handsome sheet of water which is almost concealed from view by an extremely dense planting of Scots Pine. The trees are so closely planted that all daylight is excluded from within them. Ominously worded warning signs stand sentry in the field threatening would be trespassers with prosecution. The view to the distant west is briefly of an urban sprawl, across Poynton and into Bramhall, tall buildings, indistict from this distance, loom sky-wards. Beyond the Scots Pines, the Middlewood Way, the canals ever present companion, suddenly comes into view snaking its way towards the canal. A startled cock Pheasant flies low across the pasture field from behind the towpath side hedge towards the secure gloom offered by the Pines. This most colourful and exotic of imported aliens is so commonly encountered in the British countryside that it rarely is afforded a second glance. The canal begins to widen as it continues its sweep to the left.

FOXGLOVE

The towpath bank is lined neatly with concrete as far as the eye can see into the distance as the waterway enters Lyme View Marina. The view to the east is now completely dominated by the vast bulk of Park Moor, high and featureless. A narrow strip of uneven pasture field separates the canal from the Middlewood Way, beyond which lies the cottages and smallholdings which form part of Wood Lanes, a small community within the large Parish of Adlington.

Extensive mooring bays lie to the west of the main waterway which, provide mooring for upward of one hundred and sixty boats. The deep, wooded cutting, containing the Middlewood Way with its footpath cycleway and bridleway is little more than fifty yards distant from the towpath. Suddenly, a tall mound rears up out of the strip of pasture which separates the two linear thoroughfares.The mound marks the end of a tramway where coal carried in wagons arrived at the canal side from nearby Kingfield Pit. The mound also bears the remnants of another removed bridge which once crossed the canal at this point. It was necessary for the coal to cross the canal to be unloaded from the wagons and loaded into narrowboats as as not to obstruct the busy towpath Kingfield Pit was the most southerly colliery on the extensive Poynton coal field or may be , the largest of the Adlington collieries as it unquestionably was. The coal seams were exhausted by 1888 and the mine closed and the tramway and the bridge fell into dereliction. Small pits on the eastern bank were so close to the waterway that they could almost deposit their coal into boats waiting in the wharf which has now become the extensive moorings of the marina, several acres in area. Kingfield Pit was the property of the Legh Family of Adlington Hall.

Beside the towpath, the next milestone is encountered. A rather short squat original stone,it leans drunkenly towards the hedge. Consequently, it is necessary to stoop to read "From Marple 5", "From Hall Green 21 1/4" The mooring area across the canal and its attendant, and equally extensive, car parking, reverberate with activity, the sound of people, relaxing or maintaining their prized narrowboat or cruiser, distant sawing of wood, shouting children, the smell of paint or the chugging of a manoeuvering boat.

The canal stretches out straight towards Bridge No. 18 in the distance. A short distance before the bridge, a set of steps from the tow path leads down to a

wooden cabin which, as a shop, provides the canal user, be he boat user, angler, walker, or jogger with a cool drink or ice cream in the summer months, or steaming hot soup, Bovril, coffee or tea and piping hot pies in the grip of winter. Benches, around a paved area flanked by grass which blazes with golden Daffodils in March, provide foot sore travellers with a welcome respite. Souvenirs and canal publications vie for space with baskets of fresh laid free range eggs and fresh farm milk. Beyond the cabin, a tiny lane is carried over a railway bridge which spans the Middlewood Way. This meeting place of leisure interests, cyclists and equestrian riders, holiday makers and week-end cruisers parties of competition anglers and, armies of ramblers, all converging on the tiny hamlet of Wood Lane has almost given it holiday resort status Wood Lane itself just over the Middlewood Way is aptly named as the communities heart its pub "The Miners Arms", its Methodist church, its telephone kiosk and the village stores all straddle junctions of Wood Lane North, Wood Lane South and Wood Lane West!

In front of the bridge, the canal widens out into a spacious bay "Adlington Basin". At the time of the canals completion, the area now occupied by Bridge No.18, was already the heart of the Adlington Collieries, consequently, the large wharf now occupied by the Marina and the spacious turning basin were of vital importance. A concrete launch - slipway enters the bay from the west bank. The tiny lane, having passed over the Middlewood Way now reaches up to and over the canal bridge.

The bridge itself is a return to the noble gritstone arch, the first stone canal bridge since the A6 highway crossed the canal at High Lane. No.18 is a particularly sturdy solid bridge whose stones bare deep rope cuts and grooves. Passing through the bridge, Adlington Basin and the bustling Marina are left behind, the journey across the exhausted coalfield of Poynton and Adlington is over and the next leg of the journey southwards lies ahead.

Chapter 3
ADLINGTON TO BOLLINGTON

Having passed beneath bridge No 18, a flight of stone steps lead up from the towpath to the lane above. The far bank is unlined ,with clumps of rush and Sedge grow ing out into the water. A marshy field climbs away from the waters edge. Beside the towpath, a very low, hard cropped Hawthorn hedge borders a narrow strip of lush but marshy pasture which separates the canal from the deep cutting which carries the Middlewood Way.

In the more distant west, the housing of Wood Lanes disappears slowly to give way to open countryside. In the field which rises away to the east, a flooded pit hole in visible from the canal. It is surrounded, at least in part, by Hawthorn trees, Gorse, squat Willow trees and one tall Oak which stands sentry over all. The scores of flooded pit holes to be seen in fields to both east and west of the canal are typical of many thousands to be found throughout the county of Cheshire. The vast majority of these are flooded marl pits or marl holes. Marl digging throughout the last two or three centuries was not confined solely to Cheshire, but the ample deposits of marl (which is a light clay with rich fertilizing qualities) to be found here, supported it's own industry.

Itinerant bands of marl diggers roamed the county contracting their labour to dig the marl and to spread it over as many pastures as could be supplied. It was common practice, to permanently destroy a very small portion of a field to improve the quality of many surrounding acres. The hole was dug usually in the centre of the field, but occasionally a 'double' pit will be encountered, where the marl diggers revisited a farm, years or even decades after leaving a previously flooded pit. If the first pit had provided generous quantities of marl, a second would be dug directly alongside the original one but a thin strip of land like a causeway would be left between the two.

This division was known as the 'Midfeather' and prevented the water from the original pit leaching into the new one while it was still being worked. The legacy of countless flooded marl holes have permanently altered the natural ecology of Cheshire. Although most are individually quite small in surface area, collectively, they have added many hundreds of acres of water to Cheshire, providing valuable habitat for aquatic life. Like the canal, the field pit sports it's own typical wildlife which will be representative wherever in Cheshire the pit is situated. This particular pit, just south-east of bridge No 18, displays a sign board out in the water, probably advising would be anglers that the fishing is privately controlled. The fish, encountered in a typical pit will be totally different from the canals typical species. Whereas the classic canal fish is the Roach, the most prolific pit fish is the closest cousin of the Roach, the Rudd which is totally absent from the canal.

The layman often confuses the Roach with the Rudd but the latter is a totally more handsome creature with rich blue/black back, silvery white belly and deep blood red fins. The mouth of the Rudd is oblique or somewhat underslung and upturned which marks the fish as a surface feeder whereas the Roach mainly feeds at mid-water, or on or near to the bottom. The Rudd is often the only species of fish to be found in a pit where man has not had a hand in artificially introducing other species. The other species commonly found alongside the Rudd and also found in vast numbers in the canal is the noble Perch.

The Perch is, beyond doubt, the most versatile and adaptable of all fish, in British freshwater. It is found in considerable numbers in the canal but is definitely an artificial introduction. In a rich, deep lowland pool or lake, it will breed sparingly but individual fish will achieve a considerable body size. In a closely confined water like a pit or a farm pond, it chooses to breed relentlessly, but all the fish will be found to be 'stunted' to a maximum size which is governed by the available food, above which the fish never grows. The more prolifically it breeds, the smaller the stunted size. The largest Perch are to be found either in slow flowing rivers or in deep reservoirs and meres. During the early nineteen sixties, the author well recalls being able to , kneel beneath any bridge along the canal, and upon gazing into the gloom of the deep water, seeing a sizable Perch hanging motionless in the shadowy water. Quite why this situation should be so commonly encountered can only be guessed at but, what is certain is that the catastrophic disease which decimated the nation's stock of Perch throughout the mid and late nineteen sixties took its toll on the larger canal Perch. The dark green back and sides with six to nine black transverse stripes, red pelvic and anal fins and spiny double dorsal fins all set the Perch apart from any other fish to be encountered in British waters. The Rudd and the Perch are able to find their way around the country, from pit to pit without interference by man by travelling in the form of fertile eggs stuck to the feet and legs of water fowl, predominantly ducks and to a lesser extent, Herons and Moorhens.

PERCH

Beyond the pit hole, the view to the distant east is still dominated by dark, brooding moorland. Down to the right or the west of the canal, the thin strip of lush pasture is liberally dotted with clumps of rushes , plainly, it pays the penalty for lying between six to eight feet below the level of the waterway. The canal's far bank is temporarily sheet metal lined as the eastern pasture field dips away into a small stream valley. As is usually the case, the lie of the valley is clearly defined by a line of Oak and Holly trees. Down to the west, the Middlewood Way moves further and further away from the canal, widening out the wedge of pasture which lies between, where sheep now graze. The sheep pasture gently dips down to the tiny stream which has now been culverted beneath the canal. The trickle of water is little more than a land drain but is still culverted correctly beneath the waterway as would be a major stream or river. Beyond the stream's course, the Middlewood Way moves, once more out of sight.

The view ahead now opens out to provide a distant glimpse of Bridge No. 19. Flying ducks, winging their way down the waterway, swoop low and crash down onto the water in a most undignified fashion. A line of tall, mature Alder trees line the water's edge on the canal's eastern bank, stretching away in a fairly regimented column towards the distant bridge. Somewhere, out of sight, above the fields beside the canal, a Skylark sings, an endless cascade of song which goes hand in hand with the warmer months of the year. This wonderful symphony of bird song is so much an integral part of the countryside that it becomes no more noticeable than the background drone of insects. The Skylark rises almost vertically in a hovering flight, often to several hundred feet, sustaining its clear warbling song even as it sinks gradually back down to the ground.

In the distant east, the plaintive cry of the Lapwing echoes above the rising ground. The water's edge beside the towpath is now an unruly mass of rushes, Sedges, saplings of Alder and Willows and Cow Parsley , which during April, May and June, flowers in a mass of white. Cow Parsley is the first of the parsley family to flower, most commonly seen by the roadside where its masses of flowers seem to roll like a breaking wave as passing traffic relentlessly roars by. Rough Chervil follows the Cow Parsley into flower during June and July, followed by Hogweed to continue the succession of bloom through to September. Across the canal, the pasture field is replaced by a rough bank which rises steeply away from the water. The bank is overgrown by swaying masses of Willow Herb and huge thickets of brambles. A tall hedgerow of Hollies interspersed with Oak trees towers above the bank and, through gaps in the hedge, rows of static caravans in every conceivable colour stand in strictly regimented lines.

The occasional view of caravans through the tall hedgerow, across the water reveals the large commercial caravan site at Woodend Farm which evolved from the great enthusiasm in the 'outdoor movement' during the nineteen twenties and thirties when the Pennine Foothills and areas of Cheshire close to such early tourism 'hotspots' as Lyme Park became holiday areas in their own right. A mass exodus of town dwellers, hungry for countryside recreation, would emigrate out from Manchester on Sundays and during public holidays so the need arose for inexpensive accommodation. The gradual development of the caravan made the countryside retreat more accessible to more people and this particular site was considered ideal due to its close proximity to Lyme Park, the Peak District and, the market town of Macclesfield. The proximity of the canal provided ample opportunities for hiking and angling.

Just before the bridge, the next set of stop planks is encountered in its wooden clamp. Just how often they are needed for their correct use is debatable but many a pic-nic or a rest has been enjoyed sitting above the towpath, in the shadow of a bridge, on the stop planks.

A flight of stone steps with a wooden hand rail leads up from the towpath to the track. The track leads over the bridge linking Woodend Farm and the large caravan park with Jepsonclough Farm down to the west and eventually leads to on Wood Lane South. Bridge No. 19 is another classic stone arch, a tribute to the stonemason of yester-year. Certain bridges along the canal's course display strange marks in some of the stones which are 'toolmarks' or signatures cut by the stonemason who dressed the blocks. Each mason had his own 'toolmark' just as the great wood carvers often carved their own tradmark on pieces of furinture. It has been said that the very character of the Macclesfield canal is derived from the rocky Pennine Hills for it is the stone (of the bridges, lock chambers etc) which marks its route and gives it its special quality. As the waterway was constructed so late in the canal era, it reflects the confidence of the engineers vast experience, amassed over a long period. The high embankments, bridges, deep cuttings and the magnificent group of locks at Bosley (which divide the Marple to Bosley five hundred foot level from the Bosley to Kidsgrove four hundred foot level) are obvious examples of the engineers self confidence. Brilliantly carved, exstravagently ornate, the bridges are so solid and

STOP PLANKS

permanant as to appear immortal.

After passing beneath Bridge No.19, the canal widens out to its normal width and is straight away lined at each bank, the far bank by concrete and the towpath bank by sheet metal. The reason for the lining is that immediatly upon leaving the bridge, the canal is embanked and continues to be so for the next eight hundred yards or so; half a mile of handbuilt embankment. From the canal's eastern bank, immacultely manuicured lawn sweeps away towards a beautiful farmhouse. The house is timber framed in finest Cheshire tradition and the panels between the Oak framework gleam brilliantly white. The property is roofed with stone slates of gigantic proportions which would surely flatten a dwelling of more feeble construction. Plantings of Larch trees, Scots Pines and stands of Lawsons Cypresses crowd round the tarmac drive which sweeps down to the property. Groups of Elwood and Leyland conifers partly conceal the house from view. The canal is carried well above the level of the house . Beautifully clipped grass which, in season is clothed in hugh drifts of golden Daffodils, slopes directly away from the canal's edge. Beside the towpath, a very tall and dense hedge almost hides from view the uncultivated valley which slopes gently away from the canal. Across the waterway a sizable reed fringed pool shimmers beside the house with its Weeping Willows, and the obligatory Canada Geese.

In the distant east, the moorland, which has dominated the eastern horizon right from High Lane, comes to a dramatic end where stone quarrying on a massive scale has literally taken a huge bite out of the end of the moor. Beyond the path and mountainous unkept hedge, the valley is a mixture of marshy grassland and spinneys of trees. The waterway begins to curve to the right. The garden on the left bank abruptly ends and as it does, the most curious building occupies the canals bank. In the field on the eastern side of the canal, during the nineteen fifties, wooden chalets were erected by the previously described 'outward bound' town dwellers, desperately seeking that idyllic spot for the week end away or a holiday in Cheshire's green and tranquil countryside.

Almost all of the now disused chalets have been demolished, have fallen down or have been blown down but the one which remains, at the waters edge, now in a state of total dilapidation must surely have surpassed all of the others in sheer inventiveness. Through the overgrown vegetation and complete decay, it is still recognizable as a mock Tudor chalet which "epitomizes the arcadia desires" of a town dweller. It was constructed in 1954 by a retired couple from Manchester who craved their own Cheshire cottage retreat.

The black and white architecture echoing the noble farm house next door, the once tidy cottage garden, even the outdoor toilet with a horseshoe on the door have now almost totally been reclaimed by nature. The climbing roses which once decorated the walls now reach up to and over the roof (which sags alarmingly) and are now the only things holding the building together. The two interior rooms with diamond shaped leaded windows were heated by coal fires but, as neglect has become dereliction, this last remnant of a bygone chapter in the long story in the quest for leisure, will soon be gone for ever.

The field where the chalets once stood is dotted with gorse and boggy areas of rushes and slopes steeply away from the embanked canal. The stone quarry on the end of the moor looms to the distant east but, now, a densely wooded hill moves into view in the middle distance between the canal and the moorland. The hill is known as the Oakridge, but, from the towpath, it would seem to be completely planted up with Scots Pine. The canal straightens out and both banks are lined up as far ahead as the eye can see. Tall Hawthorn and Gorse bushes, ablaze for the first half of the year, with yellow flowers, mark the eastern bank before it plunges steeply away into the valley beyond.

The valley is now thickly wooded with Oaks, Ashes, Sycamores, Black Poplars, Hollies and Alders as Blakehey Wood the largest stretch of woodland within the town of Pott Shrigley, stretches down to the waters edge. From the towpath, the eastern view is through the tree tops of Blackehey Wood, looking towards the more distant Oakridge which now obscures the view of the moorland. The melodic cooing of Wood Pigeons echo from both sides of the valley and occasionally the raucous rattle of a Woodpecker attacking a dead bough in search of grubs and larvae, bursts forth like machine gun fire.

Beside the towpath, the tall hedge ends abruptly affording an uninterrupted view down into the valley to the west. The hedge has been replaced by a most unusual "fence", a fence of stone slabs, not unlike graveyard headstones. Each stands about a yard high, eight feet apart, and have two circular holes, approximately four inches in circumference, one at the top and one at bottom. The fence, which was installed at the canals completion, marking the highest stretch of this extremely long embankment, was actually made up of materials which were both convenient and close to hand. The stone posts came from the extensive quarry on the moor and the holes originally carried two strands of steel winding ropes from a nearby colliery, strung from post to post. Beyond the stone fence, the valley degenerates into a jungle of Oaks, Hawthorns, Ashes and vast thickets of Brambles and Dog Rose where Magpies flit through the tree tops.

When the woodland to the east comes to an end, it is replaced by lush green pastures climbing up towards Normans Hall Farm. Sheep graze the sloping valley land. Scores of large Rooks probe the pasture turf in search of insect larvae and worms. The sheep and the Rooks forage together on the rising ground, intermingled like the black and white of piano keys.

Still steeply banked, the canal straightens out and the tall Hawthorn hedge once again towers above the pathway, replacing the stone fence. Tall Alder, Hawthorn and Sycamore trees line the far bank, giving the canal a sheltered passage. Where the water is sheltered from cross winds or breezes and the surface is as calm as a mil pool, small Roach can be seen to be dimpling the waters surface as they top or rise to take an insect on the surface film. The brilliant yellow of Coltsfoot growing beside the towpath, flowering from early March, breaks up the endless green. As winter draws to a close, the Coltsfoot is so eager to burst into flower that it does not even wait for the leaves to form. The stems covered with many over lapping fleshy purple scales, fairly burst from the cold ground to bare the vivid yellow/orange flower heads aloft. From April through to October the Dandelion takes over the role of the Coltsfoot, decorating the waterside with a golden blaze of colour.

The valley to the west of the canal is quite densely wooded and a stream or brook can be heard tricking and babbling somewhere, as yet, out of sight. The wayward Hawthorn hedge overhangs the towpath alarmingly. On rounding a sharp, right hand curve, the canal suddenly widens out into a bay. The waterway is instantly one hundred feet wide; quiet, calm, dark water. The bay is actuely square in construction and is the site of Ryles Wharf. This was originally owned and operated by the nearby Styperson stone quarries. This stone was greatly prized as a building stone, vast quantities being used on the building of the Macclesfield, Bollington and Marple railway (now the Middlewood Way). The profusion of trees all around the Wharf is due to the fact that the canal cuts through the valley of an ancient woodland, namely Ryles wood, which gives the wharf its name.

On completing the curve in the canal, Bridge No. 20. is ahead, surrounded and overshadowed by tall Sycamore trees. On the approach to the bridge, the first overflow sill or "wash", to be sited on the towpath side of the canal is encountered. The sill is one hundred and five feet long and the canal is contained by a concrete wall just over one foot wide and the exact height of the canals normal water level. Below this retaining sill and the towpath is a channel with a sloping bottom. It starts at three inches below canal level at the bridge end and slopes to three feet at the other end, whereupon, the excess water which escapes from the canal over the sill is culverted beneath the towpath into the stream which runs away through the wooded valley to the right of the towpath. The overflow sill runs for the width of the wharf, forming an almost perfect one hundred foot square of water in front of the bridge. A strategically positioned pathside seat stands opposite to the wharf where one can sit and contemplate the perfectly still, quiet water which mirrors the images of the towering Sycamores. Spring Bank Lane passes over the bridge as it climbs its way out of the tiny hamlet of Booth Green, on its way up to Pott Shrigley.

The actual village of Pott Shrigley, which includes the Styperson area is situated within the Peak National Park comprising "a scattered, upland village on the western edge of the Pennines." The name "Pott Shrigley" is a curious one whose origins are non too clear. It is most unlikely that the land owning family brought their name with them, this was not the way in which things were done;

quite the contrary, the Shrigleys, the earliest recorded landowners would have taken their name from locality. It seems likely that the word "Pott" comes from an old word meaning a pool (which probably refers to the low lying and marshy land to the north-west of the parish church) and "Shrigley" denotes a woodland clearing.

Bridge No.20. itself is a standard stone arch beyond which, a steep flight of sixteen stone steps lead up to Spring Back Lane. Beyond the bridge on the towpath bank, the next set of stop planks is encountered. Unusually, this set is housed, not in the customary wooden clamp but in a concrete box of building block construction and covered with a solid concrete "lid" but open to one end to make sliding the planks in and out possible. Aesthetically, this odd construction is grotesque when compared with the ususal wooden clamp but, at least, it provides a cooling seat in very hot weather. A very low hedge beside the towpath, gives a good view across undulating pasture to the west.

The woodland on the eastern bank peters out as the canal leaves the valley of Ryles Wood but a regimented row of Alder trees remain, lining the canals far bank into the distance. The Alder roots reaching out into, and up out of the water like so many sinuous tentacles, rises away to the horizon. Beside the towpath, the next milestone is situated, leaning at a crazy angle towards the hedge. It is partly concealed by Ivy which rambles over both the ground and through the bottom of the hedge. It is an original stone reading, "From Marple 6 Miles", "From Hall Green twenty and a quarter miles". The words Marple and Hall Green were painstakingly removed by chisel during World War Two to disorientate the invading enemy.

Down to the west, the pasture field, dotted with Oak trees, hosts a flooded pit hole, almost certainly another example of marl extraction. A considerable view is now available down the west where the near distance is dominated by an excellent view of Woodford Aerodrome. The extensive airfield at Woodford, some two and a half to three miles due west is not a commercial airport but a British Aerospace factory which presently employs in the region of 3,000 people.

New Hall Farm Woodford dated 1630, was purchased by A.V. Roe in 1925 for use as an airfield. From humble beginnings, the airstrip has evolved into the thriving complex which has been used for the assembly of Lancaster & Shackleton bombers. Light aircraft have been produced and the A.T.P. and 146 Airliners are currently being assembled. As an aircraft factory Woodford is probably best known as the birthplace of one of the most evocative military aircraft of the century, the awesome Vulcan Bomber.

Beyond Woodford lies the sprawl of Handforth and beyond, Greater Manchester stretches, seemingly to the horizon, with its tower blocks, factory chimneys and scores of church spires, rising from the maze. To the east, across the rising grassland, a narrow lane comes into view as it makes its way down towards the canal. In the distance, a large bungalow set in extensive gardens, can be seen to occupy the eastern bank. The canals unlined margins are indistinct with clumps of Reed, Sedge, Willow saplings and colonies of Flag Iris growing out into the water.

Rounding a curve in the waterway, the eastern bank is occupied by the gardens which surround the fine detached bungalow.Sweeping lawns dotted with shrubs and trees roll down to the water. A wooden stile is set in the hedge beside the towpath where a yellow painted arrow directs walkers towards a footpath, running roughly diagonally across the meadow to the west which passes Springbank Farm and Jepsonclough Farm on its way back towards Wood Lanes.Gazing along the line of this footpath, the view, looking north west, is clearly of Stockport. The modern bungalow on the far bank occupies the site where Styeperson quarry had its main wharf. Massive slabs of stone would be transported down to here from the quarry to be sawn into slices which were easily handleable so that they could be loaded into waiting boats. Bridge No. 21, Brookledge Lane Bridge is now directly ahead.On the approach, a lush growth of Ivy which smothers the bank to the right of the towpath swarms up onto the stonework of the bridge itself and threatens to engulf it in its stranglehold.

Although the canal travels the whole length of the large rural parish of Adlington, Bridge no. 21 is the nearest to the focal point of the parish, Adlington Hall, the seat of the family of Legh of Adlington (pronounced Lee.) Almost exactly two miles to the west of this bridge, the hall lies just beyond the main Macclesfield to Stockport road. Prior to the Norman conquest, Adlington was held by the Saxon earl Edwin, not as a residence, but as a hunting lodge in the formerly vast forest of Macclesfield. After the conquest, Adlington passed into the ownership of Hugh Lupus, the first earl of Chester and nephew of William the Conqueror. The Domesday Survey conducted after the conquest lists Adlington as "Edulvinstane".

The original hunting lodge, built for Edwin the Saxon, was constructed around two massive Oak trees which were left growing and firmly rooted in the ground. Incredibly, the same two Oaks still support the eastern end of the Great Hall. The Great Hall, as seen today, was started somewhere around the year 1480. The twin Oaks still have their roots in the ground but the trunks have been carved with an adze so that they are now octagonal. Between the trees is an organ. There is evidence that a small organ existed at Adlington in about 1640. Some years after the restoration of the monarchy, the present organ was built (c 1670) and it incorporates the console of the pre-Cromwellian instrument. It represents the largest 17th Century organ in the country. During the early thirteenth century, Adlington was granted to the De Corona family. The last member of the De Corona line, Ellen, married John de Legh in 1315. This began the association of the Legh family with Adlington which continues to the present day.

Unlike the great house previously described at Lyme, Adlington Hall, by its own admission, does not profess to be one of the great country mansions of England. Having said this, it is a strikingly handsome, yet homely building. The building, which is quadrangular in shape is a mixture of differing styles and architectural periods. The timber framed "black and white" east wing is Elizabethan. The Georgian south front, connecting the west wing with the old Elizabethan east wing, was built in the the mid Eighteenth Century. This brick and stone frontage is most impressive, its two stories being divided into thirteen bays and central to the front is a tall portico with four Ionic columns on octagonal pedestals. The pediment above is adorned with the Legh arms and below in letters of stone, "Charles and Hester Legh 1757". The entire building is roofed with flags of stone from nearby Kerridge. Continuing our southward journey through Adlington, bridge no 21 carries Brook Ledge Lane which leads from Adlington up to Pott Shrigley.

It is not only the canal traveller who can be forgiven for not realizing that he is in close proximity of Adlington, the village, but likewise, the motorist who speeds along the A523 between Macclesfield and Hazel Grove will search in vain for the 'village'. Adlington is, in fact, what historians classify as a dispersed village. It is made up of a number of small hamlets which are widely scattered over an area in excess of 4,000 acres, yet its population is slightly less than 1,000 souls. It is ironic therefore that Adlington's assessment in the Domesday Survey of 1080 refers to its 21 acres of good meadow which was the highest such figure for the entire county, indicating that, at the time of the survey, the thriving agricultural settlement of "Edulvinstane" was the most intensively farmed in Cheshire.

Another total contrast is executed as the scene beyond the bridge is revealed, a mighty Hawthorn hedgerow towers twenty feet above the canals far bank. On the towpath bank, a ramp path leads up to Brook Ledge Lane. No view to the west exists at all due to a huge thicket of Damson trees, a veritable jungle of fruit bushes which are a mass of white blossom in April. The Damsons smother a steep bank which rises up towards the mature garden of a fine detached house. It will be from this garden that the Damsons originally escaped. During late April, the Damsons shower the towpath and canal with a blizzard of confetti when the delicate white blossom falls in masses.

The canals far bank is lined by sheet metal and a marshy area lies between it and the mountainous hedgerow. This wet strip is home to Rushes, Sedges, Branched Bur Reed and Common Horse Tail. The canal curves gently ahead and is totally sheltered by a towering hedge to the left and the high bank to the right. The mature condition of the beautiful shrub garden lying beyond the high bank, adds to the sheltering effect as dark conifers rise fifteen and twenty feet above the high bank. Rounding the canals curve, a straight length stretches away into the distance. Masses of Dog Roses tumble down the bank to the towpath's edge.

Tall Sycamores rear upward from the bank, strangling Ivy creeping up their trunks and into their branches. A large detached house with brilliantly whitewashed walls and heavily slated roof is partly concealed by banks of early flowering Rhododendrons.

Pairs of patrolling Mallards dart at a wayward leaf floating on the waters surface or at a passing raft of Damson blossom assuming that everything which floats is food. A view of the fine garden reveals rolling lawns dotted with large flowering shrubs and huge drifts of naturalized Daffodils. As the Hawthorn on the eastern bank begins to thin, a strip of pasture is revealed, separating the canal from a lane which runs parallel. This is Sugar Lane which branched off Brook Ledge Lane just beyond Bridge No. 21. It runs due south through the Styeperson quarries towards Bollington and will cross the canal further along the route. Beside the towpath, the fine garden ends quite abruptly and becomes woodland and cascades away from the pathside as the ground now falls steeply away to the west.

Across to the east, Sugar Lane moves further away from the canals course and climbs upward to the quarried hillside above. Woodpeckers, attaking a dead bough in the Bartons Clough Wood to the west with great enthusiasm, echo their deafening attack through the still air. The marshy area across the canal, on the far bank is enriched with handsome clumps of Marsh Marigold, the absolute gem of the waterside. This is a widespread native plant which would not appear out of place in the most choice collection of garden plants. The brilliant yellow flowers and glossy leaves can be seen from April, the flowers lasting through to late July.

Rounding a gentle curve to the right, Bridge No. 22 is visible in the distance. The canal's banks are both sheet metal lined as, once again, the waterway is briefly embanked across a deep valley. Bartons Clough Wood fairly tumbles away from the canal's edge and, through April and May, the steeply sloping woodland floor is a wonderful carpet of Bluebells.

MARSH MARIGOLD

Beyond the canal's passage across the valley, stands Bridge No. 22. The remnants of Styeperson quarry looms in the distant east as the bridge is reached. Bridge No. 23 can be seen in the distance, framed in the arch of No. 22. The fact that Bridge No. 23 is so perfectly mirrored in the arch of No. 22 is an indication as to just how straight the length of canal between the two bridges really is. The mellow stone of the bridge harmonizes with the surrounding herbage so as to appear as a natural part of the scenery, instead of the man made edifice which it really is.

Hawthorns overhang the towpath and a flight of fourteen stone steps lead up from the path to the top of the bridge, where a rough trackway lies. The trackway forms part of a public right of way between Sugar Lane to the east and the Middlewood Way which actually runs close by to the west. Bridge No. 22 has stop plank grooves below its arch and upon emerging from the bridge, the rotting remnants of a long abandoned stop plank stand is almost lost in the pathside vegetation. The woodland no longer occupies the west bank and the east bank is taken up by the gardens and lawns of a large white house standing above a bank of brambles which reaches down to the waters edge. Looking forward to Bridge No. 23, the customary wooden seat is situated beside the towpath.

The view to the west begins to open up and the impression is that the canal is elevated as the view seems to be almost downwards across the Cheshire plain. The view is actually of Adlington, Mottram and towards Alderly Edge. The view to the east of the canal, beyond the line of Hawthorn trees which line the far bank, is of a pasture field which leads up towards a large farm house and its attendant outbuildings which appear to be in a state of semi dereliction. The building closest to the canal is the gaunt skeleton of a dutch barn with rusty corrugated metal sheets hanging from the woodwork which creak when touched by the slightest breeze. A modest quantity of partly rotted or badly weather-damaged hay finds a modicum of shelter beneath what roofing sheets remain on the old barn. The remaining farm buildings and indeed the house itself, Clarke Green Farm, would seem to be in a similar state of partial dereliction beyond which the ground gradually rises up towards Nab Head

The cutting which carries the Middlewood Way comes into view once more down to the west. Again, the two parallel trade routes of yester-year, both transporting their respective cargoes between Macclesfield and Marple are but one field apart. Across the Middlewood Way and the patchwork of pastureland, the view across Cheshire is breathtaking considering that the hills on the far western horizon are in Wales. The ground between the canal and the Middlewood Way drops steeply away from the towpath, consequently, the canal is now half embanked. On the rising ground, Lapwings search the turf for insects and grubs. A grass valley lies beyond the canal to the east where a herd of black and white and red and white Hereford cattle are watched over by a Charolais bull of monstrous proportions.

Immediately beyond the embankment, the canal widens out into a wide hole or turning hole. The wide expanse of turning space here was originally used by boats waiting to be loaded with coal from Winterfold Pit which was once the most southerly of the Adlington collieries. A great feeling of spaciousness and openness prevails as Bridge No. 23 is reached, taking in the rolling vista up to the east, of the grassy valley stretching up towards Nabhead and down to the west, over the Middlewood Way, Higher Doles Farm, and right across the Cheshire plain, into Wales. Another notable feature of the view westwards is the occasional spectacle of huge airliners climbing steeply away from Manchester International Airport at Ringway. They seem to appear suddenly as if out of the ground, already labouring upwards.

Bridge No. 23, a pleasant stone arch, carries nothing more than a grass footpath. An uneven set of stone steps lead up from the towpath to the bridge, deeply dished by the passing of many feet. The one feature which makes this idyllic, rural bridge of special note is that on top stands the remains of a huge block or cube of solid concrete which, like the removal or defacing of milestones and the pill box beside Bridge No. 13 at Middlewood, is another remnant of wartime defensive precaution. The concrete block was originally placed squarely on top of the humpback to prevent enemy vehicles from passing over. Beneath Bridge No. 23, number 24 is clearly visible some little distance ahead.

A level grass field stretches away from the waters edge to the east. Obviously not a pasture field, the lush, dark seed grass is a product of chemical control and intensive fertilizer and a far cry from the pleasant sward of pasture field with its Daisies, Clovers and multitudes of flowering and seeding herbage. Large mature Willow trees overshadow the wide waterway between bridges 23 and 24. From among the Willows, Dog Roses trail down to touch the water. Large colonies of Rushes, Sedges and Yellow Flag Iris encroach ever further out into the canal from its unlined banks, where small Roach "plop" loudly as they enthusiastically rise to take insects from the surface film, sending ripples spiraling out towards the banks.

Drawing nearer to Bridge No. 24, the far bank begins to degenerate into reedy marshland. In the bottom of the pathside hedge, an unexpected garden escapee is found making a valiant attempt to choke and ultimately displace the Hawthorn. Strangely enough, the dense patch of Gooseberry bushes do not appear at all out of place. Across the canal, the marshy area becomes ever more extensive. Amid this area of rushes and Sedges lies another flooded area, almost certainly another worked out marl pit.

As the canal begins to narrow to Bridge No. 24, number 25 can be seen very clearly ahead. Over the course of this last mile or so, this unusual situation has occurred again and again where the bridges are unusually close together and the canal is uncommonly straight in its course. A second concrete block, identical to the one of Bridge No. 23 can be seen on the apex of the bridge. The bridge itself is interesting, a low, squat stone arch which has, at some time, been 'extended' in height above the original stonework. At some later date, approximately a yard of concrete wall has been added. What can actually be seen is an original stone bridge, topped off by a stone coping then a yard high concrete wall topped by a concrete coping. Added to this, the massive concrete block on top of the bridge presents an unusual picture. Another feature of Bridge No. 24 is that no access exists between the towpath and the bridge top. So far, this is the first instance in the twenty four bridges so far encountered where there is no public right of way across the top.

Beyond the bridge, a pasture slopes away to the Middlewood Way and beyond that lies the hamlet of Whitely Green. The canal, from Bridge No. 24, curves gently to the left up to Bridge No. 25 which lies just ahead. The pasture to the west comes to an end and is replaced by a busy transport yard which, thankfully, is largely hidden behind a mountainous hedge. Row upon row of huge container wagons are packed into the available space in the yard. A whole transport fleet is almost completely concealed by the huge hedge which, here and there is reinforced by panels and interwoven fencing. Looking back now to Bridge No. 24, through its archway, Bridge No. 23 is perfectly framed and likewise, in its arch, as though in miniature, the arch of No. 22 can be seen quite clearly.

As Bridge No. 25 is neared, a yellow painted sign board on the far bank explains that the next stretch of bank is "N.C.C.C. private moorings". As with the whole of the High Lane canal arm (see chapter 2) the east bank of the waterway here up to Bridge No. 25 is held by the North Cheshire Cruising Club as reserved moorings. The busy little lane which crosses Bridge No. 25, Holehouse Lane, commences at a junction with Sugar Lane, which still runs, roughly parallel to the east of the canal. After crossing the canal, Holehouse Lane provides the transport business with its link with the outside world. Immediately upon crossing the Middlewood Way which, as ever, lies just out of sight to the west, the lane form the thoroughfare through the hamlet of Whitely Green before joining the main Macclesfield to Stockport road From the point of view of the local historian, Bridge No. 25 is one of the most interesting along the Macclesfield Canal. On top of the bridge, looking northwards up the canal, a strange inscription will be found on the bridge wall above the key stone. The passage of time has partially obliterated the poignant message which tells of fate of two young lovers whose impossible affair led to them throwing themselves from the bridge with wrists bound tightly together in the hope of finding eternal peace beyond the dark water beneath Holehouse Lane .

The message reads;

"Lovers Leap June 1894"

The further inscription below is indecipherable due to a combination of weathering and lichen incrustation.

Emerging from Bridge No. 25, a pasture stretches away from the canal's far bank with fresh young bushes of Gorse overhanging the waters edge, a vivid mass of golden flowers. A few yards out from the bridge, the next milestone is encountered beside the towpath. Again it is an original stone which almost defies reading. "From Hall Green" is almost unrecognizable and the actual mileage, i.e. Nineteen and a Quarter, is not legible at all. The other side reads "From ———", the word

Marple has been completely obliterated and again, the lettering, "Seven Miles" cannot be read at all. A thick incrustation by Lichen does not help in the deciphering of the stones' message.

To the east, a tall, stately row of Lombardy Poplar trees mark the course of a driveway which leads from Holehouse Lane to several properties at Lane Head which stands above the canals far bank. It is, however, the view directly ahead which draws the attention as a hill towers above the canal to the east with the town of Bollington nestling in its shelter. On the highest point of this hill, which is called Kerridge Hill, stands the brilliant white monument known as White Nancy. Unlike the previous landmark, Lyme Cage, with its brooding air of mystery, White Nancy is almost comical. Standing at the absolute peak of Kerridge Hill, White Nancy is visible for many miles around.

During April and May, brilliant white drifts of flowers mingle with the grasses and Dandelions of the pathside bank. The Greater Stitchwort is responsible for the frothing foam of white flowers. The leaves are narrow, stiff and lance shaped but totally lost among the bankside grasses. The pure white profusion of tiny blooms betray its presence among the encroaching grass. The waterway begins to curve gently to the left ahead, clumps of Flag Iris and Sedge venturing out into the water from unlined margins.

The bulk of Kerridge Hill looms to the south east with the strange form of the brilliant white monument catching the eye as it seems to shine with an inner light when caught by the sunlight. As the canal continues to curve, the far bank degenerates into what at first appears to be another cattle drinking hole, but continues to widen out into a bay, the original use of which has been lost with the passage of time. The whole bay is overhung from the far bank by a huge Willow tree.

The pasture on the eastern bank is divided by the remains of an ancient dry stone wall, now in a ruinous condition. At some time, a hedgerow has been planted along the line of the wall. Over the centuries, this hedgerow has died and largely disappeared leaving an odd twisted and contorted Hawthorn tree and line of mature Oaks which once dotted the ancient field boundary. In 1831, the Macclesfield Canal arrived to rudely intersect this ancient boundary. Small lambs playfully gambol through the gaps in the long crumbled dry stone wall and leap with carefree abandon over the remaining stonework. Bridge No. 26 comes into view in the distance around the continuing curve in the waterway.

White Nancy still dominates the view ahead and many interesting and contrasting stories surround the origins and the naming of the monument. Two families played significant roles in Bollington's industrial development namely the Mellors and the Gaskells and it is the Gaskells who are usually credited with the building of White Nancy. It is generally accepted that is was erected to commemorate the battle of Waterloo around 1815. Some suggest that the name

Nancy was taken from a horse which was responsible for hauling much of the fabric of the the monuments construction up the precipitous incline to the top of Kerridge Hill. Others intimate that Nancy was a female Gaskell and that White Nancy was built as a garden house or feature by the family while they occupied nearby Ingersley Hall. Even the description of the monument is no straightforward matter; the one fact which can be stressed categorically is that

WHITE NANCY

it is brilliantly white. It stands not more than twenty five feet high and resembles a bell or a thin necked milk bottle in general shape.

While looking directly ahead towards Kerridge Hill, Bridge No. 26 seems to shelter at its foot Beyond the bridge, for the first time, a huge brick chimney can be seen soaring skyward. On the approach to Bridge No. 26, the waterway is again lined with metal to both banks as it is embanked briefly across a shallow grass valley. Sugar Lane comes into view to the East, traveling along the top of the rise in the pasture as it begins its descent to cross the canal at the bridge. Sugar Lane Farm lies across to the East. From the farm yard, a stream of fat, golden brown hens spill down into the meadow beside the canal where they diligently scratch the turf in search of titbits. They mingle with the sheep to the obvious delight and entertainment of the lambs. The ground to East and West rises gently to meet the stonework of Sugar Lane Bridge, No. 26, which is architecturally, one of the finest along the Macclesfield Canal.

Sugar Lane Bridge is an exquisite example of a 'skew' bridge. 'Skew' bridges were built at an oblique angle to the canal incorporating a twist or skew in their construction to avoid the carriageway above having to negotiate a tight or dangerous 'Z' bend. The skew bridge demanded the utmost precision skill on the stonemasons part as each block of gritstone needed to be individually designed to fit to the next, the stones of the actual arch being laid at sloping angles instead of horizontally. The canals planners and engineers went to great lengths and, presumably, expense to carry what, even in the late 20th Century, is an insignificant lane across the canal. The bridge is an absolute masterpiece. It is as vital a piece of Cheshire's architectural history as any of the great estate houses or any Victorian town hall or public monument.

The hedgerow bank beside the towpath rises up to the bridge, clothed in bluebells during April and May. Trees crowd around the stonework on all sides as if to protect and watch over it and a stone ramp constructed of cobble setts leads up from the towpath to Sugar Lane. Emerging from beneath Sugar Lane Bridge, the length of canal which now lies ahead is absolutely straight and at the end of this looms the massive form of Clarence Mill. From Sugar Lane Bridge, the first real view of Clarence Mill is down through a 'tunnel' of tall trees. Tall Hawthorns and Willows on the left bank overhang the water and a tree and shrub covered high bank to the right, is clothed with masses of brambles, tangled grasses, Docks and Cleavers.

This humble hedgerow plant must surely be the commonest of wayside weeds, so common that is is easily passed by without a second glance. Its common name is derived from the hooked hairs on its fruit which 'cleave' to passing animal hair or clothes. The high bank to the east drops away suddenly to reveal an uneven, 'hummocky' field climbing away from the canal. It is obviously poor ground as it is deeply pitted and dotted by clumps of Gorse. Two of the largest mounds in the field are actually spoil heaps from a mine which was once worked beneath the field. On this occasion, the prize was not coal, but fire clay. The strong, heat-proof bricks which were the end product of the Clearance Clay Mine were used in furnace lining and for lining flues and kilns etc.

The canal is once again metal lined to either bank as it is transported over another embankment. The uneven field plunges downwards in all directions below the canal's level to form a wet swampy hollow which is more than likely a result of subsidence into the mining below. A gap appears in the Hawthorn hedge where a set of wooden steps leads down from the towpath to a narrow footpath which disappears into the trees. A painted sign board points the way through the wooded valley towards "The Vale Inn, 250 Yards". The board goes on to promise traditional beers but further warns that this is a private wood with access only to the Vale Inn. As the sheet metal lining and the embankment ends, the ground to right and left returns to canal level and the wooded clough land to the right is now strewn with scores of what would seem to be disused poultry sheds, wire netting runs and allotment plots.

Beside the towpath, a small squat version of the milestone is encountered. This is actually a quarter mile marker. These are considerably smaller stones which were once far more numerous than the larger milestones, marking as they did, half, quarter and three quarter miles but many have been lost over the passing decades. The message of the stones can be positively confusing as they do not mark anything as simple as the quarter, half and three quarter fractions between the milestones, but the number of half or three quarter miles from either end of the canal. The importance of this calculation ceased when tolls were no longer paid by commercial narrowboats.

The canal is now overshadowed by the colossal form of Clarence Mill. As with many Cheshire towns, Bollington owes its present form to the Industrial Revolution. In the case of Bollington, the prosperity came from cotton. One of the features which helped to form Bollington's destiny has been its location, enclosed almost completely by towering hills. Its beautiful stone-built houses and the remnants of its unique industrial heritage have helped toward it being designated a conservation area.

Totally without mention in the Domesday Survey, Bollington existed, from Saxon times, as little more than an agricultural hamlet and forming part of the large rural parish of Prestbury. During the latter part of the 18th Century, several water powered mills for the production of cotton cloth sprang up in the area, spearheaded by the enterprising families of Gaskell and Mellor. It was however, the Swindells family as leading cotton manufacturers who brought about the industrial heyday of Bollington. Martin Swindells, after acquiring the leases of the earlier water mills at the beginning of the Nineteenth Century, went on to build the two giant mills, one either side of the newly arrived Macclesfield Canal which, to this day still dominate the small town with their towering chimneys and their monumental proportions. The Clarence Mill, built in the late 1820's, was completed along with the canal onto which it directly fronts.

The mill was totally reliant upon the waterway for the exportation of its end product which was high quality spun cotton used extensively in the production of Nottingham Woven Lace which was transported via the Macclesfield and the Trent and Mersey Canals. The five storey main block of the mill is stone built and, from the canal, presents a staggering mass of windows. It's thirty six bays stretch across it's facade to a slightly projecting tower. The canals far bank now comprises the mills gritstone landing stage. Once alongside the main block of the building, a doorway with an ornate stone archway above, can be seen, inscribed "Brook and Swindells". The "Swindells" refers, of course, to Martin Swindells, The "Brook" was Joseph Brook who assisted in the building of the mill and was related to Swindells through marriage The customary gravel surface of the towpath is, alongside the mill, replaced by cobbles and the towpath, is now raised well above the canal's level and lined by massive blocks of stone. The remains of rails run across the wide cobbled towpath where small carts on railway-type wheels crossed the canal from the mill via a long dismantled swing bridge and crossed the towpath to tip ash and waste from the mill's two great steam engines, "Perseverance" and "Success" into an area beyond the present day towpath boundary fence.

The stretch of water which passes Clarence Mill fairly teems with ducks which must be habitually fed titbits by the mill's inhabitants. The modern day parking area in between the mill and the canal was originally an extensive wharf from which the finished cotton would leave by boat and raw cotton would arrive from Manchester docks via the Ashton and Peak Forest Canals. In addition to the cotton, huge quantities of coal to power the engines would arrive daily from the Poynton and Adlington collieries to the north and from the Staffordshire coal field to the south. The mill was last fully operational during the 1890's but continued to spin cotton right through to 1970. As with Goyt Mill near to our journey's start at Marple, Clarence Mill today houses light industrial units. As we continue to pass the mill's seemingly endless frontage, the watercourse which is still lined by massive blocks of gritstone, begins to curve very gently to the right, up to the southern end of the mill, where a tall brick chimney stands sentry over all below.

A wooden pathside seat is provided opposite to the mill from where one can sit and contemplate this massive symbol of Victorian industry. As if from nowhere, Mallards wing in to land on the water from all directions as they seem conditioned to associate stationary humans with picnic scraps. To the right of the towpath, a five bar gate with a pedestrian kissing gate next to it and a stile next to that is suddenly encountered. This provides access from the towpath to a track which runs down through the old canal side coal wharves and yards, down to the main road into Bollington. As the towpath passes the coal wharves it is festooned with mooring rings where coal laden narrow boats would once have tied up while the boatmen tipped the coal from the boats, down chutes into the yards below.

Beside the towpath in the absence of the Hawthorn hedge, a stone wall takes its place. The canal curves sharply to the right as it begins to leave Clarence Mill behind. Like the Hawthorn hedge it replaces, the stone wall is almost completely smothered by brambles and, between it and the towpath, large colonies of Butterbur grow up to obscure what remains of the wall. Butterbur, with its large Rhubarb shaped leaves (each up to 36 inches across) can easily and rapidly swamp the towpath where enough moisture is present in the ground for its extensive root or rhizome system to develop. A native of damp woodland or river banks and flood plains, it often covers areas, many square yards in extent, excluding all other plants. In March and April, flower stems grow up and appear above ground before the leaves. The stems are stout, up to 30 inches tall, and carry dense clusters of pink violet flower heads and strange cobweb-like hairs. After flowering, large, long stemmed leaves grow from the rhizome

BUTTERBUR

As the sharp deviation to the right in the waterway is completed, the canal embarks upon its journey across one of the most celebrated embankments along its course, the famous Bollington embankment and aqueduct. It is carried along, 60 feet above Bollington, across the valley of the River Dean. The Macclesfield Canal's construction was controlled by its chief engineer, William Crossley, but it was local engineer, Charles Nichol, who was responsible for the construction of Bollington's ambitious embankment. It was he who chose to span the River Dean valley with massive earth bank as opposed to a conventional aqueduct supported by arches constructed from brick or stone.

The coming of the canal not only stimulated Bollingtons local industry providing ample employment and instigating rapid population growth, but it visually changed Bollington for all time as the massive 60 feet high viaduct effectively separated one half of the town from the other. The majority of the buildings in the older section of the town, to the east of the canal, date from this period of rapid industrial expansion. The old coal yards to the west drop away into the valley and the track which left the towpath at the stile can be seen below, running through them and eventually joining the main road, at the foot of the aqueduct. The view to the east is of old Bollington with its rows of gritstone millworkers cottages, viewed through the tops of trees which stand around the embankment. Beyond the valley of Bollington, the more distant view to the east is of steeply rising ground. The much quarried Billinge Hill is in the near distance and beyond that, the view carries right through into the far away high peak district of Derbyshire.

On the open, airy embankment top, two wooden benches are set against the stone wall on a cobbled area, again, surrounded by clumps of Butterbur. Traffic can be heard passing beneath the embankment and, across the water, the progress of the road through the town can be followed. The view to the east is dominated by Kerridge Hill and White Nancy, while to the west, Bollington stretches away into the distance. Further along the embankment, the Butterbur has colonized the waters edge as well as the strip of ground between the towpath and the stone wall. The position of the actual aqueduct over the road is marked on the passage over the embankment by the bridge walls either side of the waterway in addition to the customary stone walls. Peering over the bridge wall, one looks down at the tops of street lamps. Once over the aqueduct, quaint stone cottages stand to the immediate right of the towpath where they are precariously perched at the top of this towering embankment. The waterway begins to curve quite sharply to the right.

The canal's far bank is suddenly occupied by an extensive timber yard. Beside the towpath, the stone wall temporarily gives way to a neat wooden post and rail fence set into which is a gate and pedestrian kissing gate. This gives access to a lane around which the stone collages cluster. The lane disappears from view by passing over Bridge No. 27 which suddenly comes into view immediately ahead. The kissing gate leads the walker to the front of the delightful "Aqueduct Cottage", where a tarmaced footpath runs between pretty garden flowers and shrubs, and slopes down to the first of sixteen outrageously steep stone steps arranged in flights like a staircase. A handrail appears beside a further set of twenty seven steps, which are even more steep than the previous, at the end of which the exhausted walker finds himself on the footpath beside the road at the foot of the towering stone aqueduct. The journey up the steps from road to canal is reminiscent of an assault on the north face of Everest!

On the final approach to Bridge No. 27, the stone wall reappears beside the towpath and rises up to become one with the bridge wall. The standard stone arch of Bridge No. 27 seems somewhat unspectacular when compared with its predecessor; No. 26 at Sugar Lane. Due to the sharp deviation in the waterways course since leaving the embankment, Clarence Mill has disappeared from view, behind, save for the towering chimney of brick.

Across the canal, detached houses set in ample gardens overlook the canal's passage from above. Here, on the outskirts of Bollington, for the first time since High Lane, the canal passes through a totally built up suburban area. More frequently, the larger gardens to the west bank slope down to the canal where private mooring stages occupy the bottom of the garden. As the bank begins to drop away, the extent of the densely populated area is revealed as any distant view to the west is effectively blocked by rows of houses. Gardens reach towards the towpath side, bordered by the same stone wall. Occasionally the householder has chosen to extend his garden domain by cultivating the area between the stone boundary wall and the towpath with delightful results. Even where the majority have chosen not to garden beyond the wall, the grassy bank between the stone wall and the towpath is often clothed with garden escapees. Forget-Me-Not is a common colonist, decorating the grassy wayside with swathes of blue and the various garden species of large white daisies, Marguerites etc, have often found a foothold where they are able to tower above their natural wild counterparts. Daffodils are another welcome alien beside the towpath where they have obviously been discarded as bulbs.

In place of the familiar Hawthorns and Sycamores, Alders and Elders, it is now cultivated trees and shrubs which overhang the towpath. Willow leaved Cotoneaster, overloaded with brilliant scarlet berries during Autumn hang low across the path. In one place, outside the confines of a garden, a mature flowering Cherry tree which would hold pride of place in any collection due to its great size is an absolute mass of pink and white blossom during late April and early May. The whole kaleidoscope of shapes and colours of garden trees and shrubs are paraded beside the towpath; Conifers, Forsythias, Lilacs and Jasmines vie for attention at their own particular times of the year. Even though the houses across the canal are of more modest proportions, the 'end of the garden' mooring jetty is an increasingly common feature. Beside the towpath, rambling roses and fruit trees overhang from gardens beyond the stone wall, including a Juniper of tremendous proportions which the towpath walker needs to physically brush past, so valiantly does it struggle to escape from its garden restraint.

The next milestone shelters beneath the spreading limbs of a Cherry Blossom tree. The tall original stone reads, "From Hall Green 18 and a quarter miles". The reverse side however, fails to reveal the distance from Marple which should, of course, read 8 miles. The fact that the information concerning the distance from Marple is missing due to a combination of weathering and lichen growth would intimate that maybe this stone was one of the lucky ones which was uprooted and buried at the time of the second world war which would also explain the reason for its tall and erect stature. Between the neat little houses on the far bank, White Nancy reminds the canal user of its presence.

Quite unexpectedly, the canals banks are suddenly lined by huge blocks of millstone as, once more, the ground to the right of the towpath drops steeply away beyond the Hawthorn Hedge which has, just as abruptly, replaced the stone wall. Again, the canal is half embanked. The waterway begins to curve to the left. Directly ahead, the view is dominated by the distant form of the Adelphi Mill. The straight length of canal and towpath ahead is totally overshadowed by the Mill and its famous 'Romanesque' tower.

Plantains decorate the edges of the towpath and have replaced the Butterbur in growing among the gaps between the mill grit blocks of the canal bank. The most obvious feature of the Hoary Plantain is the tall leafless spike rising from the flat rosette of leaves. The single flower head, so characteristic of the plantains, bares pinkish purple stamens in the Hoary Plantain which gives the flower head a reddish appearance, unlike the brownish flowers of the other common plantains. As the Adelphi Mill draws nearer, the pretty gardens continue to reach the waters edge to the left.

Unlike the Clarence Mill, the Adelphi occupies the west or towpath side of the canal and, as the mill draws nearer, boats are moored more or less solidly to either bank. A wide bay appears in the waterway opposite to the mill where narrow boats are moored in considerable numbers. The half embankment of the canal continues as the ground beyond the pathside hedge and fence drops away steeply. The Adelphi Mill towers ahead, a much more architectural building than the Clarence, constructed ruggedly of blocks of Kerridge Stone. The tower at this northern end of the building projects far above the main body of the mill with its bizarre mock Roman crenellations visible from much of Bollington.

The mill was built during the 1850's by George Swindells to be run by his two sons and named it Adelphi which is Greek for brothers. The Adelphi was not so completely dependent upon the canal as the Clarence, despite its proximity to the waterway, because the Macclesfield, Bollington and Marple Railway (now the Middlewood Way), which arrived in 1869 literally passed its front door. This diverted valuable business from the canal much to the annoyance of the original Macclesfield Canal Company. The mill produced cotton which was considered to be of inferior quality to that produced at the Clarence. Production eventually went over to silk then rayon and nylon before the mills eventual closure in the mid 1970's.

Beside the towpath, the Hawthorn hedge and fence end abruptly as the canal is carried over a stone aqueduct. The bridge wall beside the towpath is too high to see over and is also covered in a thick growth of ivy which further prevents a view down to the road which passes beneath the canal on its way into Bollington. Just over the aqueduct, a steep flight of fifty steps leads down the actual rampart beside the aqueduct, from the towpath to the street below. Robust iron railings surmounted by ornate finials are set into a low stone wall to separate the towpath from the mill yard. The railings are handsomely maintained with a luxurious coat of black, red and gold paint.

In the old mill yard, another fine building in the same style and the same stone as the mill houses a visitor centre which is now owned by Macclesfield Groundwork Trust. The discovery centre runs displays on Bollington's industrial heritage, the canal and railway systems and all aspects of the Cheshire countryside from a recreation point of view. The building in question was originally the gatehouse to the Adelphi and housed the offices to the mill. Beyond the cobbled yard, the more distant view to the west is a panoramic vista across the newer town of Bollington, across Bollington Cross and of the Cheshire plain stretching away beyond Prestbury. The Adelphi today in undergoing a tasteful refurbishment and redevelopment. Whereas it has housed light industrial workshops since its mid 1970's closure, a tasteful conversion of at least part of it into "The Old Mill Hotel" is proposed. Conference and banqueting facilities in addition to twenty bedrooms should secure the future of this splendid old building.

A brightly painted narrowboat can be seen moored in the bay across from the mill with an equally brightly painted sign board adjacent to it. The board advertises the fact that this craft is actually the "White Nancy" cruising restaurant.

The boat itself certainly commands attention painted as it is in green, red, yellow, blue and white. The boat's name "White Nancy" is sign written on its bright coloured panels and the information board even gives details for table reservations. A large hut which provides facilities for sea cadets occupies a space in the busy bay adjacent to the floating restaurant, The towpath bank, alongside the mill continues to be lined by vast blocks of stone, some of them seven feet long by three and four feet thick. The towpath provides numerous mooring rings where scores of narrowboats would tie up daily to offload raw cotton at the end of its long journey from the southern United States of America or from the Middle East or to be loaded with finished spun cotton before the coming of the railway in 1869.

Dozens of narrowboats continue to occupy the wide bay, many registered in Bollington and painted out in the same colour scheme. These craft represent the Anglo Welsh hire fleet operating from their offices here at Bollington Wharf. Their large car park occupies much of the remaining space around the wharf. The towering six storeys of the mill dwarf the canal and the wharf. From the towpath, one can suffer from vertigo just counting the number of flights or stages, by which a fire escape scales the main block of the mill.

The canal resumes its normal width beyond the wharf and the far bank is occupied by large modern warehouses which are partly hidden by a high wooden fence and a row of screening trees which have been planted along the waters edge. The tame Mallards which excitedly swim towards the towpath walker will actually leave the water and give chase along the towpath, as they automatically assume that every passer by leaves scraps of bread on the towpath as a natural by-product. To take this observation a stage further, assuming the passer by is not accompanied by a dog, the ducks will actually peck at the feet of the walker, providing of course, that he stands still! Beside the towpath at the waters edge, the crumbling bank lining has created a shallow or semi aquatic zone where Water Plantain has gained a foothold. The broad oval leaves, larger than and not unlike the terrestrial Dock leaf, appear from March onward. The tall slender stem rising high above a tight thicket of leaves, culminates in a pyramid of branching spikes tipped with tiny flowers. In bloom throughout June, July and August, the flowers only open during the afternoon.

Beside the towpath, the iron railings come to an end and are replaced by a tall stone wall. The strip of undisturbed grass which runs between the towpath and the stone wall is colonized with beds of stinging nettles but here and there are clumps of White Dead Nettle with its characteristic open mouthed flowers of purest white. The flowers often seen to be swarming with nectar-hungry bees from May to November. Across the canal, the warehousing comes to an end and once more, housing occupies the eastern bank. On the towpath bank, the stone wall is smothered with Ivy which, in addition to its clinging stems, baring the fibrous, adhesive covered roots and lobed leaves, has developed extensive non clinging, flowering stems where the leaves are quite unlike the classic 'ivy leaf' shape associated with the non flowering stems.

Thickets of Raspberry canes briefly colonize the grassy strip at the foot of the wall which reach out to grasp at the clothing of the passer by. Up ahead, Bridge No 28 comes into view. The high stone wall, which is summounted by a half round coping stone, still runs alongside the towpath and obscures any view down to the west. Large mature trees come into view beyond the wall and occasionally overhang it, their spreading boughs reaching across both towpath and canal. Sycamores predominate but here and there, a mature Hazel reaches right across the towpath and almost touches the water. The wall is extremely neat, being built of local stone whose blocks are uniform in size, no larger than a building brick and pointed with a dark mortar. Huge Beech trees tower above the wall and Ivy cascades over from the other side. The uppermost growth of the Ivy blooms prolifically during the autumn months. Ivy will only bare flowers where it recieves full sun. The globular clusters of greenish-yellow flowers produce copious amounts of rich nectar which is avidly mopped up by hoards of honey bees and overflies. The seething mass of feeding insects is often a spectacular and unexpected sight in late September or early October when the heat of the mid-day sun can be uncharacteristic intense. Many of the larger hoverflies on the Ivy are impossible to tell apart from the honey bees with which they share this intoxicatingly sweet bonanza. These are actually drone flies which take their name from the male Honey Bee as both insects have no sting.

A small group of the most exquisitely restored and refurbished dwellings one could wish to find, stand alongside this quiet length of canal and in the lee of the mellow stone bridge. Behind the wall which runs alongside the towpath is Tinkers Clough, an area of outstanding natural beauty. A deep clough or valley with a tiny stream in the bottom which is of great importance both to Bollington and to local wildlife as a rich natural habitat. It is colonized by an above average cross section of tree species, many are fully mature specimens which explains the woodland giants overhanging the stone wall. The clough is served by well maintained paths. Its close proximity to the canal is a matter of mutual benefit to the birds and mammals and insects of the one habitat as they can interact with those species which are native to the other. In its own right, Tinkers Clough Wood is home to the Greater Spotted Woodpecker, the Great Tit, the Long Tailed Tit, Blue Tit, Chaffinch, Treecreeper and Wren along with the more common Black Bird, Wood Pigeon and Magpie.

Across the canal, the splendid dwellings are built from the local Kerridge stone and the first to be reached could easily have been a row of cottages originally running lengthways, parallel to the canal but is now divided into just two separate homes. A beautifully formal area of garden separates the houses from the canals edge. A profusion of brilliantly coloured flowers are contained in formal beds by low walls of Kerridge Stone and the remaining space, instead of being lawned, is flagged by Kerridge flag stones. Yellow Alyssum Saxatile, white Iberis Candytuft and blue Aubretia spill from the flower beds in torrents of bloom over the mellow stone walls. An ornate balcony extends outward from a bedroom of one home; a fine wrought iron affair painted out in black and gold and supported by two horses heads carven from stone. The actual canal bank is formed by a stone jetty decorated with vivid splashes of flowers contained in stone urns and troughs. The second dwelling has a long wrought iron balcony which extends along much of the first floor level which is smothered by masses of Montana Clematis which, during May is a foaming sea of lilac/pink flowers. Along the towpath bank, the lining of stone has slipped away into the water to the extent that, in places, the towpath has needed to be shored up by planks of wood as an emergency measure to prevent it from eroding away into the canal. The limbs of the Great Beeches overhang from Tinkers Clough Wood right across the towpath and half way across the canal.

The final building in the group, across the canal, is actually positioned the other way round in that the gable end reaches toward the canal. The remarkable fact is that Bridge No. 28 abuts directly to the gable end of the cottage. The two are built from identical stone and join invisibly to give the impression that one was in integral part of the other. A name stone on the gable end reads, "Beehive Cottage, Rebuilt 1968"

A flight of twelve, heavily worn stone steps lead up from the towpath to the top of the bridge. The steps are actually built into the bridge wall and lead up to a wooden signpost which points down into Tinkers Clough Wood. On top of the bridge, a simple grass footpath leads either down into Tinkers Clough or beside the garden wall of Beehive Cottage, beneath flowering Cherry Trees and past green and gold Berberis and variegated Laurels to join a tiny lane and then to branch off due east, across fields, to Kerridge Village.

CHAPTER 4

Bollington to Macclesfield Marina

Emerging from beneath Bridge No. 28, the scene is once again leafy and peaceful. Beside the towpath, a set of stop planks is stored in a curious concrete box with solid sides. The end from where the stop planks are removed has a metal plate bolted over it so that the actual planks can not be seen at all. The stone wall no longer runs beside the towpath, it is replaced by the usual low Hawthorn hedge beyond which, the ground falls very steeply away into the valley of Tinkers Clough.

The Hawthorn hedge is interspersed by Elder bushes which during June are covered by the fragrant flat topped white flower heads. From August to September, the familiar bunches of blue and black Elderberries hang heavily from reddish/purple stems. These berries are particularly beloved by Wood Pigeons, members of the Thrush family and makers of traditional country wines. The grass beside the towpath is massed with Plantains and Daisies and the white flowers of Cow Parsley and Pignut. A belt of tall Sycamore trees and Hawthorn bushes which began at the bridge overhang the water from the far bank.

The canal continues to be half embanked for a considerable distance ahead, the ground to the west fairly plunges away into Tinkers Clough. Who could wish to be in a more peaceful spot than here? The reflections of the tall trees on the quiet water, disturbed only by the occasional dimpling of the surface by small Roach. The incessant melody of bird song is so much a part of the scene that it would be most conspicuous if it was to cease. Occasionally, a natural drama is played out. Like a great plunging glider, a Heron swoops down towards the canal with a view to landing at the waters edge to escape from the annoying Jackdaws which are persuing it, mobbing it in a way that smaller birds so often do in order to harass a flying predator. With an indignant squawk the Heron sights the towpath walker and veers sharply upwards, the great wings flailing to regain height, to the obvious delight of the Jackdaws who readily continue their aerial persecution of the bemused Heron.

Despite being awarded protected status, the Grey Heron is extremely numerous throughout Cheshire, and is well represented along the Macclesfield Canal. The abundance of pits and pools in adjoining fields make the canal an ideal habitat. The marshy zone at the canal's edge where the banks are unlined is the perfect hunting ground for the enormous bird which will be seen, if the walker spots it before it spots the walker, standing motionless, often for long periods of time, waiting for a small fish, frog, toad or newt or even water vole to come within range of the long, sinuous neck and long dagger like bill which shoots out with lightening speed to grab the prey. Often the Heron will stand motionless in just inches of water for so long that small fish swim confidently among it legs only to be caught in the downward stab of the bill.

The tall Hawthorn trees which continue to line the canals far bank are interspersed by wild cherry trees or Bird Cherries which, like their hybridized and interbred garden cousins, are a mass of blossom during April. Many cultivated cherry trees, both culinary and decorative are derived from this native wild tree. The view to the west over the Hawthorn hedge is of the deep Tinkers Clough Valley. Tinkers Clough wood is now behind us but the grass valley continues to runs parallel to the canal.

Through the dense Hawthorns and Cherries on the far bank, a beautiful stone cottage is briefly glimpsed. Suddenly the Hawthorns drop away and the view eastwards is completely dominated by the looming bulk of Kerridge hill. As the canal made its way through Bollington, it was the end of the hill, topped by White Nancy, which was prominent but now, the waterway runs parallel to the long "Saddle of Kerridge". The hill or ridge lies some half a mile distant from the canal, The densely wooded slopes hide the scars of many stone quarries. The hill seems to suddenly rear up out of the surrounding and otherwise perfectly level farmland, giving the impression that it is the result of some sudden and violent geological upheaval.

The waterway begins to curve quite sharply to the right as it moves around the end of Tinkers Clough valley. The canal's banks are lined with large blocks of gritstone around the curve. Boats are moored solidly along the far bank as the waterway suddenly opens out into what, at first, appears to be another wharf or marina.

The waterway enters a bay from which, an area of water resembling another canal arm extends away to the east beyond a curious sluice gate system. This site was originally a stone yard and a dry dock. Stone was transported down from the quarries on Kerridge Ridge by a tramway and was loaded onto waiting narrowboats.

The whole area of the dock could be drained periodically so that any stone which had fallen overboard during the loading process could be safely and profitably retrieved. Some of the quarries which formerly used this wharf are still in use but the dock is now used purely for the mooring of pleasure craft. In the distant east, at the foot of the Saddle of Kerridge are the quaint cluster of building s which make up the tiny community of Kerridge maintaining its independence from much larger Bollington. The terraced cottages are grouped tightly on the wooded hill as if seeking defence from the threat of continuing quarrying. Over the centuries, the extraction of the valuable stone has threatened to eat away the very hill itself, leaving White Nancy to gaze across Stockport and into Lancashire from an increasingly isolated position.

A long, straight length of canal stretches away into the distance. The view to the west is obscured by a mountainous hedgerow which accompanies the towpath far into the distance. Beyond the moored boats, the majority of which are registered at Kerridge,(as opposed to the Bollington registered boats back at the Adelphi Mill) farmland stretches away towards the hamlet of Kerridge. The boat owning fraternity in Kerridge have gone to considerable pains to beautify the old stone wharf with lavish beds of flowers and neatly cut lawns.

The grassy area between the path and the huge hedge is home to brilliant white drifts of greater Stitchwort in May, masses of golden Dandelions from March through to October and the equally golden Meadow Buttercup and Creeping Buttercup. Beyond the mooring wharf, for the first time since the approach to the Clarence Mill, south of Bollington, pasture land is all that can be seen beyond the canal's far bank. Just above the waters surface where the pasture rises away from the canal, the soil is dotted with the entrances to many small tunnels or burrows which betray the presence of Water Voles.

Unless the vole has been careless enough not to hide the burrow entrances with a grassy overhang as is the case here, the towpath walker usually encounters the chocolate brown vole by means of a sudden plop as it dives into the canal from the vegetation of the towpath bank when startled by the approaching footfall. The plop is followed by a 'V' shaped wake moving quite swiftly, either directly across the canal or along the near bank to the nearest hidden burrow entrance. The fact that the water vole is often mistaken for a Brown Rat and that it has ignorantly been christened "The Water Rat" detracts from the fact that it is an exceedingly handsome little animal. Its relatively short tail, blunt, chubby face and long glossy coat all distinguish it from the unsavoury rat which, admittedly, may also be encountered along the canal. The vole is active by day and feeds entirely upon bankside vegetation. The frenzied munching and chewing and shaking and rattling of the waterside sedges, rushes and reeds which is often heard by anglers for long periods of time, is entirely the work of the industrious Water Vole. The vole falls prey to the stalking Heron in large numbers, to Owls, Pike and now to the most recent newcomer to the waterside predator list; the Mink.

The grass area to both left and right of the towpath is decorated throughout the summer months by the distinctive blue flowers of the Tufted Vetch. As many as forty individual flowers make up each flower spike. Depending upon soil type, the flowers will range in colour from deep blue through various shades of china blue and powder blue to pinkish purple. The Tufted Vetch is absolutely in its element along the Macclesfield Canal and is surely one of the most distinctive plants to scramble over Cheshire's grassland and hedgerows.

The leaves are made up of as many as 30 greyish leaflets. From the tip of each leaf emerges a branched tendril which twines round neighbouring plants enabling the vetch to climb for distances of six feet or more.

The canal continues to stretch away wide and straight and occasionally glimpses through the almost impenetrable wall of Hawthorn to the right reveal pasture land stretching away to the west. Chaffinches squabble noisily in the depths of the huge hedgerow and erupt in a fluttering mass of feathers and wings to escape from the towpath walker as he brushes beneath the overhang of Hawthorn. As they dart away, the white shoulder patches and the wing bars are the only identifying features but, when seen at rest, the splendid colours of the Chaffinch, the commonest of British birds are effectively revealed. The slate blue crown and neck, the orange face and throat, the pink belly and rump and chestnut back all seem to point towards an exotic and rare migrant or passage visitor not a common resident which probably numbers seven million pairs. The Chaffinch nests in the Hawthorn hedgerow which borders the majority of the Macclesfield Canal's 27 three quarter mile length.

TUFTED VETCH

At long last, White Nancy begins to disappear from view to the north east, leaving the saddle of Kerridge stretching away southward, parallel to the canal. In the distance, a lane comes into view, approaching the canal from the east. The lane can be seen crossing the canal some distance ahead by means of Bridge No. 29 which now comes into view. The bridge which lies ahead, carrying Clarkes Lane is one of the Macclesfield Canal's more celebrated pieces of architecture. For the first time since the journeys start at Marple, the towpath is transferred to the canal's eastern or uphill bank via Clarkes Change Bridge. This beautiful roving bridge is robbed of the title of Macclesfield Canal's finest due to the fact that much further along the journey, the towpath is carried over arguably the most spectacular roving canal bridge in the British Isles. However, Clarkes Change Bridge is as individual as Bridges Nos. 1 and 2 at Marple and a splendid example of stone architecture.

Approaching Bridge No. 29, beyond the level pasture to the East, traffic can be seen making its way towards the bridge. The huge hedgerow to the right is transported towards Clarkes Changes Bridge by a bramble covered bank which begins to rise up beside the towpath.
Raspberry

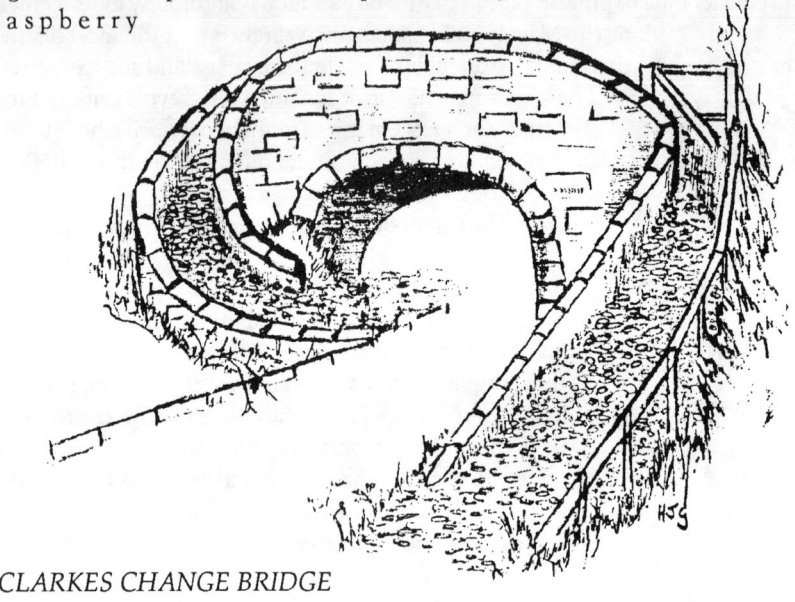

CLARKES CHANGE BRIDGE

canes grow up from the dense carpet of brambles on the bank which, particularly following a shower of rain will be seen to be crawling, in the most literal sense of the word, with shelled garden snails. Song Thrushes eat vast quantities of these shelled snails by breaking open the shells on stone 'anvils'. Quite why certain isolated pockets of ground should be colonized by thriving hoards of shelled snails instead of the monotonously common slug, which is frequently to be seen gliding across the towpath or slithering its way among pathside vegetation is something of a mystery. The Black Slug, which is a ridiculous common name for an animal which comes in a variety of colours ranging from black, brown, brick red and orange to grey, has a habit of swarming up the stems of pathside grasses and sedges, again, particularly after rain. The result of this mass exodus is that large numbers end up sticking to the legs of the passer by with slimy and sticky consequences.

During 1912, one of only two recorded instances of the canal bursting its banks occurred somewhere on the half embanked section between Bridge No. 28, (which at the time is described as being adjacent to "the Old Beehive Mill, Bollington" - not the rebuilt Beehive Cottage) and Clarke Lane Bridge. A gap developed of about forty yards wide and a telegraph pole was left hanging by its wires over the escaping torrent. Records show that much damage was done to houses in the path of the onrush and a nearby gas works was put out of order.

A pathside wooden seat stands at the foot of the rough bank in the lee of the bridge. A wooden fence is positioned across the towpath and a pedestrian gate gives access to a stone cobbled ramp which leads the towpath steeply up to the lane above. Climbing up the cobble ramp a tiny Wren darts out of a hole in the masonry where it has concealed its nest. The diminutive Wren, fully grown at three and three quarter inches, darts away out of sight delivering its explosive alarm call.

Looking northward to the west of the canal, the strange Romanesque tower of the Adelphi Mill can be seen apparently rising up from an area of pasture. As the bulk of the mill is concealed from view at this distance, the tower protruding above open grassland, presents a most peculiar apparition looking for all the world like some isolated folly. A second pedestrian gate gives access from the road to the downward ramp which, unlike the approach to the bridge, curves gracefully downwards to deliver the towpath beneath the bridge on the eastern Bbnk.Emerging from beneath the bridge is, initially, a disorientating experience. To find the canal lying to the right after so many miles is odd as everything appears to be the wrong way round.

Leaving Bridge No. 29 behind, the traveller launches off into a leafy, tranquil haven of quiet shady water and overhanging trees. A rough bank rises steeply up beside the towpath, obscuring the view eastwards. At the top of the bank, tall Oak, Ash, Elder and Hawthorn trees tower above the bridge.The western bank, across the water is a mass of trees and undergrowth, overhanging the canal and beneath them, in season, the ground is carpeted with Bluebells.

The waterway stretches away from the bridge ,wide, straight and unlined to either bank. The high bank, rising skyward beside the towpath is, during late spring, a pleasing patchwork of colours, white and blue as Bluebells and Greater Stitchwort seem to be in competition to cover the greater area of grassy bank. From May onwards, ducklings are very much in evidence. It is by no means unusual to see a female Mallard being followed by anything up to thirteen or fourteen brown and gold young - every child's favourite baby bird. The handsome drakes take little part in the child minding operation, skulking some distance away, often in all male 'gangs' of several individuals. The barbed wire fence along the top of the flowery bank is dotted with large Silver Birch trees whose spreading boughs further shade the towpath. The foot of the bank, at towpath level is marked by low and overhanging Grey Willows and Goat Willows.

Clarkes Change Bridge slowly disappears behind as if being engulfed by the abundant leafy boughs reaching toward it from all sides. While the Bluebells and Stitchwort still flower profusely, fronds of bracken push their way up through them to take over and clothe the bank when the flowers fade. Beds of stinging nettles crowd the grassy strip between the towpath and waters edge. Above them, an occasional Willow sapling grows through seeking to gain a root hold in this precarious strip of damp ground. Large Birch and Oak trees overhanging the canal from the far bank are vividly reflected in the quiet water. The grass strip between path and water is often colonized by Bush Vetch, which is almost identical in appearance and habit to the Tufted Vetch. The five of six blooms in each flowerhead invariably recieve the attentions of the Bumble Bee who find its nectar irresistible.

Often, during late spring and early summer the waters surface will be almost completely covered by Dandelion seeds, forming a scum or, more poetically, a cream topping which skates away with the faintest breeze and provides hours of entertainment for the Mallard ducklings who, during their first few weeks of life, doubtless consume a good quantity of it. Close to the waters edge, during the early months of the summer, the delicate, almost fragile flowers of the Lady's Smock will be seen in abundance. The large petals shade from deep lilac to palest pink bordering on white. An extremely common inhabitant of damp grassland, it will be encountered throughout the journey from Marple through to Kidsgrove, and also in most of the meadowland through which the canal slices. Its flowers, on fragile stems, peep above the grasses of unmown pastures until late June. The Lady's Smocks alternate name of Cuckoo Flower, refers to its habit of coming into flower to coincide with the arrival of the Cuckoo.

The canal's far bank is now completely hidden by a dense unbroken line of overhanging Purple Willows and Osiers, which hide the bank from which the grow, as they reach out to touch the water. The tiny Mallard ducklings disappear and reappear, in and out of the overhanging branches. Sprawling clumps of Honeysuckle clothe the grassy bank beside the towpath. Through occasional gaps in the Willows which line the western water line, small paddocks can be seen to lie beyond where ponies graze the poor ground between spikes of Thistles and patches of Docks. An odd Moorhen scratches around search of worms and beetles.

Beside the towpath, swaying clumps of Cow Parsley attract Hover Flies and Bumble Bees, while Raspberry canes crowd among the Cow Parsley,

LADIES SMOCK

compeating for space. Where the path side bank begins to drop slightly, a good view is had of the southern end of the saddle of Kerridge . Above the densely wooded sides, higher ground, covered only with vivid golden Gorse, rises above the trees.

The canal maintains its above average width and begins to curve very slightly to the left ahead. Buff tailed Bumble Bees disappear through the sheltering grasses into a tiny hole in the pathside bank where a young queen will have established a colony, probably in an old mouse nest which will eventually house up to one hundred and fifty individuals. The uncluttered, orderly Bumble Bee colony is a far cry from the sixty thousand which make up an average Honey Bee colony.

From April onwards, one of the most colourful symbols of springtime, the male Orange Tip butterfly will be conspicuous, visiting the pathside White Clovers and the White Dead Nettles. The males hatch well before the females and are recognised by the bright orange tips to the wings. When the females do hatch, they are unrecognizable from the numerous white butterflies as they lack the orange tips. The colourful males will be seen to be patrolling their own territory, a length of canal, into which few rival males will venture. Beside the path, stands the next milestone. Again, this is an original stone which stands tall and uncluttered by encroaching hedgerow or undergrowth. The stone proudly proclaims "From Hall Green, Seventeen and a quarter miles ". This is exceedingly difficult to read as the carved numerals have become extremely weathered and 'filled in' by lichen growth. The reverse side of the stone reads " From Marple' and the numeral 9 has been completely removed by chisel.

Beyond the milestone, the grassy bank falls away to virtual non existence, to reveal a luxuriant meadow rolling away, carpeted by golden Buttercups and Dandelions, toward the saddle of Kerridge.. The canal itself is extremely wide and, in addition to this, there is a distance of some twelve feet or more between the towpath and the waters edge which is taken up by a thick belt of Yellow Flag Iris which has created a marshy habitat by its own presence.

The Iris colony extends away into the distance and the marsh between it and the towpath is home to semi-aquatic plants such as Amphibious Bistort with its spikes of pale pink flowers throughout the summer and the Lesser Marshwort with its insignificant white flowers. The thin strip of woodland which can be seen beyond the narrow pasture to the west is actually the last visual contact with the Middlewood Way. For 9 miles, the canal and the Middlewood Way have run roughly parallel , sometimes in sight of one another, never more than a quarter of a mile apart. Once intense rivals in business but now linked by dozens of adjoining footpaths and by societies demand for leisure time in the countryside. From this point onwards, the "Way" gradually moves further and further westwards toward its end in Macclesfield.

No sooner has the view across to the saddle of Kerridge and of the flowery meadows re-established itself to the east, than the grass bank rises up again to obliterate it. Masses of Stitchwort flowers like summer snowdrifts clothe the bank. Intermingled with the Stitchwort is the more easily overlooked Speedwell. The many varieties of Speedwell are superficially similar but all are low growing, semi rambling, hedgerow plants with flowers of the purest blue.

The distant Kerridge ridge is glimpsed across open meadows as the grassy bank dips lower. It is interesting that White Nancy is now clearly visible once more. As the canal curves and bends and snakes its way along, the ridge is viewed from slightly different angles. The intense quarrying of the ridge is more evident from here due to the fact that the further southward the ridge progresses, the more sparse the formerly dense woodland which clothes the hillside becomes.

The canal begins to curve dramatically to the left. Rounding the curve, the view ahead is dominated by the appearance, to the west of the canal, of the huge factory complex of Hurdsfield Industrial Estate.

On the apex of the bend, Bridge No. 30 comes into view directly ahead. On the approach to the bridge, a splendid view of Kerridge Ridge and Kerridge village is available to the east. It almost seems that no matter how far one travels along the canal, it is impossible to get any further distant from Kerridge!

On the far bank, tall concrete posts support heavy chain link fencing. On top of the posts, three or four tensioned strands of barbed wire project outwards as Hurdsfield Industrial Estate bristles with security. On a narrow strip of grass between the towpath and the pathside hedgerow, at the foot of Bridge No. 30, clumps of White flowering Dead Nettles crowd around a set of stop planks in their wooden stand.

Bridge No. 30 presents an unusual appearance because, at the time of writing, it is undergoing complete restoration. On the north, or Marple facing side, the bridge wall is missing altogether. The stone arch spans the canal but, above the arch, there is no wall or parapet. A soil ramp leads up to the top of the bridge where an information board explains that this bridge is in the process of being restored by the Macclesfield Canal Society. In excess of four thousand pounds has been raised towards the total cost which is estimated to be seven thousand, eight hundred pounds, needed to complete the restoration; a valiant effort of fund raising and sheer hard work on behalf of the societies working parties.

Above the bridge, to the left, a wooden stile and sign post is set into a section of wooden post and rail fencing. One arm of the sign post points back along the towpath and reads "Clarkes Lane". The other arm, pointing over the stile, gestures in the general direction of Kerridge Ridge and reads "Clarkes Lane Kerridge". The bridge wall on the south, or Macclesfield facing side has been built up and finished off. It is heartwarming to see the painstaking effort and attention to detail which has gone into this project. Emerging from Bridge No. 30, a set of stone steps lead from the top of the bridge down to the towpath and, in addition to this, a concrete ramp with a wooden handrail has also been laid. Between the towpath and the waters edge, the narrow strip of ground throngs with Plantains and Lady's Smock.

The waterway continues wide with banks unlined and, here and there, clumps of Aquatic Plantain grow right out into the water. Beyond the security fencing of chain link on the far bank, a planted screen of Leylandi conifers hide the massive factories which lie beyond. The industrial estate is vast by Cheshire's standards and partly accounts for Macclesfield's below average unemployment figures.

Green Veined White Butterflies visit the Bush Vetch and the Lady's Smock beside the water.When in flight, the Green Veined White is often mistaken for the female Orange Tip. It will more often be encountered here than in gardens as it is a native of damp meadows, bogs and forest rides.

Where a gap occurs in the dense pathside hedgerow, the view across to the east is virtually unchanged. Kerridge Ridge is viewed across lush meadow land where large herds of Friesian cattle graze the rich grass, upholding Cheshire's right to the title of 'the premier dairy county'.

The waterway curves gradually to the left as Bridge No. 30 is lost from view behind.In the bottom of the pathside hedgerow, Cow Parsley and Rosebay Willow Herb guarantee a continuity of flowering throughout the months of summer. Across the waterway, the far bank is crowded with brambles and bushy Willows which partly hide the chain link fencing. Despite the layers of screen, the ominous and unfamiliar sounds and shapes of the factories are evident from the canal. Both of the waterways banks are colonized by Yellow Flag Iris which effectively narrow the canal as they reach out into open water. Gaps in the pathside hedgerow reinforce the theory that Kerridge Ridge is traveling southward at a pace equal to that of the towpath traveller. Looking out across the undulating pastureland which is dotted with ancient Oaks, White Nancy can be seen with perfect clarity.

The maze of industry on the western bank was established during the early 1960's and is largely responsible for Macclesfield's modern day prosperity, as it houses world leaders such as ICI and Ciba Geigy in the pharmaceutical industry. The strange sounds of industry which permeate the screen of trees seem alien and out of place in this world of bird song and gently lapping water. From the factories and works, a modern day factory chimney towers upward, higher than its Victorian counterpart at the Clarence Mill at Bollington.

Delicate blue Speedwell flowers ramble through the grasses of the hedgerow bottom. The canal suddenly narrows drastically to pass through the huge Mill stone foundations of a demolished swing bridge. The dismantled bridge was actually Bridge No. 31. It was removed after British Waterways Board become the owners of the Macclesfield Canal and officially numbered the bridges. The previously encountered dismantled swing bridges had all disappeared many years ago and were not existent at the time when the waterways board, as new owners, awarded each bridge its regulation blue number plate. Consequently, no bridge displays the number 31. Beside the towpath, actually in the hedgerow, stands the remains of a drain off paddle, The stone lined underground chamber, planked over with wooden boards is all intact but the mechanics of the ratchet paddle appear in poor repair. At the site of the dismantled swing bridge, just discernible in the undergrowth on the far bank is the remains of a set of stop planks. Covered by rambling brambles and Cleavers, the planks have almost been reclaimed by nature.

The original use or need for this swing bridge, along with the right of way over it from one field to the other for livestock ceased to be relevant with the coming of industrialization to Hurdsfield. The rapid deterioration and inevitable removal of the bridge can vividly be imagined. As a postscript to this observation, set in the tall hedgerow alongside the towpath and level with the swingbridge foundations, the old stone gate posts can still be seen where the field gate used to hang, along with the rusted metal hinges. It is decades now since cattle crossed the towpath, bridge and canal here to graze the land to the west. Beyond the foundations, the wide towpath is enhanced by the delicate blue flowers of the Germander Speedwell.

The vegetation in the bottom of the hedgerow is, during the summer months, frequently host to one of our most vividly coloured insects. It may be less than three eighths of an inch in total length but the Black and Red Froghopper is difficult to overlook. These strikingly coloured insects will rarely be found singly but a dozen or more will often occupy several square yards of grasses and nettles. The 'Black' of its name is glossy jet black and the 'Red' is brilliant scarlet. Touch one, particularly towards the tail end or brush against its host plant and the 'Froghopper' part of its name will be dramatically demonstrated. It will launch into a leap which is reminiscent of a bullet leaving a gun.

The land lying to the east of the canal is tranquil pasture well dotted with trees, quite unlike the stark uniformity of the modern high yield grass fields, chemically treated to provide crop after crop of silage. The most striking of contrasts however, is between the grassland to the east and the industrial metropolis to the west which lurks beyond the tall screen conifers.

Long before the warm air is filled with Orange Tip butterflies, visiting the clovers beside the towpath, an occasional brimstone Butterfly may be spotted. Flitting along the hedgerow from late February onward, the Brimstone is quite often the first and the last butterfly to be recorded in any year as it flies from late February and will continue to show itself through to its hibernation in November. The word 'Butterfly' may originate from the male Brimstones bright butter yellow while the word 'Brimstone' is an old name for sulphur. Some of these ancient meadows through which the canal passes include Buckthorn among their hedgerow trees. Buckthorn is the food plant of the Brimstone Caterpillar. Those meadows and wooded cloughs which are lucky enough to be graced by the presence of wild Primroses would not be honoured in this way were it not for the long tongues of the Brimstone Butterfly pollinating the Primrose. The early Brimstone, fresh out of hibernation is the only butterfly to ensure the safe pollination of this increasingly rare native plant.

Up ahead, the wide waterway again narrows suddenly to pass through the foundations of a second removed swing bridge. As before, this bridge had formerly been awarded a number . Consequently, Bridge No. 32 is also missing. Masses of pathside Lady's Smock flowers in a profusion of pink, soften the sober grey of the Millstone blocks of the swing bridge foundations. When Hurdsfield Industrial Estate arrived on the scene, the right of way across the canal over Bridge No. 32 was rendered obsolete and the bridge removed. The old stone gate posts where the field gate once hung are again visible in the hedgerow. Unlike Bridge. no. 31, the old field gateway has not been obscured and blocked with Hawthorn. Instead, a wooden post and rail fence has been built across the span of the posts and a sturdy wooden stile has been set in it. The stile gives access to a public footpath which winds its way pleasantly across the meadows beyond in a very unhurried manner, where large horses stand in quiet contemplation beneath ancient Oaks; heads to the tree trunks as if meditating.

The footpath meanders away in the general direction of Kerridge Ridge. Beyond the stone remnants of Bridge No. 32, the waterway resumes its normal width. The mountainous hedgerow beside the towpath towers aloft while, its base is host to a mass of billowing white Cow Parsley which, in its own right, has achieved an excessive size, flowering at chest height to the towpath traveller. Beyond the swing bridge foundations, a natural thicket of Brambles, Willows, Rowans and Dog Roses partially screen the high chain link fencing behind which the densely planted Leylandii conifers continue to screen the industrial complex. No sooner has the waterway returned to its customary width than, once more, it narrows drastically to pass through the foundations of a third dismantled swing bridge.

Unlike the previous two, this bridge was removed prior to the official numbering of the bridges by the British Waterways Board. Consequently, this bridge is not, nor ever was No. 33! Without doubt this is a rather confusing state of affairs, considering that the last numbered bridge was the partly restored No. 30 and the next to be encountered will be No. 33! As the stone foundations are reached, the tall security fencing which has been a feature of the west bank for a considerable distance, disappears, veering away at a right angle to the canal, marking the end of Hurdsfield Industrial Estate. As the security fencing drops away, a more distant view westwards becomes available for the first time, of a tower block looming upward from Hurdsfield's other estate, its densely populated housing estate.

The west bank, beyond the dismantled bridge is occupied by an area of public or common ground which is kept mown, presumably by the council. Here the population of the vast housing complex which lies beyond can wander freely or exercise their dogs.

The eastern meadow banks up toward the stone built Shoresclough Farm beyond which, Kerridge End marks precisely that; the culmination of Kerridge Ridge.. Across the water, the west bank is occupied by the first modern overflow sill to be encountered. Constructed entirely from concrete, the intricacies of its operation are hidden due to the fact that it is situated on the opposite bank. The water level concrete sill can be seen to be removing excess water by splash or wave action, presumably down into a run off channel.

Up ahead, the canal begins to curve gently to the right. Behind, the vast industrial estate falls away into the distance.Through a gap in the pathside hedgerow, a brief glimpse of a small stream is caught as it is culverted beneath the canal.Some few yards further along the towpath, the remains of a drain off paddle is encountered.The stone lined chamber with wooden planked cover is intact but the remnant of the ratchet system by which the excess water would be released and channeled into the stream course before passing away beneath the canal, does not appear to have been operated for decades. It is logical therefore, to assume that the modern overflow sill on the opposite bank has taken over the role.

The waterway continues to curve to the right ahead and the far bank is lined by sheet metal as the canal suddenly opens out into a wide hole or bay. The waterway is at least one hundred feet wide at the wide hole and beyond it the mown grassy area is used as a football pitch which is in more or less constant use throughout the year.

Ahead, stands the next bridge, No. 33, a return to the stone arch. Beside the towpath, a low grassy bank rises up on the approach to the bridge which seems to shimmer with the blue of many thousands of tiny Speedwell flowers. The bridge carries only foot traffic, providing a footpath link from the intense housing development which lies beyond the playing fields to the canal towpath Just a few yards out from the bridge, set in a sea of Brambles and Vetch flowers, beside the towpath is the next milestone; a short, squat original stone which reads "From Hall Green 16 and a quarter miles" and "From Marple 10 miles". Beyond the milestone, swarms of Bumble Bees and Honey Bees crowd the blue flowers of the Vetch. The meadow which rises away beyond the low hedge is a mass of seeded Dandelions, Plantain flower heads, Buttercups and splashes of Red Clover. The Red Clover is the most precious of pasture plants, nourishing the soil with nitrogen, providing superb nectar for honey and being valuable fodder for livestock in its own right.

Several tower blocks now rear above the sea of distant housing which is

Hurdsfield . By comparison, the agricultural land to the east along with scattered rural dwellings make up the area known as Higher Hurdsfield. The rural settlement of Higher Hurdsfield has long struggled to retain its individuality from Hurdsfield which technically is absorbed into the fringes of Macclesfield town. In 1286, the village was known as Hyrdesfield meaning "Open Land at a Hurdle". Higher Hurdsfield's first mention as a separate entity appears in 1301. The arrival of the canal completed the isolation of Higher Hurdsfield. In fact the actual boundary between Higher Hurdsfield and Macclesfield had to be altered. The boundary had always been Higher Fence Road but the toll bar was removed by a few yards to the other side of the canal.

The canal's towpath bank continues unlined, Yellow Flag Irises extending out into the water. The far bank, out of necessity, remains metal lined as the ground beyond drops sharply away. The wide waterway remains half embanked on its way to Bridge No. 34. The combined height of the pathside bank and the hedge on top ensure that no view to the east is available. On the approach to the bridge, the sheet metal lining of the far bank comes to an end as the waterway opens out into what was once a wharf. The area of the old wharf is marked by the canals banks being constructed from huge blocks of mill grit. Several locally owned boats enjoy permanent mooring in the disused wharf.

As the bridge is neared, traffic can be seen and heard commuting between Hurdsfield to the west and Higher Hurdsfield and Kerridge End to the east. Beyond the stone lined wharf, the canal narrows to Bridge No. 34, where a row of terraced houses on the west bank follow the busy road towards Hurdsfield. In the shadow of the bridge, a ginger and white cat sits on a grassy patch across the water, mesmerized by dashing and darting Mallard ducklings which are tantalizingly beyond its grasp. It looks on in utter disbelief and total frustration as they scuttle in and out of the shadow of the arch of the bridge, swimming in endless circles around their mother. The wide carriageway above necessitated Bridge No. 34 to be built somewhat wider than normal; a 32ft length of canal passes beneath its arch. Upon passing beneath, we discover that the original bridge has, in more recent times, been further extended in width adding an extra 8 or 9 feet in concrete.

RED CLOVER

Emerging from the bridge, a pathside wooden seat gazes across the water to where the far bank is again lined with massive blocks of stone. The extensive wharf which widened the waterway prior to the bridge now opens out again beyond it .A century ago, the majority of Macclesfield's coal would arrive at these busy wharves either side of the Macclesfield-Hurdsfield-Chapel En Le Frith road bridge as it was originally named. The wharves were operated by J Needham who owned, among other collieries, the

Red Acre Pits, some 5 and a half miles back along the canal between Poynton and Adlington. At the time of writing, new houses are being erected on this southern half of the Needhams Wharf. The new 'cottage style' homes, as a brash advertising hoarding describes them, are certainly desirable and attractive and each dwelling boasts its own mooring rights as each new garden terminates at the waterside mill stone bank lining. For the duration of the wharf, the towpath bank is similarly lined with the sturdy mill grit blocks.

Beyond the wharf, the waterway begins to curve sharply to the right. The canal is overshadowed from both sides now by housing. Mature dwellings occupy the west bank but, beyond the pathside hedgerow, an, as yet uncompleted housing scheme is currently invading the eastern bank. It must not go unrecorded that, some half a mile away, due west, the Middlewood Way or the old Macclesfield, Bollington and Marple railway which has been the canals constant, if often unseen traveling companion now reaches its terminus in Macclesfield.

Many of the gardens which reach down to the waters side on the west bank do so by various ingenious terraced rockeries and flights of steps and often with a jetty or mooring at canal level. Where the pathside bank is not so high, the new housing development on the east bank further crowds the canal with encroaching suberia. Already the next bridge is visible ahead. The multiplicity of colourful garden plants and trees spilling out from the waterside gardens cast dazzling and vivid reflections on the water. Nearing Bridge No. 35, the high pathside bank begins to drop away, revealing the housing estate, compact, neat little boxes built far too close together.

The waterway which has remained unlined since leaving Needhams Wharf narrows to meet Bridge No. 35. The most noticeable feature of the bridge is the pink colouration of its stone which indicates that the millstone grit came from the nearby Teggs Nose quarries. Like the Styeperson Green stone from the Styeperson quarries several miles back, the Teggs Nose Pink was highly prized for its individuality. Bridge No. 35 is also notable as being another very fine skew bridge. No. 35 may not quite match Sugar Lane Bridge, (No. 26, just North of Bollington) in the exquisite angle by which it carries its carriageway across the canal but is, in its own right, a masterpiece. The beautifully engineered blocks of stone, each individually cut and angled beneath the arch, are accentuated by the pink colouration. A flight of cobbled steps with a wooden handrail lead up from the towpath to the top of the bridge.

The housing which encroached upon both banks prior to the bridge, disappears without trace beyond it. By contrast, the canal's west bank is now occupied by a meadow, which slopes gently away from the canal, grazed by a herd of Fresian cattle. The waterway curves sharply to the left, sweeping away the claustrophobia of the dense housing. The Friesian cattle in their glossy black and white livery, slurp loudly at the canal water, consuming gallons at each visit. No sooner does the canal complete its sharp deviation to the left than it begins an equally sharp one to the right.

The Willow Herb, Brambles, Dandelions and Lady's Smock at the foot of the hedgerow is alive with buzzing and droning insects. Beside the towpath, the remnants of an old drain off paddle is set in the hedgerow. A crowded farm yard lies somewhat below the canal's level from where the heavy, sweet aromas of cattle and of silage compliment the rural surroundings. Farm yard buildings crowd towards the hedgerow. An old brick built barn, crammed full of sweet scented hay briefly rears above the towpath. A brief glimpse of tower blocks to the more distant west serves as a harsh reminder of our close proximity to Macclesfield with its constantly escalating population.

Pied Wagtails skim low over the waters surface then veer upwards to perch in the overhanging branches of a waterside Hawthorn tree, their constantly bobbing tails wagging in unison. The commonest of our native wagtails takes its name from its pied plumage; black above, white below, white face patch and black chin and bib. The Pied Wagtail is frequently encountered in farmyards, towns and open country but especially beside water where the canal provides abundantly rich pickings for its insect diet.

As the right curve is completed, not only does the next bridge come into view, but also a panoramic view down to and across Macclesfield is suddenly available. On the final approach to Bridge No. 36, a school playing field occupies the land on the canals west bank. Bridge No. 36 is a modest stone arch which again displays the unmistakable pink hue in its stone. The bridge carries no path or track or public right of way of any kind. No ramp or other facility link the bridge with the towpath save for a well trodden foot way where generations have scrambled up the bank and squeezed between bridge wall and Hawthorn hedge. Beyond the bridge, iron railings along the waters edge on the far bank separate the canal from the sports field beyond.

The more distant view down to the west, as the waterway begins to curve, is of the tower blocks which overshadow the streets of traditional housing. As the canal continues its passage around the curve, it opens out, once more, into the wide expanse of another wharf which is home to Peak Forest Cruisers and has been since the early 1970's. The extensive Buxton Road Wharf was formerly one of the busiest along the canals route, dealing with the majority of Macclesfield towns incoming and outgoing goods.

The canal is wide enough here to allow scores of narrowboats to occupy the extensive moorings which are available in the wharf and to moor solidly along the towpath bank awaiting a turn to move across into the wharf and still enable a clear and unobstructed thoroughfare to run along the centre of the waterway. The extensive parking area beyond the waters edge on the far bank now used by patrons of Peak Forest Cruisers was once the goods yard for the busy wharf. Boats are moored solidly along the towpath bank as the completion of the curve reveals the red brick "Hovis" mill up ahead, towering above Bridge No. 37, Buxton Road Bridge. The canal, beyond the wharf, continues stone lined to both banks and remains a sufficiently generous width for both banks to be more or less permanently moored up with a clear central channel for passing boat traffic.

Mingling with the multitudes of bold Mallards which constantly weave in and out of the moored boats looking for an impromptu meal, is the stately Mute Swan. It glides serenely, keeping a watchful eye on the ever hungry ducks, using them as look outs, making sure that their next meal is homed in upon. Food may appear via the towpath or from the duck feeders on the top of the bridge or, as a by product of meal preparation aboard a boat. It would be a misrepresentation to state that the Mute Swan is common on the Macclesfield Canal, but were it possible to cover the canal's whole length at one go, maybe half a dozen birds would be discovered at any one time. At points such as here, where so many boats are constantly occupied, chances are, a swan will be encountered all year round. An odd pair of birds may turn up anywhere, even on some of the more remote rural lengths where they will have 'stopped off', probably on a lengthy flight between lakes or between the numerous meres for which Cheshire is so famous.

The canal side is far too busy a place for the swans to choose for the construction of their gigantic nest and the rearing of their young. These normally placid birds require copious amounts of free space during the breeding period as they become extremely aggressive and totally intolerant of disturbance. The physical nature of the canal (long straight lengths of obstacle-free water) make it ideal for swans either landing or taking off. Both of these activities require stretches of water of almost aircraft runway proportions, particularly the latter. A swan flying low along the canal, skimming the bridge tops, is a memorable sight. A powerful yet graceful spectacle. The mighty wings throbbing with that emotive and unmistakeable sound. The Mute Swan is actually the world's second heaviest flying bird, the first being an African Bustard. The towpath walker, angler or pleasure boater will testify that the Mute Swan is misnamed. It

MUTE SWAN

will hiss and snort in anger or annoyance and will even trumpet weakly.

The waterway remains stone lined right up to Bridge No. 37. Unlike the majority of the canal's bridges, Buxton Road Bridge displays a concrete, pebble dashed face as opposed to the normal mellow gritstone in its variety of shades and colours. The actual Buxton - Macclesfield Road, the A537, is without question, the busiest highway to be encountered since the A6 at High Lane. Macclesfield town centre is less than ten minutes walk down to the west. If the A537 is followed in an easterly direction for less than three quarters of a mile, it begins to climb steeply into the rugged and desolate landscape of the Peak District National Park. The craggy hillsides, often mist shrouded, crumbling stone walls, sparse vegetation and very few trees represent a stark contrast to our leafy journey along this lush and tranquil waterway.

One and a half miles up the road from Bridge No. 37, Teggs Nose Quarry can now be visited as a fascinating country park. At the quarry face, a display demonstrates how the stone was obtained and what its principal uses were prior to the end of the quarry's working life in 1955. Upon the north face of the bridge is a plaque which, itself, is dated 1981 and commemorates the opening of the Macclesfield Canal on November 9th 1830. The official opening ceremony was an elaborate affair. A procession of boats set out from either end of the canal, 25 boats from the Marple end and 52 from the south. The lead boats from each end carried the directors and committee members of the newly formed Macclesfield Canal Company. Behind the leading boats came others carrying the committees of the other major canal companies and also brass bands. Many of the others were trade boats carrying coal, lime, salt, stone, grain, cotton etc., representing the various commodities to be carried by the new waterway. The two processions met at Macclesfield and, headed by the Macclesfield cavalry, the proprietors and officials walked in procession to the town hall to "a splendid banquet".

The whole of Buxton Road Bridge seems, at first glance, to be of concrete construction. The canal passes through an arch of considerable length, again concrete, only the towpath itself is constructed from blocks of mill grit incorporating stop plank grooves. Now, exactly 10 miles, 7 and a half furlongs from our journeys start at Marple, the heart of the town is reached from which the canal takes its name.

Macclesfield is automatically associated with the silk industry, the first silk mill being built in 1743, but, prior to that Macclesfield existed as a market town of medieval origins. This medieval core of the town which centres upon the parish church, town hall and market place is still very much the focal point of a town which appears to have spread and shifted in diverse directions. The position of the medieval town upon the bluff of an escarpment hints at its defensive positioning. From the valley below, the view of the church is breathtaking in more ways than one as it is only accessible by way of a steep climb up precipitous cobbled walkways.

The ancient township of Macclesfield was in existence at the time of the Domesday survey and was awarded its Charter in 1261. The parish church was founded in 1278, but was largely rebuilt in the 18th Century and again in 1901. The oldest section of the church surviving today is the Savage Chapel on the south side built between 1501 and 1507 by Thomas Savage, the Archbishop of York. Macclesfield's early industrial growth was centered upon the Park Green area which lies to the south of the old town where the availability of water power, provided by the River Bollin, encouraged the building of mills. Consequently, Park Green emerged as a second Macclesfield town within the township as a whole, with its own principal buildings, churches and large houses. It is in this area that the instigator of Macclesfield's industrial growth established his business. Charles Roe opened his silk button and twist operations in 1744. During the following century, the town was the very centre of England's silk industry.

Architecturally, Macclesfield appears overwhelmingly Georgian with the dignified mill in Park Green dating from 1785 and the town as a whole is famous for its profusion of splendid Georgian doorways. Throughout the town, typical Georgian doorways are to be found in a tremendous variety of styles. Park Green House displays a fine doorway, a house built by Charles Roe for the vicar of Christ Church. Christ Church was founded by the benefactor Charles Roe, but it was another industrialist, John Whittaker who build Macclesfield's vast four storey Sunday School to accommodate 2,500 pupils in 1814; it is this building which has become the Heritage Centre and where the history of Macclesfield and the development of its silk industry can now be discovered.

Charles Roe was involved with early attempts to include Macclesfield within the national canal system. It was he, along with Sir William Warren, then Lord of the Manor in Stockport and Poynton who, in 1763, attempted to persuade the Duke of Bridgewater to extend to Macclesfield, the projected Stockport branch of the Trent and Mersey Canal. Roe had copper works in Macclesfield, Bosley and Havannah near Congleton. The ore came from Anglesey and North Wales by boat to the River Weaver and from there, it had to be hauled by road into Cheshire. This unsatisfactory method could have been avoided if the ore could have reached Macclesfield by canal. Warren was anxious to have a better outlet for his Poynton coal but the canal was considered non feasible and came to nothing.

In 1765, Roe and Warren began to explore the possibility of a canal linking Stockport via Poynton to Macclesfield and the Weaver. The route was to take in Knutsford, Alderley Edge and Mottram St. Andrew with the southern branch following the River Bollin to Macclesfield, and the northern branch passing through Poynton to Stockport. On this occasion, a bill was passed through the House of Commons, but had difficulties with the House of Lords and, consequently, the bill never reached the statute book. A further idea was considered then dropped during 1765 to connect the industrial towns of Congleton, Macclesfield and Northwich. The completion of the Trent and Mersey Canal in 1777 still left Congleton and Macclesfield without water communication. All in all, a dozen or more schemes had been aired in greater or lesser detail for a canal serving Congleton and Macclesfield over a period of sixty years before the Macclesfield Canal materialized.

Beyond Bridge No. 37, the canal instantly widens right out and the towpath is totally overshadowed by the "Puss in Boots" public house, whose 'beer garden', is actually seats and tables set out on the extra wide towpath. The "Puss in Boots" is an old stone building which has been much refurbished to cater for Macclesfield's canal borne tourist industry. A wrought iron staircase makes its way up the gable end of the building in stages or flights from towpath level to the lounge entrance.

The canal's far bank is stone lined beyond which, a wharf area is constantly parked solidly with cars using Macclesfield's Marina. Boats moor solidly along the towpath bank in addition to the far bank. Many are visiting craft from far afield; Macclesfield's holiday makers! Beyond the "Puss in Boots", the towpath returns to its customary width but, in the place of the usual hedgerow, a low stone wall runs alongside it. Against the stone wall, the next milestone is overhung by rampant Privet which invades from gardens beyond. The lettering on this original stone is almost completely unreadable. "From Hall Green" can just be made out but the figure "15 and a quarter miles" is completely lost. "From Marple, 11 miles" is just visible on the other side.

The ever widening waterway is overshadowed by the huge brick Hovis Mill building on the west bank. The large open area of wharf between the Buxton Road Bridge and the Hovis mill was originally known as Vernons Wharf, the same Lord Vernon of Higher Poynton whose colliery empire dominated the Poynton coal field. Much of the coal which was loaded into boats at Mount Vernon canal arm would be unloaded here for distribution throughout Macclesfield.

The massive brick structure of the Hovis Mill towers five storeys high above the canal, surmounted by a brick chimney. The profusion of mooring rings set in the towpath reflect the importance of this former corn mill. The mill was built in the late 1820's to coincide with the canals opening in 1831 so that it could benefit from the bulk transport of its grain and wheat. The special germ flour for which the mill became famous was first produced in Macclesfield in 1885 by Richard Smith. The nutritional advantages of incorporating the wheat germ with the flour which was the basis of the Hovis principal, and which remains relatively unaltered today, was orginally treated with much scepticism and opposition.

The Hovis mill, consequently, can be considered to be the birthplace of the firm of Hovis. The name "Hovis" is derived from the Latin "Hominis Vis" which means "power to man". The company became major employers in Macclesfield until the firm moved its milling operation to Trafford Park, Manchester in 1914. The Macclesfield mill continued to be owned by the same company, becoming, firstly its tin and bag producing plant then later, its publicity works. It is still possible to make out the the words "Publicity Works" which were once painted boldly across the mills frontage, overlooking the canal. As with all of the previously encountered canalside mills, the Hovis building now houses light engineering and office units.

Alongside the mill, the waterway is exceptionally wide, wooden jetties projecting out into the canal from the far bank, against which boats in abundance are moored making Macclesfield Marina one of the busiest along the canal's length. An amazing variety of dogs will be met along the canal ,especially in the more built up areas. Most encounters are friendly, often encouraging a pat or a smile from the towpath traveller. Some thing which does not bring about a smile though is the behaviour of some of the dog owners. Dog fouling is a serious problem which many otherwise intelligent dog walkers seem to turn a 'blind eye' to. This is sadly all to true as parents of some visually handicapped children will be aware. The practise of allowing dog faeces to remain on the towpath allows the parasite Toxicities to thrive in the soil where it can remain active for years. This parasite can easily be picked up on the hands or feet, and if accidently passed on to young children can actually cause blindness.

This problem needs to be taken seriously by all dog owners who should carry the necessary scoop facilities and not pretend that it has nothing to do with their dog. It certainly is not the poor dogs fault, who is only doing what comes naturally. More education in this area would help remove this very smelly problem from our canals,parks and other grassy areas. Apart from the ignorance of letting this continue, often signs will be seen waning of fines for dog fouling in public places. Perhaps the provision of 'poop' dust bins in strategic places would help? Whilst on the subject of dog ownership, it is the law that any dogs, especially large ones, must be kept under control in public places, which of course, includes the canal towpath.

CHAPTER FIVE
MACCLESFIELD TO OAKGROVE

At least sixty moored boats constantly occupy Macclesfield Marina at any time of the year and often many more will crowd the expansive sheet of water in front of and beyond the Hovis Mill. Ducks find the intense habitation by man greatly to their benefit and are accompanied by the Mute Swan which glides majestically between the moored craft diligently tracking down that free meal.

The stone wall beside the towpath retains the neat lawns and prim gardens which slope steeply away from it toward the modern housing scheme. Gaily coloured flowers and shrubs frequently spill over the wall from the gardens; the bright pink clusters of flowers which smother the Rosa Rugosa or shrub rose, tumble towards the towpath, striking a parallel with the frequently encountered wild Dog Rose or Briar Rose from which it is directly descended. The pathside wooden seat, set in it's neatly cobbled area is strategically positioned to enable the resting walker to contemplate the comings and goings within the crowded marina. The sights, sounds and smells of boat painting, galley cooking and boat swilling are lived out all day long.

The waterway and towpath begin to curve gently to the left. At the foot of the stone wall and encroaching outward, threatening to engulf the towpath is a plant of nightmarish proportions which would go largely unnoticed in a primeval swamp or some steamy jungle. It is, in fact, a gigantic representative of the varied and diverse Polygonum family, a plant which was introduced to these shores by some intrepid Victorian plant hunter, that valiant breed of explorer who risked life and limb to secure specimens of exotic flora to add to the collections of botanical wonders housed in the elaborate gardens of gentlemen's country houses and the great estates. This particular Polygonum will be found in damp areas or waterside or swampy situations in gardens laid out in the 1840's and 1850's, often in huge uncontrollable colonies. It reaches 7 to 10 feet in height with large leaves and thick, hollow stems.

Where it has innocently been introduced to the suburban garden, it is rapidly identified for what it is, an invasive alien and is quickly uprooted (no simple task) and thrown promptly over the garden wall, as is the case here where, were it not for the relentless trampling of feet, year in, year out, it would rapidly swamp the towpath. As the waterway continues to curve and the marina is slowly but surely left behind, the canal begins to narrow, stone lined to both banks. Once around the curve, bridge No. 38 is visible ahead. Beside the towpath, a narrow strip of grass, overgrown by Nettles and Cleavers grows next to the stone wall, at the top of which, a huge Privet hedge totally hides whatever lies beyond. The Hovis Mill disappears from view as the curve is rounded.

On the approach to bridge No. 38, a quaint cottage is encountered beside the towpath. Originally built by the Macclesfield Canal Company, it housed an employee whose task it was to monitor passing boat traffic and to calculate cargo size and loading and to work out the appropriate tolls. A tiny postage stamp lawn beside the towpath then a metal hurdle fence separates the public right of way from the diminutive cottage garden. Against the whitewashed walls of this picture book dwelling, clipped Forsythias, Day Lilies, Escalonias, winter flowering Jasmines and the obligatory rambling Roses are all squeezed into this tiny space epitomising the classic cottage garden in miniature. The name plate on the cottage wall reads "Canal Side 1". A huge Montana Clematis which cascades down the wall beside the cottage, flowing with pink flowers, completes this idyllic scene. Tall, blue flowering Dutch Iris cluster around the squat front door which is two good strides away from the towpath. The waterway, alongside the toll house is as narrow, by comparison, as it was wide some moments ago alongside the marina. The extreme narrowing of the waterway was intentional, forming a bottleneck to prevent any boats from passing through without being assessed for payment.

Originally, a small pedestrian bridge had existed immediately beside the stone bridge, No. 38, to allow the toll keeper access to both banks in pursuit of his duties. The unusual iron work which is to be seen, set in the mill grit lining blocks of the towpath bank, is actually the remains of the footbridge locking mechanism. The high stone wall which extends between the toll keeper's cottage and the bridge continues to be overhung by masses of Privet and Laurel. Bridge No. 38 is another example of a skew bridge which, again, has a marked pink pigmentation in it's stone. For reasons unknown, the inside of the bridge arch has been lined in concrete. This arch spans a sixty feet length of canal; were it much longer, it would qualify as a tunnel. Immediately beyond the bridge, a low wall beside the towpath leads to a flight of stone steps which curve gracefully up to the road above.

Across the canal, a yard with garages and outbuildings occupies the western bank. Beside the towpath, a second canalside cottage has, like the toll house, no access onto a road but has it's only link with the outside world via the stone steps which lead up to the bridge top. The waterway begins to curve once more to the right. Upon the completion of this curve, the next bridge is clearly visible ahead.

From the completion of the curve up to bridge No. 39, the far bank is occupied by another example of extremely tasteful modern housing. Built as one long building in reclaimed brick, the seven dwellings enjoy an idyllic waterside situation. A balcony at first floor level, overlooking the waterway is an added bonus which all of the seven units can benefit from. Apart from the above average architecture, high quality building and tasteful setting, the feature which makes these particular canal side homes unique is that, incorporated into the waterside garden of the first one is Macclesfield's last surviving canal crane, now fully restored and painted out in green and red. The area now occupied by these new buildings was formerly another thriving coal wharf where the crane earned it's keep unloading the laden narrowboats. Although it is now nothing more than a garden ornament, it's future is secure. The wharf was kept busy during it's working life, handling large quantities of coal which was employed in the smelting process at Charles Roe's copper works situated in nearby Windmill Street.

Large unkempt Elder bushes dangerously overhang the towpath on the approach to bridge No. 39. A pathside wooden seat suddenly appears, set well back against the stone wall which still runs alongside the towpath but is otherwise lost amid the dense pathside shrubbery. The bench, set in the customary cobbled area, looks out across the canal to the dwellings which occupy the old wharf. Tubs and containers dotted around the stone wharf containing brilliant scarlet Geraniums in summertime complement the mellow old stone and the soft textures of the reclaimed brick work. The white painted wrought iron patio furniture and the gay colours of the Violas and Pansies which crowd around the proud old crane seem to contrast with the leafy seclusion which one experiences sitting on the pathside seat surrounded by Elders and Privets and overshadowed by the tall Sycamore trees which stand beside the bridge, their great spreading boughs reaching out across the canal.

Bridge No. 39 is a standard stone arch, low and unobtrusive and again, tinged pink.Beyond the bridge, gardens reach down to the water's edge from the far bank and, beside the towpath, the same stone wall continues to run alongside.Boats are sporadically moored to either bank well into the distance where bridge No. 40 is plainly visible.Where a view is briefly glimpsed over the pathside stone wall to the east it is across an undulating grass field to more distant housing. Gardens reach the canal's edge on the west bank for the entire distance between bridges 39 and 40. Approaching bridge No. 40, it is noticeable that it stands considerably taller and is entirely more prominent than No. 39 which was somewhat diminutive and was dwarfed by encroaching trees. No. 40 is a sturdy structure, robust and rugged, through the arch of which, bridge No. 41 can be seen.

Immediately prior to No. 40, a set of cobbled steps with a wooden handrail lead up to Windmill Street above. A wooden gate at the top of the 27 steps gives access to the street which coined it's name from the working windmill which was incorporated into Charles Roe's copper works. A wooden seat is provided in the shadow of bridge No. 40, situated between the cobbled flight of steps and the bridge itself. The wall behind the seat joins the stonework of the bridge and is clothed during the months of early summer by one of our most pretty of wild flowers, one which is frequently encountered along the Macclesfield Canal.

The delicate red flowers, shading to pink of Herb Robert appear from late May through to September. In addition to the decoration and interest created by the flowers, the deeply divided fern-like foliage and hairy stems assume a fiery red with the coming of Autumn. The native Herb Robert is widespread in shady places, on hedge banks and walls or in woods. The plant, said to take it's name from one Robert, an early duke of Normandy, is a member of the Cranesbill family, all reasonably common wild flowers of similar appearance whose hybridisation over several centuries began to furnish the gardener with the basic stock from which that most popular of garden, greenhouse and conservatory plants, the Geranium, arose.

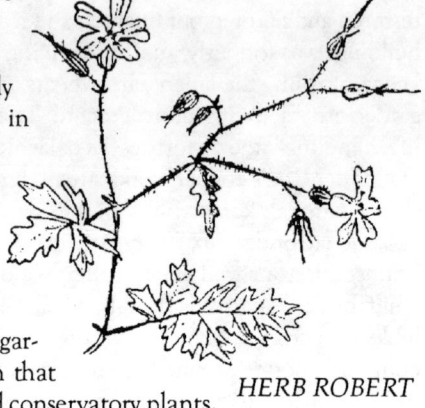

HERB ROBERT

Pausing for a moment to rest upon the wooden seat, bridge No. 39 is still clearly within view to the right. No. 40 overshadows the seat and No. 41 is beyond, but a short distance southward. Passing beneath the archway of No. 40, the pink colouration of the Tegg's Nose stone has not been hidden or tarnished by the 170 years of weathering and atmospheric pollution experienced since the stone was dressed. Emerging from the bridge, we are confronted by a situation so far not previously encountered during our journey. Between bridges No. 40 and 41, no view of any kind is possible to either left or right due to high stone walls which commence, either side, from the stone work of bridge No. 40 and extend to meet up with and merge into the structure of No. 41.

In essence, the waterway passes through a deep stone corridor which seems strange and somehow cold after the sweeping rural views or the suburban gardens, this is featureless and a little claustrophobic. The wall which towers above the towpath bank must be at least 25, maybe 30 feet high, although it seems more like 100. Across the canal, the wall which overshadows the west bank is somewhat lower, possibly 18-20 feet in height. The canal itself is lined with blocks of stone throughout this brief passage between the towering walls. Again, the telltale pink hue is discernible in the stone all around. Less than one hundred yards of canal separates the two bridges which could be described as being joined or linked as the walls on either side of the waterway are as one with the fabric of the bridges.

Bridge No. 41 is quite unlike any other along the Macclesfield Canal in that the waterway makes no attempt to narrow to pass beneath it and the towpath is similarly unaffected. The arch of the bridge is a huge yawning span and is also very high. The towpath walker, if an adult of average height, will occasionally feel tempted to bow the head slightly to pass beneath the customary arch, here, the arch itself rises to 14-18 feet above the water. When the actual height of the bridge wall is added to the excessive height of the arch, a picture begins to emerge of the giant proportions of bridge No. 41 which appears quite out of character with the Macclesfield Canal's normal architecture. One could argue convincingly that such a bridge was constructed to span the canal at some later date or as an afterthought, as the waterway does not appear to have been tailored to fit the bridge. It's proportions were so grand that it could have carried a major highway, now diverted or a busy railway, now dismantled but the bridge is most definitely original and never carried either road or rail. It remains an architectural odd ball and the most enduring example of Tegg's Nose stone as the pink beneath it's huge arch is exquisite.

Beyond the curious bridge No. 41, the mountainous wall continues to tower above the towpath bank but, across the water, a modern building in monotonous new brick occupies the site of another bygone wharf.. This less than inspiring building comprises flats and garaging for the occupants and, when compared with the elegant development which occupies the wharf adjacent to bridge No. 39, is very uniform in appearance and architecturally bland. In place of the brilliantly coloured geraniums in tubs and urns, on this canalside jetty, we have laundry hanging out to dry! The buildings almost totally conceal Richmond Hill wharf which was Macclesfield's last operational coal wharf which only closed for business in the mid 1970's. By comparison, the huge wall to the left could never be described as uniform or bland due to the diversity in size and shape of the blocks of stone and the differing colours and tints and graining of it's texture. Also nature makes continuing efforts to colonise even this towering man made rock face.

Here and there, Honeysuckle, rooted in the strip of ground between the foot of the wall and the towpath, attempts to scale the heights. In odd places, growing actually from the crevices between the mill grit blocks, Feverfew flowers profusely during June, July and August. Few wild flowers are prettier than Feverfew, in fact, it is grown in many gardens as a border flower where is seeds profusely. In the wild, it frequents waste ground and hedge banks but has a curious affinity with walls and other precarious situations where it must both struggle for nourishment and cling on to survive. It is densely covered with daisy-like white flowers with bridge yellow centres. It was not for it's decorative appearance that it was introduced into the British Isles by medieval herbalists but for the powerful drug it contains which was used, as it's name implies, to reduce fevers and to relieve headaches.

Leaving bridge No. 41 behind, the canal begins to curve sharply to the left ahead. The building which occupies Richmond Hill wharf is replaced by an odd assortment of sheds and yards. Ivy leaved Toadflax is another pretty plant which finds the pathside wall to it's liking. This is another widespread flower which was introduced into the British Isles, in this instance, from the Mediterranean some three hundred years ago. Although found throughout the length and breath of the country, Ivy Leaved Toadflax will grow only on old walls, a habit which serves to limit it's distribution. A suitable wall will often be heavily draped with this delicate but persistent trailer whose stems root at intervals loosely into the masonry. It's small leaves resemble those of ivy in shape but the exquisite flowers are similar in form to those of a Snapdragon; two projecting lips and a backward pointing spur in a shade of lilac with a yellow centre.

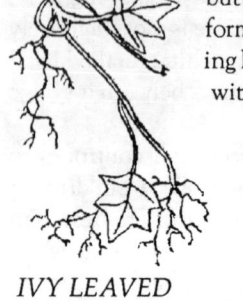

IVY LEAVED TOADFLAX

Suddenly, the canal's far bank is lined by sheet metal as the waterway is half embanked, the ground beyond the metal lining falls away quite steeply, affording a panoramic view down to and across Macclesfield. In fact, this is almost like a carefully stage managed encore prior to the final curtain because, no sooner is the town of Macclesfield spread out in all it's variety with fine views of the old Sunday School building housing the heritage centre and at least five church towers, than the canal promptly bids farewell to the largest town along it's route and heads determinedly for open countryside.

The waterway is wide and straight on it's passage across the half embanked section. A huge container depot lies immediately below the canal's bank to the west, although only the roofs of the warehousing can be seen from the towpath, so steeply does the ground fall away. The towpath bank is now lined by large slabs of stone where the Ivy Leaved Toadflax from the high pathside wall has successfully seeded as it grows from the joints between the ground level blocks.

The wall abruptly comes to an end, giving way to an equally high grass bank which sports a low stone wall along it's top. The grass bank is home to Plantains, Sorrels and red Clover, providing superb habitat for a multitude of insects and small mammals. In places, Bilberry bushes and wild Heathers grow patchily on the steeply sloping banks, indicating where the poor soil is acid enough to allow these two plants of high moorland to eke out a living. The Bilberry is actually a member of the same family as the Heather and is the only representative to shed it's leaves in winter time.

The canal and towpath begin to curve once more to the left ahead, leaving behind the final view of Macclesfield. Where the high pathside bank drops sufficiently for the briefest of glimpses to be available for the first time over the stone wall, a distant view eastward is still impossible due to a banky meadow which rises up beyond the wall. The sounds of ewes and lambs which graze this steeply sloping meadow marks a welcome return to more pastoral surroundings, not encountered since Hurdsfield. The half embanked situation continues for, as the container depot falls away from the west bank, it is replaced by housing and gardens which are all but out of sight from the canal and towpath, so steeply does the ground drop westward. Occasionally, the rough bank which separates the towpath from the stone wall degenerates into a mass of Brambles, Willow Herb and Nettles. The pasture land to the east continues to rise, if not quite so steeply, away providing perfect ground for the flocks of sheep which browse the slopes.

Across the canal, the ground drops down to allotments serving Macclesfield's suburban fringe. Rows of greenhouses and potting sheds in various shapes and sizes are just visible below the level of the canal's embankment. Between the towpath and the stone wall, thickets of Raspberry canes provide a wide range of birds including the Mistle Thrush, Dunnock, Blackbird, Song Thrush and Bullfinch with a luxurious feast of succulent fruit in late summer, a harvest which may provide a juicy snack for the passing towpath traveller.

Woody Nightshade twisting and twining it's way through the Brambles and onto the stone wall just several yards beyond the last of the Raspberry canes provides a total contrast. The display of blue and yellow flowers in mid summer is followed by the berries which are green at first, ripening to yellow and finally to deep red. The much less common Deadly Nightshade has black berries which are far more toxic than those of the woody Nightshade but all parts of the plant are capable of causing sickness.

The sheet metal lining of the canal's west bank ends, consequently the embankment comes to an end and a stone wall begins, virtually at the water's edge behind which, a pasture field stretches away. Hereford and Charolais cattle gaze over the wall at passing boat traffic with mild disinterest. At last, with not a single building in sight ahead, the canal is back in open countryside. An unhindered length of waterway stretches away into the distance with the slightly ramshackle stone wall bordering the pasture on the west bank and the rather tidier wall separating the towpath from the sheep meadows on the eastern side.

Some considerable distance ahead, the next bridge is just visible. Interestingly, the bridge will prove to be No. 43, not No. 42. As no evidence remains of No. 42, the circumstances surrounding it's disappearance will remain a mystery. Between bridges 41 and 43, the waterway never attempts to narrow down to pass through the site of a dismantled swing bridge.

The grassy strip between wall and path now throngs with Red Campion, another example of a native hedgerow flower which is rarely 'weeded out' of gardens, should it seed there by chance, for it is tall, handsome and covered with masses of red flowers in May and June. The Red Campion will, on

RED CAMPION

occasions, grow alongside it's cousin, the white Campion and the two will readily hybridise producing plants in a wide range of pinks.

Quite suddenly, the pathside wall is replaced by another towering example, equal in proportions to the huge wall which spanned bridges 40 and 41. From towpath level, it rears to a height of twenty five feet or more and is smothered in a rampart covering of Ivy. The wall on the west bank also increases in height as does the bank upon which it is built, the overall effect being that of entering a cutting within which, bridge No. 43 is surrounded by walls of mill grit. The red Campion, in places, strays across to the canal side of the towpath as well as the wall side. As the red Clover is in flower during the same period, the towpath is reminiscent of passing along a red corridor with soft red walls and crimson carpet.

The mountainous wall appears to increase in height, the nearer it gets to bridge No. 43; great stone buttresses every so often lean to it from the towpath. Decades of growth of Ivy with thick woody stems cascade down the buttresses which support this huge wall. Feverfew again puts in an appearance, growing between the large blocks of stone of the wall, it's gay white and yellow flowers adding light to this craggy cliff face of a wall. Ivy scrambles upward from ground level and flows downward from somewhere above. The high walls either side of the waterway merge into the stonework of the bridge which still bears the hallmark of having originated at the Tegg's Nose quarries. Bridge No. 43 is an excessively tall, sturdy and robust structure, an impression which is accentuated by the merging of the huge buttressed wall. In the shadow of the bridge, a set of stop planks are housed in a recently constructed breeze block and concrete container.

The clean bright concrete top indicates that the structure is very recent but, it is a sad reflection that it has already had sufficient time to accumulate a proliferation of graffiti in a kaleidoscope of lurid colours and symbols. It is only as the arch of the bridge is approached that it becomes clear that bridge No. 43 is actually a roving bridge. Beyond, the towpath is returned to the west, right, or downhill bank.

This situation confirms that Macclesfield town is well and truly behind us. Although the vast majority of the 27 3/4 miles of towpath runs on the western bank, through the major trade centres such as Macclesfield and Congleton and between bridges No. 1 and 2 at Marple, this bank is often occupied by wharfs, hence the need to swap banks. This was to originally allow the horses which powered the haulage, unimpeded to pass along the waterway.

Passing beneath the arch, the gravelled towpath becomes a cobbled ramp which snakes sinuously upward and round to the bridge top. A wide cobbled walkway leads across the top where a low wall gives a clear view southward of the canal with it's towpath restored to the normal side for the first time since Clarkes Change bridge on the outskirts of Hurdsfield. The high northward facing bridge wall however permits no view back up the waterway in the direction of Macclesfield. The cobbled ramp which leads steeply down to the towpath on the western bank does so in a graceful curving descent.

BRIDGE NO 43 AT GURNETT

The instant that the cobbled ramp becomes ordinary towpath, the next milestone stands prominently as if welcoming the traveller down from the bridge. An original stone, the distance from Hall Green which should read 14 1/2 miles has been defaced but, "From Marple 12 Miles" is clearly legible. Beyond bridge No. 43, the canal retains the slightly claustrophobic feeling of a sheltered passage as high walls continue to tower above both banks.

The high wall beside the towpath is at least twenty feet tall with the delicate flowers of Germander Speedwell lapping against the foot and Feverfew growing out from the stones well above head height. Masses of Ivy cascade downwards while a thick carpet of the brightest blue Speedwell decorates the thin strip of ground between the towpath and the wall, complimenting the pink of the stone in a way that only natural contrasts can achieve. Across the waterway, a wall of equal proportions is separated from the canal's edge by a belt of tall trees which form a solid, regimented line right from Bridge No. 43, well into the distance. Ahead, the waterway begins to curve quite sharply to the right, remaining heavily shaded and tranquil, protected and contained within the sheltering walls.

The tall trees across the canal, balance precariously on the narrow strip of ground which forms the canal's east bank, between the water's edge and the high wall. Likewise, the towpath traveller experiences a feeling of being 'hemmed in' on an unusually narrow towpath between the water's edge and the equally lofty wall to the right. The waterway has deviated now to the extent that bridge No. 43

is lost from sight. Eventually, the wall on the far bank begins to fall away taking the towering trees with it, allowing light to flood in to brighten what has almost been a tunnel passage. Quite abruptly, the pink wall beside the towpath ends and a set of 37 steep steps lead down to a road which passes beneath the canal via Sutton Aqueduct.

Having emerged suddenly from a deep cutting which ran through the foothills of an area of steeply rising ground known as Gurnet, the canal now spills out into a natural valley, that of the river Bollin, which is occupied by the hamlet of Sutton. Sutton Aqueduct is stone built and carries the canal over Byrons Lane which leads from the Lyme Green area of Macclesfield up towards either Sutton Lane Ends or Langley. Directly beside the aqueduct is an ancient hostelry, "The King's Head", in fact, the towpath traveller looks down, almost directly onto the stone flagged roof. The brilliantly whitewashed walls tend to slightly disguise the great antiquity of this old inn. The sign board fixed to one gable end proudly proclaims that this building has been an established coaching inn and smithy since 1695. An information board at the top of the 37 steps, leading down the side of the aqueduct, advertises the King's Head, promising traditional ales, food and hospitality. On it's way across the aqueduct, the towpath is exceptionally wide and the waterway is lined with concrete blocks.

Were it not for the sound of traffic using Byrons Lane, the aqueduct could be crossed almost unnoticed as the view of the lane below is totally hidden by a Hawthorn hedgerow which chooses this inappropriate moment to put in a long awaited reappearance beside the towpath hiding the bridge wall and the view westward. Across the canal, the opposite bridge wall is also hidden rom view by tall fronds of bracken which grow between it and the water's edge. The view which is available to the east is of the smoking chimney pots of a row of quaint cottages which line the lane on it's passage up through the valley. In addition to the sound of traffic passing beneath the canal, the entirely more musical sound of swiftly running water also drifts up to the towpath.

In addition to the lane, Sutton Aqueduct also spans the river Bollin. The young river is little more than 15 feet wide here. It's rushing flow and it's general appearance indicate that it has not travelled far from it's source. As a wide, slow water course, it will eventually discharge into the Manchester Ship Canal, having drained the majority of eastern Cheshire. It's waters will ultimately find their way to the sea via the river Mersey. Once the passage across the aqueduct is complete, an overflow sill or wash is incorporated into the canal's far bank where the excess water is channelled steeply down a sloping, curving course built from stone setts and is deposited into the Bollin, just prior to it's passage beneath the aqueduct.

Beyond the overflow and the aqueduct, the view eastward, out across the heavily flagged roofs of the cottages and across the wooded valley of Sutton is of hilly ground which rises towards Langley. Down to the west, beyond the aqueduct lies the extensive "Macclesfield Garden Centre". This horticultural paradise has it's access on Bullocks Lane which leaves Byrons Lane some 100 yards below the King's Head. The newly arrived Hawthorn hedgerow which ran beside the towpath across the aqueduct is now replaced by a barbed wire fence which draws the attention of the towpath traveller down into the garden centre below.

Due to the scale of this embankment, the garden centre lies far below the level of the canal. The canal's elevated position provides a view directly down into the greenhouses and shops of the garden centre where hundreds of trees and shrubs and plants stand in regimented rows. The nursery proprietors have made ingenious use of the steep embankment beyond the barbed wire fence, planting it with shrubs and trees of every conceivable shape, size, colour and form. Conifers of every kind, Wigelias, Rowan, Laurels, Larch, Lime, Broom, Escalonia, Potentilla and Azalia all clothe the huge embankment, providing a splendid display of mass planting and a superb advertisement for the garden centre.

Brooms galore can be seen in staggering range of colour variations, pinks, purple, reds, pink and yellow, pink and cream, pink and white, growing alongside the natural yellow. The canal itself becomes half embanked as the ground to the west continues to drop steeply away while that to the east returns to canal level. The ground on the far bank is actually the remnants of the ancient parkland belonging to Sutton Hall, now a hotel and restaurant. Quite apart from the tiny settlement of Sutton sporting a seventeenth century coaching inn, the site currently occupied by Sutton Hall, the hotel, dates back to a far earlier period.

As far distant as 1098, Hugh Lupus, Earl of Chester, founded the monastery of St Werburgh in Chester. The manor of Sutton was one of the places mentioned as an endowment to that monastery. By 1153, the family of Sutton still held the manorship, at this time under Hugh Revelic, sixth Earl of Chester and from that time on, the family continued to hold it in uninterrupted succession for twelve generations. An entirely separate branch of the Sutton family from Leicestershire inherited the lands and the hall around 1500 and continued for a further five generations after which time, by the death of Richard De Sutton, "slain in a tumult in Chester!" the estate passed to Sir Humphrey Davenport of Bramhall. From this family, it passed to Sir Rowland Belasyse, ancestor of the Lords of Fauconberg. During the Victorian period, the building and what land remained was owned by the lords of Lucan and it is from this period that much of the present fabric dates. From the canal, virtually no part of the building of Sutton Hall is visible through the numerous original parkland trees which, by and large date from the early Victorian period when the concept of the landscaped park and such features as avenues of Beeches and Limes were very much in vogue.

From the towpath, it is the huge, mature Horse Chestnut trees, planted singly to enable them to eventually achieve their classic shape and size, which catch the eye, their huge canopies providing shade and shelter for cattle and sheep and their flamboyant candles of white flowers, so conspicuous during May. The barbed wire fence continues to the right of the towpath, beyond which, Bullocks Lane can be seen, down to the west, beyond the garden centre, running roughly parallel to the canal.

By the dawn of the twentieth century, Sutton Hall had degenerated into little more than a farmstead although remnants of exquisitely carved wood panels from the older buildings were incorporated into the Victorian house which bares no resemblance to the massive baronial pile which it replaced. A chapel had existed, incorporated within the original building since being established by Sir Richard De Sutton in 1153. By the Victorian period, the later chapel, built at the end of the sixteenth century by the Fauconberg family was in a sad state of dereliction and was used as stabling and timber storage. This latter chapel contained a priest's house. Prior to it's desecration, the pews, the rich marble slab covering the alter and other valuables were removed to Chelford Chapel and the vaults, containing the remains of many family members were filled in!

The canal curves very gently to the right while, to the west, Bullocks Lane moves closer and closer to the canal. Across the canal, cattle graze among the giant Beeches and Horse Chestnuts. Among the trees, a post and rail fence on the east bank marks the passage of the drive to Sutton Hall. Upon the completion of the canal's curve, the next bridge comes into view ahead. A coincidence exists between the hamlet of Sutton and the fact that the Macclesfield canal; one of the last canals to be cut, should pass through it. James Brindley, Britain's pioneering canal engineer moved to Sutton to live in 1733, aged 17.

He worked in the area as an apprentice Mill and Wheelright. He eventually moved to nearby Leek in Staffordshire, building various water mills for corn and flint. After surveying the various suggested routes for the Trent and Mersey canal in 1758, he went on the become the engineer on Britain's first major canal, the Bridgewater. He spearheaded the canal boom in the 1760's and was working on the Trent and Mersey when he died in 1772; over half a century before the Macclesfield Canal was cut through his former home. One further coincidence is that Brindley was buried at Newchapel, near to Kidsgrove; the terminus of the Macclesfield Canal.

Bullocks Lane crosses the canal at bridge No. 44 which lies directly ahead. Immediately prior to the bridge a half or quarter mile marker stone is set beside the towpath, beneath the barbed wire fence. A set of shallow wooden steps leads up to Bullocks Lane from the towpath. Sutton's ancient history can be traced back to beyond the period of the Norman Conquest. The high ground to the east, beyond Sutton Lane Ends is Ridge Hill. A moated manor house once occupied the Ridge Hill area whose lands were in the possession of a branch of the Legh family (pronounced Lee) ,the Legh's of Ridge. It was from Ridge Hall in Sutton that, during the early eighteenth century, the remains of three monoliths or stone crosses were removed to Macclesfield where, they eventually found their way into the public park. These stone monoliths were widely believed to be Mortuary Stones which had marked the resting place of Saxon nobles or chieftans. It was also understood that at the time of religious unrest during the reign of Henry the Eighth, the memorials had been disfigured and their inscriptions obliterated.

As a matter of far more recent history, bridge No. 44, carrying Bullocks Lane, is another splendid example of canal architecture. Built as an exquisite skew bridge, the angle at which Bullocks Lane crosses the canal is fantastic. Architecturally, bridge No. 44 is on a par with No. 26 at Sugar Lane, north of Bollington; a monument to the stonemason of yesteryear. Beyond the bridge, a jungle of Brambles and red Campion almost conceal a set of stop planks.

Dog Roses, overhanging the towpath pluck painfully at the passer by. When decorated by their pale pink flowers through June and July, they bring a great beauty to these pathside banks. During the same months of the year, the grassy areas to right and left of the towpath are frequently adorned by the massed canary yellow flowers of Meadow Vetching. The yellow vetches seem to take over the flowering period from the blues which tend to be a little earlier. The Meadow Vetchlings flowers of purest yellow, often number anything from five to twelve squeezed onto each stalk. It is a prolific plant of grassy places and will be encountered all along the canal's length. Although it bares forked tendrils, it tends not to climb as vigorously as it's various blue cousins, preferring to use surrounding plants purely for support. It will continue to beautify these grassy areas well into August in most years.

Beyond bridge No. 44, the rough bank across the canal, a mass of brambles, is brightened by the stately spires of Foxgloves, flowering well above the tangling throngs, in both pink and purest white, vividly reflected in the dark water.

In the heat of a summer afternoon, the towpath traveller may be treated to the appearance of the Banded Demoiselle, Britains largest Damselfly at approx 3 1/4 " inches and a creature of striking beauty. Due to its robust size, it flies more powerfully than its cousins of lesser stature. When disturbed, it will lift strongly from the canalside The male Demoiselle appears almost exotic as he reveals the dark blue almost black patches which adorn his otherwise transparent wings. The flickering of the four bold patches (one on each wing)accentuate the fluttering style of flight which is so characteristic of the Damselfly order.

The canal stretches away in a long unhindered length. The rough ground on the east bank is now replaced by a meadow, across which, Bullocks Lane can be seen, moving further away from the canal's course, making it's way towards Lyme Green. The pathside shrubbery is largely made up of Hazel, one of Britain's most common of hedgerow and wayside trees yet rarely to be found along the canal's course. To add further to the variety of pathside shrubbery, a thicket of Blackthorn replaces the Hazel. In early spring, the Blackthorn is covered by brilliant white blossom which temporarily detracts from the long, impenetrable. The fruit of the Blackthorn is the blue-black, bitter sloe, commonly used to flavour gin.

Eventually, this varied hedgerow colony begins to give way to a neater, more orderly Hawthorn hedge beyond which a meadow stretches away westward. Across the water, meadowland stretches away eastward. This rich grazing land once made up the agricultural holdings of the Sutton estate. The canal here marks the boundary between the Sutton lands to the east which, at the time of the canal's arrival, were held by the Lords of Lucan and the extensive lands held by the Earl of Harrington to the west. The unusually straight length of canal which stretches away ahead, does so into the settlement of Lyme Green.

During the warmer months of the year, the canal and it's surroundings provide a perfect habitat for the vast numbers of Swallows and Swifts which throng our summer skies and fill the air with both their pleasing twittering song and their spectacular and breathtaking aerobatics. The canal is particularly attractive to these most familiar and well loved of visitors because both Swifts and especially Swallows feed on the wing by means of insect collection during low level flight. The birds also drink on the wing, skimming rapidly over the canal's surface.

In the case of the Swift, the swarms of insects which throng several inches above the water during warm weather are funnelled into the large gaping bill by stiff bristles around the mouth. When feeding young nestlings, food is stored in a throat pouch which often bulges with gorged insects. These aerobatic birds on sickle wings swoop along the canal at great speed seeming to derive exhilaration and boundless pleasure from swooping through and over the bridges. Their lives are spent, in the fullest sense, upon the wing, alighting only to feed the young, they collect nesting materials and even mate in flight.

The Swift, the duller of the two species, will normally be seen from April through to September. Considering that the Swallow is considered to be the harbinger of summer, the first birds often arrive from their African winter vacation as early as May and stay with us until mid October. The speed at which the bird flashes past the would be towpath ornithologist provides precious little opportunity for identification but, for the record, the Swallow is the one with the russet throat, white marks on the tail and long tail streamers.

SWIFT

To further confuse the matter of identification, as a very rough guideline, in the canal's urban stretches, the numbers of birds will be greatly swollen by the presence of

House Martins. Not a bird of open farmland, this one time cliff face nester now requires human dwellings upon which to construct it's elaborate nest. A smaller bird than the Swallow or the Swift, the House Martin has a noticeably shorter tail and a distinctive white rump.

SWALLOW

Sorrell and Red Clover in flower beside the towpath, Willow Herb and Red Campion dotted in the grassy banks, Woody Nightshade and Honeysuckle rambling along the hedgerow create an ever changing procession of colour; a naturally diverse garden. The meadows which occupy the canal's eastern bank are another favourite territory for the wandering groups of Canada Geese, particularly during the winter months. Like the favoured meadows around Poyton and Adlington, considerable numbers of geese choose to pair up and breed here. Down to the west, the southern tip of Macclesfield is still clearly visible across rolling meadows carpeted with white and red Clover and drifts of yellow Buttercups. The expansive meadowland to the east is grazed by herds of continental beef cattle, Charolais, Simmental and the occasional white faced Hereford. Away to the west, the busy A523 road which links Macclesfield with Leek in Staffordshire comes into view for the first time while the ground to the east rises away to hide the departing view of Bullocks Lane.

A large Heron which had been fishing in the canal's margin, within feet of the cattle on the east bank, takes to the air upon the approach of the towpath traveller. It flies no more than twenty yards further up the waterway and alights once more to continue it's business. This procedures is repeated several time until, with a raucous shriek of utter annoyance, the great bird wheels around and cunningly lands some thirty yards behind the intruding human. A considerable distance ahead, bridge No. 45 comes into view. Down to the west, a large white painted pub, The Star Inn, stands prominently beside the Macclesfield - Leek road. It has been calculated that within the area of Bollington and Macclesfield alone, almost ninety public houses are within reach of the canal towpath!

As bridge No. 45 is neared, the floodlights at Macclesfield football ground can be seen down to the west and it becomes abundantly clear just how busy the A523 road really is. On the final approach to bridge No. 45, the pasture on the far bank gives way to gardens reaching down to the water's edge. The grassland to the right rises up to meet the busy trunk road where an incessant steam of traffic pours across the bridge. A pedestrian footbridge of concrete construction is slung across the canal alongside the original bridge with it's two lanes of highway. Away to the east of the bridge, alongside the A523 lies the community of Lyme Green. The wide stone bridge itself is built at a slightly skewed angle to the canal although almost unnoticeable when compared with the previously described bridge No. 44.

Immediately beyond, a flight of steps lead from the towpath to the busy road. Beside the towpath, the customary hedgerow is replaced by a wooden post and rail fence beyond which, rough, coarse grassland slopes away westward to Lyme Green industrial estate or business park. Similarly, across the canal, a rough bank of overgrown vegetation leads up to scattered workshops and light industrial units. The wide waterway curves slightly to the left, beyond which, a long straight length of canal presents itself. The Hawthorn hedgerow returns beside the towpath, increasing in height, preventing a view down to the west. On the eastern bank, the industrial units eventually give way to pasture rising away from the canal's reedy, unlined margin. The towpath bank is now stone lined, wild drifts of Docks, Sorrell, Nettles and Buttercups, invading the strip of ground between the bank lining and the towpath.

Where a limited view is available, over or through the pathside Hawthorn hedge, it could hardly be described as aesthetic, it is of an extensive scrap yard where hundreds of decaying cars are piled high in precarious stacks, a mournful sort of place where the luxury limousine and the humble family saloon share a common and undignified end. Between the canal and the area occupied by the scrapyard, an Inter-City express train will frequently be seen, speeding either towards or away from Macclesfield, running alongside the waterway is the mainline Manchester - Stoke railway. Beside the towpath, the next milestone is encountered. This is the first new stone to be found since the very first one at Marple junction. Cut from Kerridge mill grit, just like the originals, the inscription, (clearly legible for a change) reads "From Hall Green 13 1/4 miles" and "From Marple 13 Miles". A handsome reproduction of the original, even down to the style of the letters and characters.

The canal continues extremely wide. The rushy margin at the far bank gives way to a meadow which rises away, festooned with Buttercups. A curious feature of this particular length is that the waterway needs to be sheet metal lined on the towpath side because the footpath is noticeably several inches below water level. Beyond the hedgerow, a rough area of marshy grassland slopes gently down towards the busy railway line. Skylarks constantly perform their own particular brand of aerobatics above the long, unkempt grassland which obviously meets their requirements for nesting and breeds the right kinds of insect food.

As the sheet metal lined waterway deviates once more, bridge No. 46 is visible ahead as the canal and railway line move closer and closer together. A beautifully wide stretch of water leads up to the next bridge, the arch of which is mirrored perfectly in the placid water. To the left of the bridge, farm building cluster around a modest stock yard, cattle stand around the foot of the bridge and have eroded the canal bank with their constant trampling.

Bridge No. 46, a modest stone arch, carries an unmade trackway serving several farms. Immediately beyond the pathside hedge, below canal level, a fenced off corner of a field is crammed to capacity with hen sheds, mostly improvised some with attached wire netting runs. The poultry enclosure is home to fowl in abundance and of every kind one can imagine. Muscovy Ducks, fancy Pigeons, Marran Hens, Rhode Islands Reds and Bantoms of mixed and dubious pedigrees. What little space is not occupied by feathered inmates is occupied by wheelbarrows, galvanised water and corn dispensers, mobile chick enclosure and even a small muddy pond where the ducks dabble. The stonework of the bridge displays deep rope cuts and grooves beneath it's arch. Immediately beyond the bridge, a short flight of steps lead up to the track above.

The railway line now runs almost directly alongside the canal. Beyond the railway track, occupying many acres to the west lies Danes Moss, poetically described at "Macclesfield's last wilderness". Danes Moss is one of Cheshire's most important peat bog areas which has, justifiably, been designated a "SSSI" (site of special scientific importance). Exploited for centuries for fuel, the peat was dug commercially and formed a thriving business by the Earls of Harrington. Thankfully, what relatively small proportion of the moss remains is now a conservation area. As the last great ice age receded, the retreating glaciers gouged deep depressions into the softer, more alluvial lands of lowland Cheshire. Over many centuries, these areas filled with dead and decomposing vegetation which eventually formed thick layers of peat. The area of the moss probably existed as a wet and swampy wilderness by the formerly vast forest of Macclesfield. By the Saxon period, the inhospitable moss was supposedly occupied by the Danes from where they conducted their piratical raids throughout the Saxon occupied county.

An interesting little book entitled "Notes of the Antiquities of Macclesfield" written during the 1860's mentions "some very interesting relics left by the Danes have, at different times, been discovered here". The same Victorian writer, namely I A Finney puts forward an interesting and colourful if unproven explanation, regarding the origins of Danes Moss:

> "The site is supposed, by some, to have been an immense forest, and would seem to have been deluged or otherwise destroyed by fire, or some natural cause, as large trees have been frequently found embedded in an accumulation of animal matter of a decayed nature forming a mass of turf which has been used for many generations as fuel for fires."

With the coming of the canal in 1831, the Earl of Harrington's lucrative peat fuel business began to collapse as coal, carried by the waterway in vast quantities, became readily available. As the peat industry died a natural death when it found that it could not compete with the canal's endless supply of coal, the versatility of the raw peat came to it's rescue and Danes Moss continued to be exploited. This time, the justification for the peat extraction was in the name of fertiliser. The canal snakes it's way across the moss continuing to adhere religiously to the parish boundary.

Beyond bridge No. 46, a narrow strip of waste ground, no more than ten yards wide separates the canal from the railway line. When the railway arrived in 1848, unlike the canal, it crossed the moss in more or less a straight line, disregarding any parochial boundaries. The dividing strip of waste land is a jungle of grasses and Great Willow Herb.

The waterway curves to the left as the railway line and canal seem to move evermore closely together. A Hawthorn hedgerow begins beside the towpath, intertwined with Dog Roses, which screens the view of the railway. When an Inter City express roars by, the ground seems to tremble because, the hard core embankment upon which the rails are laid, in turn is laid across a section of peat bog. The majority of the buildings on the east bank are of relatively recent construction. When the Harrington peat business became totally non viable, the old works were converted to the production of animal glue from bones.

This singularly antisocial industry generated much ill feeling and hostility. Production expanded to include the grinding of bones for fertiliser and eventually moved into the processing of slaughter house waste. This downward spiral culminated in actual damage to the canal and it's environment with vast amounts of water being removed for use in the processing, this water being returned to the canal in a disgusting, oily, polluted mess. Thankfully, by the 1950's, this environmentally damaging industry found itself in serious decline, the site gradually being redeveloped. As the curve in the waterway is rounded, the pathside hedgerow increases in height, further obscuring the view of the railway.

Across the canal, the unlined east bank is increasingly colonised by beds of sedges and, beyond the sedges, Willows have been allowed to grow up, screening the engineering works. For the first time, in the distant South East, the next dominant landmark comes into view. Like the cage at Lyme Park and White Nancy at Kerridge the visual feature which accompanies the next section of our journey is a manmade landmark standing on high ground. Unlike the ancient Lyme cage and the curious, early 19th century White Nancy, this one is very much a product of the late twentieth century, the telecommunications tower juts a clear 286 feet above Crocker hill.

As the buildings on the east bank are left behind, the flowery pasture which replaces them is grazed by horses. The pathside hedgerow is replaced by a post and rail fence which reveals the railway, still running parallel to the canal. The jungle of vegetation which separates the railway line from the towpath is extremely valuable as a wildlife habitat for it is totally impenetrable and is never disturbed.

The low growing Willow bushes, Great Willow Herb, Brambles and Nettles present an unapproachable barrier to those passing along the towpath on foot.

Small mammals in particular need the shelter and privacy provided by this linear oasis, sandwiched between the canal on the one hand with it's traffic made up of the unhurried passage of the cruising narrow boat and the railway on the other with the Inter City commuter train tearing along at speeds approaching 100 miles per hour. The Bank Vole, the Common Shrew and the wood mouse all benefit from the protection which they are denied in open farmland. Scores of small Roach dimple the canal's surface as they rise to take Mayflies from the surface film. Again the waterway curves gently to the left. The ground on the east bank is occupied by a boarding kennels, an observation which is confirmed by a chorus of barking and yapping.

A sharp curve sees the railway disappearing rapidly from view as the canal veers away on one of it frequent deviations. On the apex of the curve, the waterway narrows suddenly and drastically to pass through the mill grit mountains of another swing bridge, the difference being that, for the first time since the start of the journey, this bridge is still in existence, if swung permanently open. The swing bridge itself is in good repair and appears to be complete but out of use. It proudly displays it's British Waterways blue and yellow number plate, this being bridge No. 47. The bridge shows no sign of having been used for some years but it's robust timber construction seems to be sound if in need of a coat of paint.

Beyond the swing bridge, the waterway resumes it's customary width, overhung by large trees from the far bank. A large shrub rose on the far bank grows right down into the water, it's big, bold pink flowers break up the solid green of the canopy of trees. Tall Alders overhang the canal from the unlined east bank to the extent that their foliage touches the water and, in turn, their sinuous, tentacle like roots protrude up from the water. A lush grass field stretches away from the canal's far bank, sloping gently upwards to the east. Swallows and Swifts skim inches above the grass of the meadow as they do above the canal collecting insects which hover just above the grass. The canal is wide and dark, tranquil and shaded as it passes through these tree lined banks. Through gaps in the pathside shrubbery, dense birch woodland can now be seen occupying the area vacated by the railway. The woodland floor beneath the birch canopy is largely clothed with grass but, here and there, where the trees grow more thinly, allowing shafts of sunlight to penetrate, tall Foxgloves reach upwards with tall spires of flowers.

Further along, Oak, begin to overtake the Birch in terms of dominance, overhanging the towpath. When the hedgerow or shrubbery is replaced by a barbed wire fence, a fine view is available down into the dark woodland where the canopy now excludes a greater amount of daylight as the more vigorous Oak predominate. The waterway curves gently to the right and beyond the curve, the view directly ahead is dominated by the bulk of Crocker Hill with the Post Office

Telecommunications mast reaching upwards a further 286 feet. Friesan cattle graze a pasture on the canal's east bank which sways gently with oceans of golden Buttercups. The water's edge, where the cattle drink, has been trampled, in places, into muddy quagmire. Beside the towpath, the view into the cool, dark depths of the Oak wood where very little direct light now penetrates, is unhindered by a hedgerow or even a fence now, the woodland and pathway being separated by a deep drainage channel with dark stagnant water lying beneath a scum of duckweed and green algae.

The strip of ground between the bank lining and the towpath is host to a thick belt of common Horsetail, a nonflowering plant which is a survivor of a very primitive group of ancient plants allied to ferns. The ancestors of the humble horsetail included tall forest trees whose fossilised remains formed the vast underlying coal fields of east Cheshire and North Staffordshire which, in turn, led to the Macclesfield Canal coming into being as a means of transporting this rich and valuable commodity. The modern day Horsetail grows from a deep spreading rhizome which, as any unfortunate gardener will testify, is almost impossible to eradicate; traces of Horsetails's rhizome roots being found to depths in excess of six feet beneath the surface of the soil. The rhizome sends up unbranched brownish fertile stems during April which are tipped by a spore bearing structure which resembles a cone. These die after a few weeks and are replaced by the taller green sterile stems with their narrow grassy leaves in layered whorls.

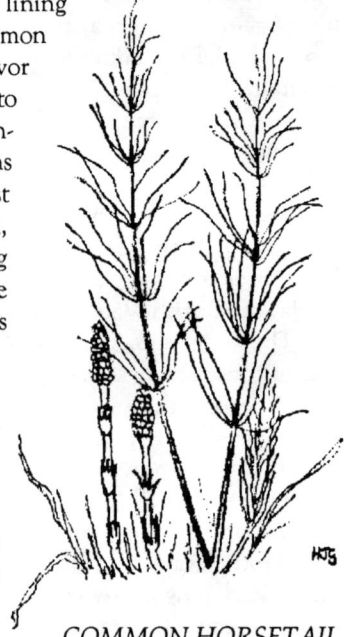

COMMON HORSETAIL

As the canal's course straightens, traffic can be seen ahead travelling along the A523 Macclesfield - Leek road. The whole view ahead opens out as the canal embarks upon the single longest half embanked section throughout it's length. The mixed Oak and Birch woodland begins to move away from the side of the towpath where a narrow strip of grassland takes it's place. To the right of the towpath, a strip of Clover dotted grass is bordered by a barbed wire fence beyond which the ground is embanked away into the ever widening strip of pasture. From the canal's far bank, grassland climbs away towards the Macclesfield - Leek road. The canal stretches away, curving very gradually all the time to the right forming a gentle crescent across the valley, dissecting the old estate of the Earls of Harrington.

Down to the west, the Oak and Birch woodland has now moved further westward almost out of sight, it's place is taken by a patchwork of grass fields which are dotted by ancient Oaks and Ashes. Stunted Alder trees continue to dot the canal's far bank as the busy A523 runs nearer and nearer to the watercourse. 200 yards along the half embanked valley, a squat 1/2 or 3/4 mile marker stone stands in the grass beside the towpath surrounded by carpets of red and white Clovers. Increasingly, the traffic, speeding it's way along the A523 between Macclesfield and Leek, can be seen and heard clearly from the towpath and the hedgerow which separates the grass meadow from the highway is now immediately beyond the east bank. Down to the west the pasture below the grass embankment is grazed by a small herd of plump, glossy black Aberdeen Angus cattle.

A further hundred yards along the half embanked section, the waterway narrows to pass through the tell tale mill grit bank linings of another removed swing bridge. This particular one has disappeared in fairly recent times because it was actually bridge No. 48. The only evidence today of bridge No. 48, apart from it's massive bank stones which will survive for as long as the waterway remains, is an isolated set of weathered stop planks which stand on the canal's far bank in their wooden clamp. On closer observation, stop plank grooves will be seen to be incorporated in the mill grit foundations.

Accommodation bridges, in the form of wooden swing bridges, were in frequent use along this particular reach of the canal as it continues to dissect the ancient Harrington estate. Three hundred and fifty yards along the valley, a stone wall rises directly up from the water's edge on the far bank, separating the waterway from the A523 road which now runs directly alongside. Five hundred and fifty yards along, the half embanked valley temporarily comes to an end. The barbed wire fence is once more replaced by a low, neat Hawthorn hedge. Beyond the hedge cluster sheds and outbuildings which belong to a delightfully simple stone cottage which lies ahead.

At the water's edge on the far bank, the opening to a stone culvert is set slightly back forming a small sheltered bay in miniature, overhung by fronds of fern. The culvert is actually the first water supply to the canal to be encountered sine the commencement of the journey at Marple. Here, water from Sutton or Turkshead reservoir reaches the canal directly after passing beneath the A523 road via this sturdy stone culvert. According to the bill to parliament which was drafted by Thomas Telford and his assistants when originally seeking the enabling act for work to begin on the Macclesfield Canals' construction, there was to be one reservoir at Pott Shrigley, two at Sutton and two at Bosley to supply water to the section of the canal which lies at the 500 foot contour, i.e. Marple to Bosley. Needless to say, the 400 foot level, i.e. Bosley to Kidsgrove, was kept sufficiently 'topped up' by the 500 foot level and the constant use of Bosley locks. The only reservoir near to Pott Shrigley is at Styperson, supplied by rivulets. It is quite possible that at one time this was used to supply the canal but today there is no evidence of a feeder or any connection with the canal of any kind.

At Sutton, there is only the one reservoir which is fed by the Rossendale Brook, a tributary of the river Bollin, but no evidence of there ever having been a second. Likewise, at Bosley, there is only one reservoir, much larger than that at Sutton. In addition to the fact that only two of Telford's projected five reservoirs were eventually constructed, the original Macclesfield Canal Company found that when the canal reached it's full operation, they had an excess of water from the two reservoirs. Sutton held approximately 92 million gallons when full compared with the much larger Bosley, covering 86 acres and holding 402 million gallons. In the early years, the canal companies revenues were boosted by the selling off of excess water. Between the years 1844 and 1846, 200 million gallons at 2d per 1000 gallons was sold to Manchester's Gorton reservoir prior to Manchester acquiring previously unavailable supplied from the Lake District. Directly beyond the mouth of the canal feeder, a black painted sign board set of the far bank warns oncoming boat traffic in bold white lettering, "Slow, Pontoon Bridge 50 yards".

Beside the towpath stands a quaint canal side cottage built from mellow stone, dating from the time of the canal's construction. The modest two storey dwelling with it's brick chimney stack and tiny windows was originally built by the Macclesfield Canal Company for it's employees. The fact that the cottage was totally cut off by the canal, having no access to any roadway or driveway was of little concern to it's original tenants as their vital supplies were constantly brought in by passing boats. Macclesfield was easily accessible due to the fact that continuous boat traffic passing the front door was infinitely more regular and reliable than the equivalent public transport today. The tenants day to day requirements were, available several hundred yards walk away in Oak Grove (for example - The Inn!). However, with the cottage now in private ownership, a solution to the lack of access, particularly in the event of an emergency, needed to be found.

The problem was resolved by the canal's present owners, British Waterways Board, consenting to the installation of a pontoon or floating Bridge. This bridge is permanently moored alongside the towpath bank except when in use. Hoards of Mallards and their kin throng around the Pontoon bridge and sunbathe or simply doze on the grass beside the towpath. Across the canal from the cottage, the strip of ground where the user of the Pontoon bridge alights upon the far bank is denoted by a further "Private Property" sign. Beyond this, a neat hedge and gate give access directly to the Leek - Macclesfield road.

On the continuing curve, the next milestone is encountered. The squat original stone reads quite clearly, "From Hall Green 12 1/4 miles, "From Marple 14 miles". The half embanked situation resumes beyond the cottage as the ground to the west drops steeply away down into a grass valley. Beyond the canal's far bank a mixed hedgerow of Hawthorn, Ash and Sycamore screens the canal from the almost incessant traffic on the A523. Across the road enormous mature trees tower above the roadway, casting a great shadow over both road and canal. Horse Chestnuts, Oaks, Beeches and Larch, all obviously artificially planted, flank the A523, preventing any distant view to the east. Beside the towpath, set in the hedgerow, a drainoff paddle is situated from where it can discharge excess water, via a stone lined channel, into a brook which meanders along the bottom of the grass valley to the west.

The wide, dark waterway now curves gently to the right ensuring that a distant view directly ahead is always tantalisingly out of reach. Every slight deviation of the canal is now copied faithfully by the road alongside, as anyone familiar with the twisting, snaking drive through the tree lined valley of Oak Grove will testify. The dense, unkempt nature of the pathside hedgerow with wild Dog Roses twining and clambering and often overhanging the walkway, largely hides the panoramic view down into the extensive grass valley beyond.

Rounding the latest curve in the canal, boats are often moored, sometimes solidly, nose to tail along the towpath bank as the waterway makes the final approach into the hamlet of Oakgrove. The final straight into Oakgrove lies ahead, at the end of which, the pedestrian section of Oakgrove's rather complicated bridge system can be seen. The length of canal up to the bridge is, more often than not, solidly moored with boats, regardless of the time year. In many ways, Oakgrove is a curious little settlement. It is best described as a hamlet for it fails to qualify as a village. Prior to the arrival of the canal, it was nothing more than a tiny settlement within the extensive Harrington estate. The hamlet was not attached directly to any manor house as the Earls of Harrington were absentee landlords, actually residing near to Derby.

The settlement never clustered around either a church or chapel so the honour of being the nucleus of the hamlet goes fairly and squarely to the Inn; formerly the Royal Oak, now the "Fools Nook". When the canal arrived, with it's business traffic, Oakgrove became an important halt, originally sporting several busy wharfs including that owned by nearby Gawsworth Hall. One of the most consistent contradictions concerning Oakgrove it it's very name. According to the Ordnance Survey map, "Oakgrove" is currently the correct title. Many local people persistently refer to it as Fools Nook (now the pub name) - the author included.

During the canal's commercial heyday, both of these titles were abandoned in favour of "Sutton Stop". To further complicate the issue, the land which lies between the canal and Sutton reservoir is, most definitely, Sutton Oaks. In truth, the settlement as a whole is made up of less than a dozen buildings and the first of these to come into view from the canal is a converted and refurbished lodge which stands across the A523 road, a glorious building in stone, in front of which, an old fashioned road sign board confuses the passer by even more by informing that he is currently passing through Sutton Oaks!!

The next building to come into view, again, a distance away across the A523 is the brilliantly whitewashed inn. Not only does the inn's name echo a previous period in the hamlets history but it's lounge has been christened "Fools Paradise" and it's bar, "Anglers Nook". The ground to the west, behind the dense pathside hedgerow, continues to fall steeply away where glossy coated black and white Friesian cattle graze the lush valley pasture. Mooring rings feature in the towpath with increasing regularity, the nearer one gets to Oakgrove bridge. The celebrated swing bridge comes into view, alongside the already visible pedestrian footbridge. This is now the sole example along the whole of the Macclesfield Canal of a fully and constantly functional swing bridge which, day in and day out, is operated in the way in which it was originally intended.

On the final approach to the bridge, the canal's far bank is taken up by a stone jetty or landing stage, reminiscent of a railway station platform. A canal side cottage with tiny leaded windows and heavily slated roof backs onto the water side on the far bank immediately prior to the bridge. The towpath bank remains sheet metal lined right up to the huge mill grit blocks which line the passage of the canal through the swing bridge. While swung shut, the swing bridge carries Woodhouse End Road across the canal, from it's junction with the A523 Leek - Macclesfield road, to it's terminus, two miles to the west in Gawsworth village. The bridge itself has a tarmacadam surface and white painted guard rails. Boaters wanting to open the bridge to pass through firstly have to operate red and white painted barriers, identical to railway level crossing barriers, which drop down to seal off Woodhouse End Road whilst the bridge is open.

The towpath traveller crosses the road and immediately passes beneath the pedestrian foot bridge which is slung across and above the canal alongside the swing road bridge which is numbered 49. This footbridge stand high above the canal and towpath on two stone supports. Immediately east of the swing bridge is the junction of Woodhouse End Road and the A523. Across the busy carriageway, beside the inn, Radcliffe Road leads up to Sutton reservoir. Just 10 minutes walk from the Fools Nook inn up the steep gradient of Radcliffe Road, the picturesque Sutton or Turkshead reservoir is reached. Just beyond the road junction, behind the inn, Blackberry Cottage compliments the cluster of choice buildings which make up this tiny settlement. It's brick wall are clad in ivy and above it's high gothic gables is a huge ornate chimney stack.

Sutton reservoir nestles in a picturesque valley. Radcliffe Road arrives directly at the eastern end of the reservoir where the view westward, along the whole length of the water is dominated by the ambitious dam. In the northern corner of the reservoir, the canal supply feeder begins it's brief journey via a valve system. The reservoir is frequented by numerous water fowl and, consequently, is popular with ornithologists. It's facilities are amicably shared by Turkshead Sailing Club and the well managed Angling Club who enjoy the bountiful coarse fishing which is provided by the moderately deep, sheltered water. Membership of the angling club is kept at a regulation 36 members so that in the unlikely event of every member wishing to fish simultaneously, the available banks would hardly be crowded. In direct contrast to the canal which it feeds, the reservoirs coarse fish generally achieve a very sound average size. Tench, which are infrequently encountered in the canal despite being regularly introduced run to 3 or 4 pounds in weight. Bream achieve a similar high standard and a splendid long standing Pike record in excess of 27 pounds has remained unsurpassed for many years.

Directly beyond the Fools Nook foot bridge, a wooden fence stretches across the towpath. Set into the fence is a narrow pedestrian gate giving access to the towpath beyond. This measure limits access to the towpath by both horse riders and cyclists, both activities being prohibited. Directly having negotiated the wooden fence and gate, a drainoff paddle is encountered beside the path. The excess water which the paddle deals with is directed into a stone lined brook course which, for some distance, runs parallel to Woodhouse End Road on it's journey westward towards Gawsworth. Across the canal, opposite to the drainoff paddle is the now overgrown site of a major wharf formerly serving Gawsworth Hall.

Lying almost exactly 2 miles due west of Oakgrove, the village of Gawsworth, very beautiful and historic is, very much unspoilt. Although Gawsworth lacks the profusion of small cottages and friendly farmhouses which so characterises the Cheshire village, this is more than compensated for by the grandeur of it's Hall and it's Church which as a group, overlook a chain of quite, placid lakes and pools. The jewel in Gawsworth's crown is without doubt, Gawsworth Old Hall, a perfect example of Black and White, half timbered architecture which has been the seat of the consecutive lords of the manor since the Norman period. The house, as seen today, is largely of late fifteenth century date and is a truly breathtaking sight when viewed across the mirror calm of the manorial fish pond which lies between it and the tiny lane.

The interior of the hall is overwhelmingly homely and is still very much a family residence. In addition to the intimate rose gardens and the sunken gardens where open air Shakespeare and opera are performed in summer, within it's grounds can be seen the remarkably well preserved tilting or jousting ground where medieval knights would test their skills and, within the walled park area, the spectacular amphitheatre where tournaments would be staged. To the western side of the hall is the family access from the house to the church as, throughout recorded history, the lords of the manor have always been patrons of the church. The monuments within the church to the Fitton family (Lords of the Manor from 1316 to 1662) epitomise the bond between the church and the manorship.

The church stands adjacent to the hall on slightly rising ground overlooking it's own shady, tree lined pool. The fabric of the church, a mixture of red and buff-coloured sandstone, is largely of 15th and 16th century origins. Of the previously mentioned internal memorials, the one to Francis Fitton is rather gruesome as along with the customary effigy, it incorporates a skeleton. The memorial which depicts Mary Fitton is rather more conventional, it is she who is commonly associated with Shakespeare, supposedly being the "Dark Lady" of his sonnets. Directly across the narrow lane from the church is the old rectory. The present rectory, adjacent to the church yard is another very fine building, dated 1707.

Also dating from the early 1700's is the New Hall which is a large, stately Georgian mansion which gazes with quiet serenity across the middle pool towards the Old Hall. It's builder was Lord Mohun who along with the Duke of Hamilton featured in an infamous duel which was staged in London in 1712. The animosity arose when both had married co heiresses to the Gawsworth lands and a dispute developed regarding property. The result of the duel could have done little to resolve the original problem as both men were slain by one another! The two halls could not possibly be more different in style. The new hall is in seven bays of red brick with very little external decoration. To the east of both halls is the higher pool where plump trout leap clear of the placid water to take insects above the surface film.

South of the village, "The Harrington Arms" epitomises the old fashioned English pub. This fascinating building stands, completely isolated, at a junction of various minor lanes, some half a mile from the actual village almost as if it feels humbled by the grand buildings which cluster around the nucleus of the village. The inn is brick built in three stories with a heavy stone flagged roof. The ivy growing up the brickwork almost totally conceals the pubs frontage and a cobbled entrance area completes the scene. The rooms inside are tiny and sparsely furnished. There is no place here for the gaudy reproduction horse brasses or mock cottage style pub furniture so frequently encountered in 'country inns'. Hard wooden benches and unpolished tables are dotted around. The tiny bar is little more than a passageway and the beer is transported up from the cellar in jugs, not a single pump will be seen. The inn is also a farmhouse, the two business running simultaneously and seemingly in unison. A visit to the gents outdoor facilities entails a journey across a corner of the farmyard which lies to the rear of the building. The pubs name "The Harrington Arms", reminds us that the Earls of Harrington held lands in the townships of Sutton and Gawsworth in addition to Bosley where a second Harrington Arms inn will be encountered.

Having briefly discussed the historic village of Gawsworth, despite it technically being out of view from the canal, it would be gross negligence to omit a mention of "Maggoty Johnson". To the north of the church, Maggoty Lane winds it's way towards the main Congleton - Macclesfield road. Beside the lane, a spinney which covers a small area of gently rising ground is marked by a National Trust sign set beside a stile, giving access to Maggoty Johnsons Wood.

Maggoty Johnson or Samuel Johnson, often referred to as "Lord Flame" held to accolade of being the last professional court jester in England who lived and worked at Gawsworth Hall up to the time of his death in 1773. He was wildly eccentric and reputed to be possessed, a trait which led to him being buried in unconsecrated ground in this secluded spinney. He even composed his own lengthy but entertaining epitaph which will be seen inscribed upon the tombstone. A stone slab of similar design and dimensions next to it is not a second tomb but bares an inscription engraved upon it by the lady of the manor at the time of Johnson's death who was reputedly indignant about the wording on the original tombstone.

It has been suggested that Oakgrove's previous name of Fools Nook may refer to the fact that jesters from the surrounding estates converged on this area annually or there may have been some more direct connection between the place and Samuel Johnson, maybe he originated from what is now Oakgrove, perhaps we shall never know?

Chapter 6
OAKGROVE TO BOSLEY

Beyond the swing bridge and footbridge, a strategically positioned pathside seat is available for those who wish to sit and observe the comings and goings around the hamlet of Oakgrove Mooring rings continue to be set in the towpath at regular intervals, guaranteeing abundant mooring facilities for Oakgrove's 'tourist trade'.

A tall hedgerow, mercilessly strangled and choked by Cleavers and Dog Rose accompanies the towpath, hindering a view westward into the deep grass valley beyond. The canal enters a long sheltered passageway as it travels the length of the Oakgrove valley. Tall Sycamores and Ashes overhang the towpath while Alders line the canal's far bank creating a dark and shady tunnel. The Leek - Macclesfield road still runs directly parallel to the canal although it now does so behind the dense belt of trees plus a stone wall which combine to cushion the sound of traffic.

The wide canal stretches away into the dark leafy tunnel. Beyond the busy roadway, the hillside rises steeply away completely clothed by trees. The whole scene is reminiscent of a wooded alpine mountain pass. The waterway curves gently to the right as the roadway begins to climb steeply away out of the valley, leaving the canal to snake its own course through the cool shady passage.

A brief clearing on the far bank may originally have been the site of another wharf. It is now clustered with sheds and covered parking for an assortment of agricultural implements. Down below the huge hedgerow, the deep grass valley to the west, grazed by herds of dairy cattle, is almost completely hidden from view. The meandering stream still winds its way along the bottom of the valley having picked up excess canal water from several drain off points. Cow Brook gives its name to a sizeable farmstead through which it passes some distance ahead to the south. It continues, moving southwards, picking numerous tributaries until it forms the principal water supply for the extensive manorial lake at North Rode. From North Rode Manor, it forms the lakes outflow and continues, ever more substantial, before joining the river Dane near to Colley Mill.

As the canal continues to curve away from Oakgrove, massive Black Poplar trees tower almost 90 feet above the canal from a regimented planting on the far bank. The tall straight trunks rising like tapering columns topped by lush crowns of leaves which tremble in the faintest breeze.

By now, the A523 road has risen away out of sight but continues to run parallel to the canal if well above it and the sound of traffic is ever present. A refurbished stone house of admirable proportions occupies the far bank, sandwiched between the canal and the A523. The property has been virtually rebuilt during the last decade in very traditional style with heavy stone mullioned windows with leaded glass and a long metal balcony which overlooks the canal. Beyond the stone house, the towering Black Poplars reappear, looming above the wide, dark canal. Beyond the Poplar stand, the far bank becomes dense, mixed woodland of Ash, Alder and Sycamore which slopes steeply upward.

During the summer months, the undergrowth beneath the trees which reach down to the water's edge is lush green with fronds of bracken. During the early part of the year however, whilst the boughs of the Ash and Alder are still devoid of foliage, a succession of plants make the wooded slopes of Oakgrove valley an ever changing carpet of colour. From late February, through March and April, patches of white flowers decorate the otherwise bare woodland floor beneath the barren trees and reflect in the quiet water. To discover a carpet of Wood Anemones is a delight. The large white flowers which normally hang their heads, respond immediately to the appearance of the sun, raising their heads with petals outstretched, closing with each passing cloud or with the onset of evening.

WOOD ANEMONIES

It is during April, May and early June however, that the canal's wooded eastern bank throughout the valley becomes a stunning spectacle. Nowhere along the Macclesfield Canals' length will Bluebells be seen in such fabulous profusion. As the bank slopes steeply upward towards the now distant A523, it is frequently a solid mass of dusky blue. The optical effect on the otherwise dark water of the canal, being transformed into a photographic reflection of the carpets of Bluebells is breathtaking.

During the summer months, the almost oppressive green of the tree canopy and the carpeting Bracken is occasionally and vividly broken up by the brilliant purple of Foxgloves growing from the far bank, duplicated by their reflection in the water. Here and there, the grassy area beside the towpath is decorated by the vivid yellow of the Meadow Vetchling.

The canal widens slightly and a marshy area on the canal's far bank suggests that at one time this may have been a wide turning or winding basin. Over the decades, this has slowly been reclaimed by nature as it is now, little more than an extensive Sedge bed, providing extra cover for nesting Ducks or skulking Moorhens. The massive Rhubarb like leaves of Butterbur grow on either side of the towpath, excluding the usual pathside grasses.

During April, May, June and July, the canal's far bank here is home to a fairly common plant of damp and shady places but decidedly uncommon along the Macclesfield Canal. Although this particular plant flowers prolifically and beautifully, it is often its aroma which first brings it to the attention of the passer by. The flower heads of Ramsons can carry up to twenty five star shaped flowers of the purest white, so white in fact that they almost appear blue-white. These are held above the broad, bright green, glossy leaves. Ramsons is a vigorous plant, often dominating its chosen habitat, usually a river bank, to the exclusion of everything else. Crush or in any way disturb the stems or leaves however, and the smell of garlic can be overpowering. Prolonged exposure to the smell can become nauseating. Even from the towpath bank, with the Ramsons bed out of the way of disturbance on the far bank, the heady aroma wafts across the canal in oppressive waves.

RANSOMS

Up ahead to the right and left, trees press inward. They overhand the water giving the impression that the canal is running through a forest which, given half a chance, would absorb it into its green depths. Even the herbage either side of the towpath has achieved gigantic proportions. Grasses stand in excess of four feet high, Docks flower at almost six feet high alongside the Cow Parsley flowering at head height. The huge Ash trees overhang the water to the extent that it is almost possible in places, to touch the extremities of the overhanging boughs from the towpath bank. Almost imperceptibly the trees begin to thin out, the more delicate Silver Birch beginning to take over from the robust Ash, Alder and Sycamore. Beneath the Birch canopy, the summer undergrowth of Bracken grows ever more lush and thick. Likewise, in the spring, the carpets of Bluebells are able to achieve almost total ground cover.

After what seems like an eternity of travelling through this leafy tunnel following the waterways dead straight course, the canal curves gently and, as it does, the next bridge comes into view ahead. It comes almost as a relief to encounter the first stone bridge, No. 50 since Lyme Green.

An unpretentious stone arch, beautifully built, its mellow old stone blending harmoniously with the vegetation around it. Bridge No. 50 is unspoiled as it carries no roadway and is far enough removed from any habitation to have almost become as one with its surroundings. Quite abruptly, the crowding tress fall away and the final approach to the bridge is reminiscent of having emerged from some subterranean passageway. The massive hedgerow which has accompanied the towpath almost without a break throughout Oakgrove valley continues right up to the stonework of the bridge.

Masses of blue Vetches scramble through the Nettles and Docks which grow against the stonework of the bridge. An obscure flight of stone steps lead up to a partly hidden wooden fence which is set in the hedgerow. The steps are totally disused as the fence at the top prevents an access to the cow track which passes over the bridge. The initial impression upon emerging from bridge No. 50 is of once again, being in a sheltered cutting with trees, shrubs and herbage pressing in from all sides.

Roach plop at the water's surface as they rise to take either a drowning and struggling aerial insect or maybe an insect or beetle whose native habitat is the water surface. These natural denizens of the surface film are not only in constant danger of becoming a meal for the canal's numerous Roach and Perch but actually compete directly with the fish for food as they too scavenge the water surface for other insects who have unwittingly entered an element which is alien to them.

The Pond Skater spends its whole life patrolling the surface film, supported by its four long legs while the two short front legs hold its hapless victim which it proceeds to eat by means of a sharp beak. By comparison, the whirligig beetle chooses to congregate in large groups which gyrate over the water surface particularly during the summer months. The habit of whirling in intricate patterns is considered to be beneficial to the beetle in a number of ways. Their mazy gyrations are primarily important in the location of food but, as the beetle is a creature which is habitually found among scores if not hundreds of its own kind, it is essentially an early warning of imminent danger. As soon as one beetle is aware of the presence of an intruder, it begins to swim wildly about, thus warning the other members of the group who begin to do the same. If the threat develops into an attack by a predator, the beetles simply disperse, some diving below, others scattering wildly.

Across the canal, a rough bank of Brambles, Willow Herb and Foxglove leads up to the cattle track which is transported over the bridge. To the more distant east, pasture land rises gently away towards the wooded slopes of Whitemoor Hill. Tall Ash trees tower above the cattle track on the eastern bank and, as the bank beside the towpath begins to drop away, another track is visible running along the back of the hedgerow towards the bridge. These livestock highways which have been trampled into the landscape over the centuries often resemble a quagmire during the wetter months of the year by the constant trampling of many cloven hooves. In summer, the air will be thick with flies as the trampled surface of the track bakes hard into something resembling a lunar landscape, pockmarked with deep footprints and punctuated by patches of rich green manure which is almost pure grass and which swarms with countless thousands of yellow-brown dungflies.

In the bottom of the hedgerow, the next milestone stands partially hidden.

An original stone, it reads, "From Hall Green 11 1/4" and "From Marple 15 miles". Beyond this milestone, the ground falls steeply away westward again to return to the half embankment which has been a feature of the western aspect for almost two miles.

Ahead a diminutive stream is culverted beneath the canal. It is a spur of Bosley Brook which runs down towards the canal through Whitemoor Hollow, the gap which is visible between Gawsworth Common and the wooded Whitemoor Hill. Once it has passed beneath the canal's embankment, it flows westward to join Cow Brook prior to its passage through Cow Brook Farm which lies directly to the west, before continuing its journey to North Rode. From the canal embankment onwards, boats are moored with increasing regularity to both banks. When the passage across the embankment is over, permanent moorings in the form of wooden jetties and mooring stages are spaced out along the far bank. The extensive outbuildings of the large farm which provides the permanent moorings, spill down towards the canal on the eastern bank occupying an ancient site known as Cowley.

Whitemoor Hollow, a deep yet narrow valley between Whitemoor Hill and the wooded flanks of the much quarried Gawsworth Common is plainly visible to the more distant east beyond the farm buildings at Cowley. From the moorings, the ground rises steeply up to the farm buildings where Swifts and Swallows duck and dive among the sheds and barns, harvesting the millions of winged insects which haunt the summer air. The waterway curves sharply to the left, Willow Herb crowding the towpath from either side. Across the canal, a lean farmyard cat sits on top of the silage clamp wall, waiting patiently for the appearance of a careless mouse or young rat.

Poultry sheds come into view where proud Bantom fowl strut and parade. From this tranquil setting, the explosive barking and yapping of a pair of seriously demented black and white Border Collies accosts each and every passer by. The two bundles of sheer vitality and energy bound towards the canal from the farm, stopping just inches short of the water's edge where they defiantly bark and chase up and down until the passer by is out of sight. The well appointed farmhouse stands proudly above the canal, its dark brick walls liberally clothed with Ivy.

Directly ahead stands bridge No. 51. The perfect stone arch is overhung by an Ash tree of majestic proportions. From the towpath, a set of 15 stone steps lead up the side of the bridge to a wooden stile which gives access to the tiny lane above, a single track by way which leaves the A523 at Whitemoor, runs westward to Cowley, and joins Woodhouse End Road on the journey between Oakgrove and Gawsworth. Beyond Cowley Farm Bridge, another classic scene change is executed. With unlined banks, the waterway which reached Cowley moments before via a sweeping embankment, now enters a deep cutting.

As the canal curves its way through this particular cutting, a high grass bank rises steeply away from the canal's furthermost edge where young beef cattle graze the steep incline. Grey roan Shorthorns, Charolais and white faced Herefords momentarily pause in their otherwise incessant grazing to watch the passage of a chugging narrow boat with mild disinterest. The customary hedgerow rejoins the towpath as the canal straightens out and heads determinedly onward across open country.

The Sedge beds which now line both banks of the wide waterway conceal nesting water fowl and completely hide feeding Water Voles . From March to October other creatures which, by their vivid colouring, would seem to have evolved with attraction or display as their priority as opposed to concealment also frequent the Sedge beds. The areas of lush vegetation which are sometimes typical of the canal's margins are of vital importance to the several species of Damsel Flies to be encountered. One of the commonest species nationally and often the earliest to be encountered in spring is the unusually coloured Large Red Damsel fly. With a wingspan of 1 3/4 inches, its body colour varies from a bright orange to deep crimson.

It is the Common Blue, Blue Tailed and Azure Damsel flies however which are synonymous with the rushy or boggy edges of Britain's canals. Often, on a bright sunny day, the insect in flight will at first appear as a long needle of brilliant fluorescent blue, hovering above or among the Sedges, twinkling and glinting in the sunlight, before the dark head or the semi-transparent, veined wings become visible. The Sedge bed habitat is important to the Damsel fly species for, unlike the much larger Dragonfly, their flight is quite weak, fluttery and not unlike that of a Butterfly. For this reason the Damselfly restricts itself to this confined habitat where it darts at smaller insects on or among the plant stems. Further to their feeding requirements, the sedge bed is vital to the insects reproduction as the female deposits her eggs either on a submerged plant stem by lowering her long abdomen into the water or, in some species, even inserts the eggs into the plant stem by the cutting of a small incision.

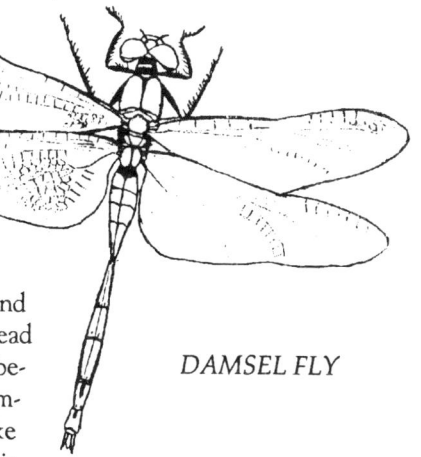

DAMSEL FLY

In the distant east, across rolling pastures, dotted with large Oak and Ash trees, lies the wooded Whitemoor Hill. The view to the distant west opens up for the first time for several miles. Across a patchwork of fields and hedgerows, maybe half a mile away, the course of the Stoke - Manchester railway can be seen for the first time since the two linear thoroughfares parted company at Danes Moss. The canal curves ever so slightly to the right and as it does, the pasture land on the eastern bank is replaced by an area of hard grazed paddock type ground where two ponies eke a living. A nicely proportioned snow white riding pony is constant companion to a fat, glossy black Welsh Cob with shaggy mane, fringe and tail and built like a barrel; it resembles an oversized Shetland.

The waterway continues to curve to bridge No. 52, Crow Hole or Crow Holt bridge which stands directly beyond. Set well back from the canal, beyond the pony meadow is a fine farm house which has obviously been much refurbished; Crow Holt Farm. Up ahead, the modest stone arch of bridge No. 52 is totally overshadowed by the tall Poplar trees which stand beyond. On the final approach to bridge No. 52, the canal's far bank is lined by a narrow sedge bed where a Moorhen sits tightly upon her floating platform nest. She and her nest bob and pitch with great force with the passage of each narrow boat. She would probably have enjoyed as much privacy and peace if she had chosen to nest beside a major oceanic shipping lane! With each boat out of sight and earshot, the female, in full summer plumage, comprising glossy feathers and bold red mark over her beak steps off the still pitching nest to examine her second brood of the season. The tiny blobs of sooty black which greet her appear remarkably well considering their constant buffeting.

Passing beneath the arch of bridge No. 52, a short, uneven flight of six stone steps lead up to a concrete driveway which links the singularly isolated Crow Holt to Cowley by way of the track running back, almost exactly to the previous bridge, No. 51. The ground on the eastern bank is now made up of neatly mown, undulating grassland, spreading downwards from the large farmhouse, right to the water's edge. A landscaped planting of mature Poplar trees overshadow the waterway.

From Crow Holt Bridge, the canal curves away to the left between margins of sedge. Throughout the month of summer, the sedge beds are gaily decorated, as is the grassy strip beside the towpath, by the vivid yellow flowers of another prolific native wayside plant which is well represented along the entire length of the Macclesfield Canal - the Birds Foot Trefoil. The Trefoil is a true grassland plant which, over the centuries has shown an affinity for roadsides and byways. It forms large clumps in situations not unlike the equally common Vetches. The bright yellow flowers are every bit as prominent as those of the Meadow Vetchling which it so closely resembles. Those with a keener botanical eye will identify Birds Foot Trefoil and the Greater Birds Foot Trefoil. The latter has been noted around Hurdsfield and Lyme Green and also much further south.

The grounds of the large house on the far bank are replaced by a grass field which slopes away eastward. Extensive pastures stretch away westward towards the distant railway line and, beyond, a more far reaching view is available down into Cheshire.. The view is of Cheshire at its most unspoiled and uncluttered. No town or village offends the eye. The vista takes in the southern half of the parish of Gawsworth and the more distant parish of Marton.

A larger fish jumps unexpectedly, causing a loud plop and a considerable commotion of ripples race outwards towards both banks. This could be a large Roach or a good Perch finding a sizeable insect on the surface film or it could be high sprits or possibly it could be an attempt to dislodge a parasite from its skin such as a fish louse or fluke.

The canal curves gently as it becomes metal lined to cross a minor valley, yet, within thirty yards it once more enters a cutting. When a view westward is available once more it is of expansive grass fields, many acres in area. The larger and more heavily cultivated the field, the more featureless and aesthetically barren it becomes. Where many seasons dressing with nitrogen rich fertiliser has destroyed the ever changing succession of beautiful meadow flowers and herbs, they are replaced by acres of monotonous lush green grass. Out in the very centre of the grass field, the only feature in a green ocean of maybe 30 acres in extent is a tiny cluster of distant trees which have miraculously been allowed to remain in this high production, no nonsense environment, evidence of an old marl pit, a relic of a bygone era of pastoral land management. Beyond the belt of Willows and Sallows(also known as Crack Willows because of thier brittleness), which currently line the far bank, pasture land gently climbs away towards Whitemoor Hill.

To the west, the monotonously bland grass field is replaced by pasture fields of similar proportions where a large herd of Fresian cattle noisily snort and munch their way through copious amounts of sweet pasture. The waterway curves gently to the right ahead, the margins continually lined by beds of Sedge. Quite unexpectedly, a pathside wooden seat which is set in its customary cobbled area to prevent it being engulfed by encroaching vegetation, is positioned beside the hedgerow. This is the first seat to be encountered which is nowhere near to a bridge, neither does it overlook a marina or wharf or any other feature as is usually the case. It is nevertheless a welcome vantage point where the footsore traveller can rest quietly amid the splendours of rural Cheshire at its most tranquil. The waterway maintains its gentle curve to the right well into the distance, unhindered by either bridges or buildings.

The extensive sedge margins are frequented during the summer months by a small visiting bird which is more often heard than seen. The Sedge Warbler breeds most readily in Reeds and Osier beds or ditches overhung by bushes and finds the quiet tree and sedge lined canal margins much to its liking. It will also nest in standing crops and young forestry plantations. The song, a hurried series of harsh, chattering notes is usually delivered from the top of a reed or bush and contributes largely to the incessant chorus of bird song which is synonymous with a summer journey along the canal. Visually, the 5 inch, mostly brown bird is notably unspectacular. A streaked back with a reddish rump and creamy eye stripe do little to assist in its identification from a distance. The courtship display of the male bird is probably the most identifiable feature, it flies vertically upward, singing, then descends on spread wings and tail. Looking out across the dairy herd grazing to the west, another telltale clump of trees towards the centre of the field points to the position of another old marl pit.

Considerably further westward, far beyond the railway line, the ornate, square sandstone tower of Gawsworth church is plainly visible . For the first time, the western horizon is decorated by arguably the most impressive landmark in the Cheshire countryside, if one of its more recent arrivals. The massive and somewhat bizarre bulk of the Mark I A Radio Telescope at Jodrell Bank, between Withington and Goostrey, is visible from much of the Cheshire Plain. In fact, there are few places where its huge white bowl, 250 feet in diameter cannot be seen.From any of the higher ground within or surrounding Cheshire, Jodrell Bank is the first landmark to be picked out from the otherwise flat and fairly one dimensional patchwork of fields and hedges. The telescope, along with its diminutive neighbour, the Mark II Radio Telescope, are the basis of the University of Manchester Astronomy Laboratories, positioned intentionally well away from Manchester itself in a quiet backwater of Cheshire, to aid, as far as possible, the detection of radio emissions from outer space. The telescope was commissioned in 1957, the vast 250 feet diameter bowl, supported by a drum shaped steel framework and held aloft by two massive towers of steel girders can be pointed at any part of the sky. As far as our canal journey is concerned, this particular landmark although only occasionally visible due to its conciderable distance away, will accompany us virtually all the way to our journeys end. The prominance of Jodrell Bank as a landmark is of little wonder when one considers that its height is almost identical to that of St Paul's Cathedral in London!

The gentle curve in the waterway continues as the canal's course almost describes a shallow crescent across the landscape. Crocker Hill suddenly looms starkly due east now that Whitemoor Hill has fallen behind. So much closer now to the canal than when it first came into view, the bleak nature of Crocker Hill, almost totally devoid of tree cover, accentuates the towering spire of the telecommunications tower.

The trees which have lined the far bank for so long come to an end as an overflow sill occupies the canal's eastern edge. This overflow or storm weir channels its excess water down a purpose built stream course which is promptly culverted beneath the canal and appears simultaneously to the right of the towpath. The stream strikes off determinedly westward to eventually join Cow Brook. To coincide with the overflow sill on the far bank, a drain off paddle and valve is situated beside the towpath. It is equipped with its own stone built water channel which spurs into the stream course. Should the drain off need to be used either for rapid release of water to prevent flooding or to drain this section of canal for repairs, its sudden influx of water is directed into the stream course to prevent major flooding of the surrounding land.

Up ahead, bridge No. 53 comes into view. Beside the towpath, Cranesbill grows in profusion in the hedge bottom. The common Cranesbill is a close cousin of the previously encountered and described Herb Robert. It is easier to see features which are associated with the garden Geranium in the Cranesbill; the soft, rounded leaves which are lobed are more Geranium-like than the fern-like leaves of the Herb Robert although the lilac/pink five petalled flowers are almost identical. In fact, the Cranesbill is far more common as a garden subject than in its native environment for its pretty flowers and hardy perennial habit make it an ideal herbaceous border plant. In the wild, the Cranesbill will be found in several distinct variations, for example, the Mountain Cranesbill, the Doves Foot Cranesbill, the Dusky, the Cut Leaved and the Shining Cranesbill. Garden centres and nursery growers also offer a staggering list of variants and sub-species to suit every taste and situation.

Bridge No. 53, a beautiful stone arch emits an aura of isolation. It carries no roadway and no human habitation could be described as being particularly close by. A fine, mature Ash tree is the bridges only companion, overhanging and protecting it. The next milestone stands, literally in the shadow of the bridge. This tall original stone is a fine example of one which, amid frenzied preparations for an invasion which never happened, proved to be too large to uproot and bury like some of its contemporaries. Instead, its fate was to be totally defaced to obliterate the information which its sole purpose was to impart. The northern facing side reads "From Hall Green —" and the figure 10 1/4 miles is totally non existent. However, the southern facing side reads "From Marple 16 miles" and is a perfect example of restoration as the whole face has been rendered with concrete at some point and the new characters have been carved into the concrete re-facing.

The canal narrows to pass beneath the bridge which holds the accolade of, not only being the 53rd since Marple junction but is the last one to stand at the 500 foot contour; beyond here the canal will begin its descent to 400 feet above sea level. Beyond bridge No. 53, the character of the surroundings begins to change. A set of stop planks stand beside an immaculately clipped Hawthorn hedge.

The ever changing procession of sweet wild flowers, herbs and grasses which have graced and decorated our journey from Marple and also our hypothetical journey through the flowering seasons is abandoned here in favour of a neatly mown grass strip on both sides of the towpath. Boats are often moored here overnight, marking the end of the arduous, time consuming and occasionally traumatic journey up through Bosley locks. Sedges still form the only lining to the canal's banks. Beside the towpath, a large sign board announces "British Waterways Board Moorings".

The hedge beside the towpath is subject to the same care which is lavished upon the grass, being clipped like a garden boundary. Up ahead, a stone cottage comes into view beside the towpath. Built by the Macclesfield Canal Company as the Lock Keepers Cottage, it still serves its original purpose. In the distance, Bosley top lock comes into view. The stone and gravel towpath which has brought us from Marple disappears, to become one of mown grass. A further information board goes to some considerable lengths to explain the procedure for obtaining the necessary permit to make use of "Bosley Top Lock Long Term Moorings". Mooring rings, embedded in blocks of concrete, are set at regular intervals in the wide grass path.

The tall Hawthorns fall away from the far bank where a sedge margin leads to a pasture which rises gently away from the canal, grazed by fine dairy Fresians. These tranquil pastures stretch away eastwards towards the looming bulk of Crocker Hill and the telecommunications tower which still dominates the horizon. The canal widens right out into an expansive sheet of water prior to passing into the mill grit confines of the top lock chamber where, by comparison, it narrows again to just one boats width.

The necessity for the wide lagoon is two fold, as a turning area allowing boats to jostle for position immediately prior to the lock and also, it is here that the main water supply for the Macclesfield Canal enters the 500 foot level. Away to the far left, across the wide waterway, the feeder from Bosley reservoir reaches the canal, after a jouney of two miles. Upon leaving the reservoir, via the dam, the water splits into two. Within yards, half of the available water forms a continuance of Bosley Brook. This is one of the three water sources which feed the reservoir, namely Swallowdale Brook which enters the reservoir at the south east corner. The other two sources are Shell Brook and Bosley Brook which enter at the north east corner.

Upon leaving the reservoir, Bosley Brook continues its course to join the river Dane, seemingly unhindered by its passage through the 86 acres and 402 million gallons of Bosley reservoir. The half which comprises the canal feeder runs firstly south then west around a hillside, under the Leek - Macclesfield road and then north to join the canal. With regard to the relative positions of the reservoir and the canal, it would, logically, have been far simpler to run the feeder in a straight line to join the canal below the twelfth and final lock but this would have been totally ineffective. It must be remembered that lock No. 12 lies almost 116 feet lower than the top lock, consequently, it was necessary to direct the feeder along this twisting, contorted journey to ensure that it fed the 500 foot level and not the 400 foot.

A blue and yellow information board,(British Waterways Board colours), is set on the far bank which is now reminiscent of an island as it is bordered on the one side by the canal as it reaches the top lock and by the feeder on the other. The board announces quite simply "Bosley Locks".

Chapter 7
BOSLEY LOCKS

It is by no means unusual to hear the locks at Bosley referred to as "The Famous Bosley Locks" or, "The Celebrated Bosley Locks". They are described as being the most attractive flight on the whole of Britains' canal system. The positioning of the flight, causing the minimum of inconvenience to the business traffic for which it was designed is technically brilliant.

The canal, commencing at the junction of the Peak Forest Canal at Marple which lies at 500 feet above sea level, joins the Trent and Mersey Canal at Kidsgrove at 400 feet, so the drop of 100 feet is unavoidable. Nevertheless, Macclesfield, Bollington, Poynton, High Lane, Hazel Grove and Marple could trade with the entire Manchester area without the transport line being slowed down by having to negotiate the lockage. Likewise, Congleton and surrounding areas enjoyed a direct thoroughfare with the Staffordshire potteries and coalfields on the one hand and the remainder of Cheshire including the salt towns of Middlewich and Northwich on the other, via the Trent and Mersey.

The lock keepers cottage, built from rustic faced mill grit hardly inspires the adjectives pretty or quaint, being a somewhat severe and bland little building; singularly lacking in imaginative features on the part of the original architect. The clustering tin roofed outbuildings do little to add to it's romantic charm. The tiny front garden which lies behind a low stone wall cries out for an old fashioned rambling rose in pink or red or a few Lupins or Hollyhocks which are sadly lacking. The keepers cottage is situated directly alongside the top lock. On the island of ground between the feeder and the canal, a solitary brick building of modern construction which is actually ladies and gents toilets stands alongside a set of stop planks. The tiny windows of the cottage look towards the top gates of lock No. 1.

Beside the towpath, a waterways information board explains in some considerable details the workings of a lock using diagrams and goes on to credit Thomas Telford with arguably the finest set of locks in existence. It goes on to explain that the gritstone locks lift the Macclesfield Canal 118 feet in one mile and perfectly illustrates Telford's preference for grouping his locks in flights. The fact that all of the locks have paired gates or, in other words, double gates at either end of each lock chamber is pointed out as representative of an unusual feature among narrow locks where it is usually the bottom gates only which are double. The information board goes on to explain the use of side ponds which will be found by the side of each of the locks with the exception of this one, No. 1. The side pond here has become a landscaped sunken garden attached to the Lock-Keepers Cottage.

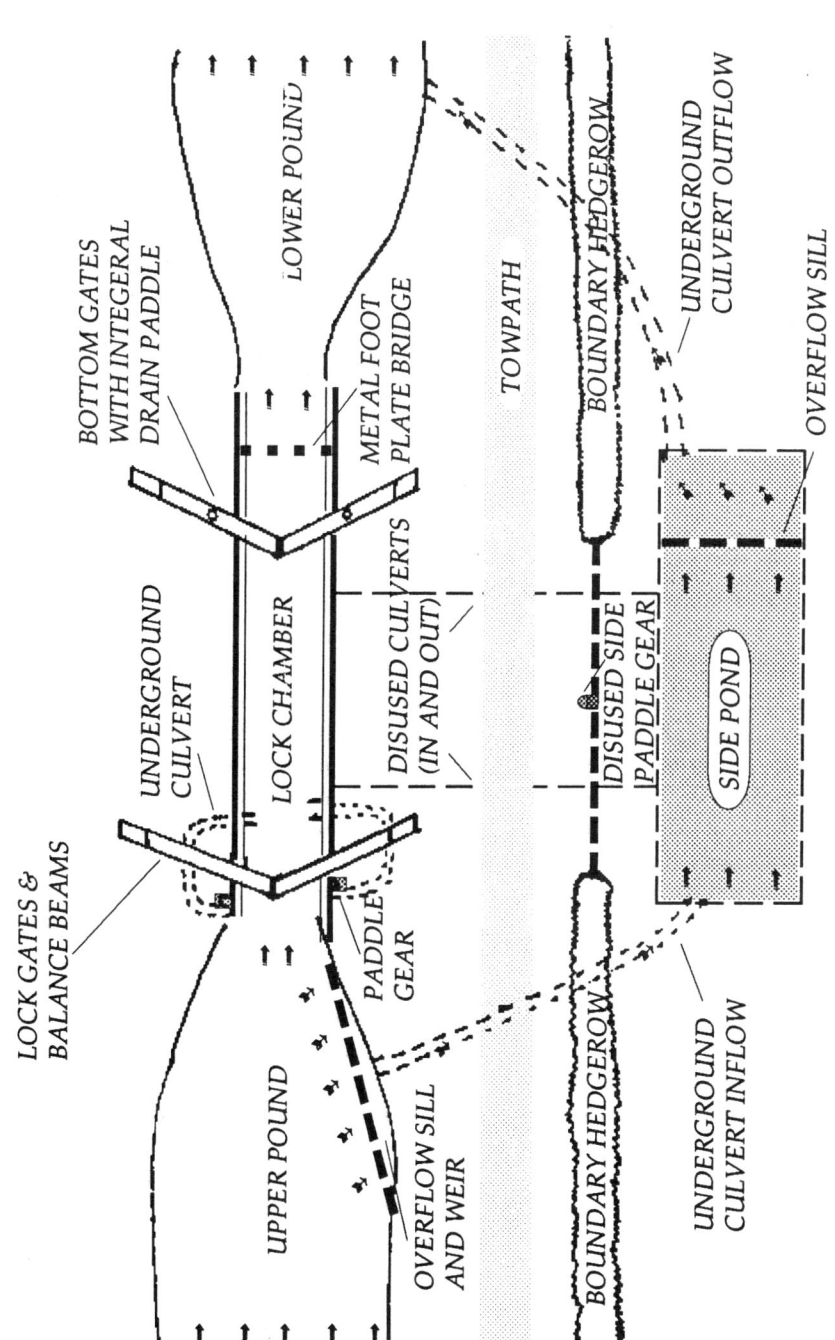

The use of the side ponds has changed since the canals' working days but, even today, the object of their existence is as a water saving device. Originally, half of the water in each lock could be emptied into the pond and the remainder out through the bottom gates into the canal. When working uphill, the lock could be half filled from the side pond and merely 'topped up' from the canal, thus cutting down on water wastage by 50%.

As to the actual functional features of lock No. 1, the first to be encountered is the bypass weir. A bypass weir precedes each lock. Constructed entirely from mill grit it is positioned at the canal's edge beside the towpath and enables excess water to be channelled around each lock, preventing the canal level from rising too high and pouring over the lock gates. The excess water runs over a regulating stone sill in the canal and into a stone channel from where it is culverted beneath the towpath into the side pond which lies off to the right of each lock, below towpath level.

The side ponds are, in turn, constructed entirely from stone. They are rectangular holding devices, consisting of a bed of gritstone flags or setts and contained within a low stone wall. They are built to hold a volume of water up to approximately 12-18 inches deep. When excess water is culverted in via the bypass weir, it flows over a sill in the side pond into a further culvert whence it passes beneath the towpath once more. Beyond the lock chamber, re-enters the canal at it's new lower level below the lock. Immediately beyond lock No. 1's bypass weir, the top lock gates mark the canal's passage through the mill grit chamber. The gates themselves are not original due to their almost constant use throughout the year. They are in need of regular maintenance and periodical replacement. The wooden sections, including the long and heavy ballence beams are kept well painted in regulation black and white. Either side of the top gates, one on each bank, are the paddle gears which open the underground culverts to fill the lock. These work along the same principles as the drain off paddles which have frequently been encountered throughout our journey.

At the downward end of the lock chamber, the bottom gates incorporate the mechanism for emptying the chamber. In the place of the underground culverts, the paddles for the emptying process are built into the actual gates so the winding gear sits on top of the gates themselves. Immediately beyond the bottom gates, a short metal plate spans the width of the lock chamber, a distance of less than 9 feet, which, with a hand rail, forms a footbridge enabling the lock operator instant access to either bank while his vessel lies within the sealed chamber. Alongside the lock chamber, the lock-keepers sunken garden is separated from the towpath by a wooden fence. The water which is culverted into it from the top locks by pass weir flows straight through to be culverted back out beneath the towpath to re-enter the canal below the lock.

Directly beyond the top lock lies bridge No. 54. The bridge a modest stone arch, carries Daintry Road which leaves the A523 Macclesfield - Leek road at Marsh Head, to the east. From Bull Gate Farm, the lane passes over the canal feeder from Bosley reservoir which is culverted beneath it, crosses bridge No. 54 then, continuing westward, crosses the main line railway before travelling the width of the parish of North Rode to join the main Congleton - Macclesfield road between Eaton and Gawsworth. Alongside the bottom lock gates, the towpath splits into two, one half drops steeply down to the canals' new level beyond the lock while the other climbs gently to a wooden gate which gives access to Daintry Road.

Following the path down to the canals' new level as it is about to pass beneath the bridge, a flight of thirteen very worn and dished stone steps on the opposite bank coincide with the plunging footpath, giving access from the lock to the bridge on the opposite bank. Once through the arch of bridge No. 54 the scene changes entirely. From the hemmed-in feeling of being trapped between the lock and the bridge, the wide open space which is enjoyed now is a considerable contrast.

The length of the canal which stretches ahead is excessively wide and absolutely dead straight. The sheet of water between each lock is, through necessity, wider than the normal canal to help it to absorb the sudden influx of water which floods in with the operation of the lock above. The bypass weir eventually delivers this excess water down to the next level via the side ponds but the immediate influx is taken up by the extra width.

The length of canal between locks 1 and 2, or the pound, to give it it's correct title, is a long one, lock No. 2 being visible a considerable distance ahead. In relation to the wide waterway or pound, the towpath follows suit, being extremely wide and beautifully mown to a turf finish which would put a sports pitch to shame. In the distance, the black and white painted ballence beams of lock No. 2 stand proud above the water and beyond them, the canal drops away out of sight. In total contrast to the mown grass of the pathway, the bank to the right sports long seeded meadow grasses, Plantains, Cow Parsley and even clumps of Raspberry canes.

As the lock-keepers cottage, lock No. 1 and bridge No. 54 disappear behind, the view to the east continues to be totally dominated by the huge presence of Crocker Hill with it's weird, high-tech monument. Below Crocker Hill, in the near distance, lies Bull Gate Farm whose pastures roll down to the canals' far bank. Up ahead, however, the view is now completely taken up by a newly appeared landmark. Rising to just over 1000 feet above sea level, the Cloud is one of the most exciting and dramatic high ground feature in Cheshire. It rears abruptly out of the Cheshire Plain, a gritstone fault which, when surveying the line of the canal, Telford referred to as "The Adjacent Mountain".

Apart from the visual impact, the Cloud influenced the character of the construction of the canal in more practical ways, providing much of the mill stone for the bridges, bank linings and, of course, the locks on this section. The stone quarry on the Cloud must have been an absolute hive of industry during the canal and lock construction. Scores of men would be engaged in the actual quarrying of the stone and, as the stone was rough dressed at the quarry, as many men again would be involved in this operation. It is said that 10 full-time blacksmiths were employed on the Cloud quarry sharpening stone punches, bezels and other chisels used by the dressers. This pattern of stone availability is repeated over and over again along the canals' course. The waterway's close proximity to the mill grit ridge to the east was an extremely advantageous coincidence. The Macclesfield Canal coincides with the so call Red Rock Fault which is, in simple terms, a north/south fracture in the earths crust which is reputed to have taken place some 180-190 million years ago whereby the red sandstone rocks which underlie the Cheshire Plain were downthrown in relation to the gritstone rocks to the east forming the ridge or upheaval of gritstone which typifies the eastern aspect. As the bank beside the towpath begins to lower, the hedgerow drops accordingly to allow a view westward across pastures grazed by flocks of sheep. Increasingly, boats will be encountered, temporarily moored to either bank, awaiting their turn to descend through lock No. 2

The pound begins to narrow up ahead as it approaches the lock. Directly

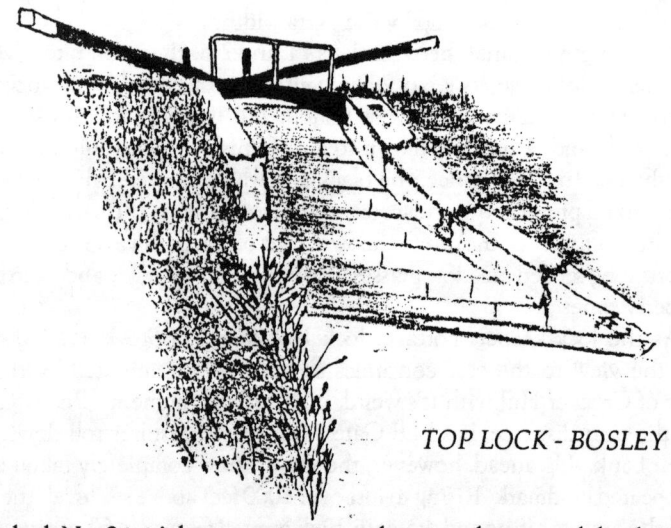

TOP LOCK - BOSLEY

prior to lock No. 2 is it's bypass weir, situated against the towpath bank where the flood of water between lock No. 1's bottom gate, and lock No. 2's top gate, is culverted away beneath the towpath It will. emerge, off to the right in the field, in the old side pond. The pond lies below towpath level alongside the huge mill stone lock chamber. In common with the previous one, lock No. 2 has it's own set of stop planks which stand on the other side of the chamber on the eastern bank. A small sign indicates that these particular lock gates were installed in 1978.

Looking over to the right, the excess water gushes from below the towpath as lock No. 1 is emptied via the stone culvert of No. 2's bypass weir, swelling the volume of water already in the side pond, forcing it out over the ponds overflow sill from where it is returned to the canal below. In keeping with the general standard, the whole area around lock No. 2 is kept painstakingly tidy, and neatly mown. Beyond the bottom gates, the towpath tumbles down a steep incline to rejoin the waterway at it's new level, beside the wide pound which lies betweenlocks 2 and 3.

Arriving at the new level, lock No. 3 is but a short distance ahead . The margins of the water which lies between are sedge lined. On the eastern bank of the widened pound, beef cattle graze the lush pasture. Distant clumps of trees and shrubbery which stand out prominently towards the centre of the cattle pasture hint at the existence of several old marl pits. Dark dots or specs in the pasture around the pits prove to be a dozen or so Moorhens feeding from the turf which proves conclusively that the old marl holes are flooded. The view to the distant east from this particular position reveals the indistinct outline of high ground lying far beyond Crocker Hill. This proves to be a brief glimpse of high moorland stretching away towards Wildboarclough, Wincle and Algraeve in the Peak District.

Down to the west, the sheep fields slope gently away in the direction of North Rode. The sedge margin across the canal is host to a giant among native plants. Although it is rarely thought of as flowering, it does so, high above the purple flower head of the reeds. The Bulrush or Reed Mace is the classic waterside plant although it is more often associated with swampy ground in lowland areas, it is found in isolated habitats along the canal . It stands head and shoulders above the sedges and reeds which have provided it with a hospitable foothold. The frequently overlooked male flowerhead sits like a golden plume at the very top of the stiff stem, often 7-8 feet aloft while, directly below this is the instantly recognisable female flower head, the familiar long brown sausage packed with tiny florets.

Immediately prior to lock No. 3, its bypass weir jettisons the volume of water which was held within lock No. 2, beneath the towpath and into the side pond to continue it's complicated journey down to 400 feet. The deep lock chamber which devours the largest of narrow boats is lined by massive blocks of mill grit from the quarries on the Cloud. The lining stone displays very little evidence of wear and tear after more than 160 years of monotonously repetitive soaking and drying, bashing and scraping by

REED MACE

boats and baking by the sun and desiccation by wind and frost.

Beyond the bottom gates and the metal plate footbridge which spans the downward end of each lock chamber, the towpath, once again spills down a steep incline to the next water level. As before, the distance between locks 3 and 4 is short, the two being separated by the now familiar reed-lined wide pound. Even in a pound as short as this, boats are often encountered, temporarily moored, forming an orderly queue, awaiting their turn to descend or climb their way through the flight.

Lock No. 4's bypass weir deals with the unstable volume of water between the two locks as the canal narrows to enter the top gates. The immaculately kept grass around the lock shows off it's functional mechanics to perfection. The free standing paddle gear for operating the underground culverts which are in more or less constant use every day, are kept well lubricated and neatly painted in black. The long ballence beams on the lock gates are perfectly turned out in black and white, even down to the individual number stencilled onto the beam.

In between the towpath and the side pond which lies beyond and below is a section of low, neatly clipped hedgerow at the base of which stands another half or quarter mile marker stone. The sheep in the meadow have access to the side pond as a drinking water supply by way of a gap in the low stone wall which surrounds the holding area. Beyond lock No. 4, the towpath drops steeply down to the new water level which stretches away towards lock No. 5.

To reach lock No. 5 which lies some short distance ahead, the towpath traveller passes beneath the heavily overhanging boughs of several large Oak trees which grow in the hedgerow line. The first one to be reached is a huge tree which is obviously of great antiquity. The massive gnarled trunk hints at a lifetime spanning many centuries. On closer inspection, the ancient trunk proves to be almost totally hollow, a disability which seems not to drastically affect the tree's general foliar health. It is obvious that this particular hedgerow with it's attendant Oaks is infinitely older than the canal. The line of the canal here must have accurately coincided with an existing field boundary. In the main, the canal-side Hawthorn was planted by the canal engineers at the time of the canal's completion. The canal would, as often as not, dissect a landowners meadow, therefore it was the responsibility of the canal company to plant stock proof boundary hedges. The next tree down is of similar mountainous proportions but is either not of the same great age or has been uncommonly lucky to resist the ravages of the many hundreds of creatures which are dependent upon the great British Oak.

In common with lock No. 1, the next bridge lies directly beyond lock No. 5. Even from a distance, it is clear that bridge No. 55 carries a very busy road; the A54 which runs between Congleton and Buxton. Bridge No. 55 could also be described as providing the main public access to Bosley locks. The unusually spacious towpath fairly throngs with people for most of the year. Those who find it difficult to walk for any distance will often choose this point to visit for a picnic beside the canal as the whole spectrum of canal atmosphere can be experienced. The position is completely rural, well away from any town. That special sensation which one enjoys only when beside water is heightened by the ever present drama of the functioning locks being played out almost constantly. Many come here just to observe the working of the locks and, an entertainment it can most certainly be! The panic and struggle accompanied by embarrassment and frustration which often typifies the first time lock operator is in total contrast to the unhurried professionalism of the seasoned boater whose cool, calculated operation beautifully compliments these superb monuments to the British canal engineer.

Often, an artist will be encountered, immortalising the scene in oil or in pencil. Whatever the reason for being here, this 'heart' of the locks is, arguably the most visited point along the whole of the canal's course. As the pound begins to narrow to arrive at lock No. 5, the bypass weir evacuates the excess water from the pound beneath the towpath. In this most picturesque of spots, closely mown grass, weathered mill stone and the deafening roar of water gushing from the stone culvert into the side pond strangely harmonise.

Passing the top gates with the twin ratchet paddle gears, the side pond lies down to the right alongside the lock chamber. This particular pond is unlike the previous ones in that it is surrounded by a higher wall due to the fact that a cottage and it's attendant out-buildings cluster tightly around and overlook it. In fact, buildings are also grouped around the bridge, accentuating the impression that this tiny area is a focal point for a miniature settlement, an oasis of habitation within an otherwise rural desert. A large farmhouse fronts onto the A54 just to the west of the bridge and, a short distance up the road, to the east, a converted farmhouse stands sentry in a similar position.

The real focal point, in truth, was actually a long forgotten railway station halt on the dismantled Leek to Macclesfield railway which formed the Churnet Valley Line. The cottage which overshadows the side pond occupies a triangular plot of land on a junction of the A54 and the tiny "Station Lane" which formerly provided access to the long lost station but now provides ample roadside parking for the scores of cars which convey the numerous visitors to this popular spot.

The Churnet Valley railway originally parted from the main line Stoke - Manchester line via a spur less than a quarter of a mile away to the west between the locks and North Rode Manor. From here, it ran through the parish of Bosley, through Rushton Spencer and eventually alongside the whole 3 1/2 mile length of Rudyard Lake, one of Staffordshire's most famous beauty spots. During the canal's working life, the cottage beyond the side pond was a thriving smithy. The same importance was held by a strategically positioned canal-side smithy as is held today by the modern service areas beside our motorways.

Beyond the lock chamber and the bottom lock gates the towpath splits into two once again. One path climbs up to a wooden gate on the roadside the other plunges downward to join the canal at it's new level, at the foot of the lock gates as it is about to be transported beneath the arch of bridge No. 55. As a result of the immediate proximity of the lock to the bridge, any boat waiting to ascend the canal by entering the lock has to wait it's turn beneath the actual arch of bridge No. 55. The bridge itself is noticeably broader, than many of late which indicates that the A54 was a highway of considerable importance at the time of the canal's completion.

The fact that Thomas Telford in his planning and surveying could never have visualised the volume, or in fact, the type of traffic which his canal bridges would one day need to carry, is a living monument to the vision of the canal engineers of yesteryear. Once again, beyond the bridge, the scene is very different from the claustrophobia of the lock and the bridge being just feet apart. The waterway widens right out and stretches away in a straight unhindered length with the next lock only just visible in the distance.

Immediately out from the bridge, the canal's width is highlighted by the presence, on the far bank, of the remnants of a formerly extensive stone lined wharf. The wharf was one of several along the canal to be actually owned and operated by the Macclesfield Canal Company themselves. It would have originally enjoyed a business liaison with the nearby Churnet Valley railway line. Today, the old wharf is overhung by two splendid Weeping Willow trees which have been fortunate in attaining maturity in a situation which has enabled them to achieve their classic form and proportions. Their delicate leaves reach down to touch the water in abundance where a narrow boat is frequently moored, shaded by the cascading foliage. Beyond the old wharf, neatly mown grass and fine gardens stretch away to several well appointed dwellings. Fancy white doves perch on the ridge of the heavily slated roofs of the outbuildings. Their home is a delightful, snow white dove cote which stands nearby. Beyond the pathside hedgerow lies a working farmyard.

Across the canal, the brilliant white Fantails peck at ants which stream from cracks between the paving slabs which form meandering pathways between raised beds of fragrant Roses and golden flowering Hypericums. Once the towpath has carried the traveller beyond the old wharf, upon glancing back, an idyllic scene is left behind. The bridge, framing the lock chamber and gates in it's arch is overshadowed by the towering Willows. A meadow on the eastern bank slopes away towards Crocker Hill whereas the view ahead is completely dominated by the craggy slopes of Cloud End which briefly, during late summer, is aglow with the regal purple of acres of flowering heather.

Growing beside the grassy towpath at the water's edge the curiously pretty Lady's Mantle with it's tiny greenish flowers forms localised colonies. The flowers are totally without petals and are coloured only by their yellowish stamens. The large, lobed leaves are said to resemble mantles or cowls, hence the common name. Its limited distribution along the canal is due to the fact that it grows more luxuriantly at higher altitudes but it's presence here is a welcome addition to the wonderfully diverse waterside flora.

Once again the waterway is squeezed into another lock chamber. Beyond the bottom gates, the customary iron footbridge spans the width of the chamber for the benefit of the lock operator. The footplate of each bridge is made from iron grilling, the holes allowing water to drain straight through, thus minimising the danger of a boatman slipping and falling into the chamber. As the towpath drops to the canal's new level, a reasonable length of water stretches toward lock No. 7, providing boat traffic with ample space in which to manoeuvre.

Of all the diverse craft which throng the inland waterway system and come together here to negotiate Bosleys lockage the most distinctive and characteristic are the preserved or restored narrow boats. Tailor made to move effortlessly within the arterial system of canals, their dimensions would seem ridiculous if viewed, for example, amongst sailing craft on some open sheet of water. Up to 70 feet long yet only 6 feet 10 inches to 7 feet wide, the narrow boat provided a tremendous carrying capacity which could travel at an acceptable speed with a minimum of motive power- the draught horse. The comparative ease of movement and accuracy in steering was achieved by the graceful and streamlined fore and stern ends.

The hey day of the working waterways saw largely all male crews working very practical and utilitarian craft. It was only as the paid crew began to be replaced by the operators wife and family and the boat became both home and business that it became the object of decoration. The feminine influence upon the spartan living conditions which had been endured by the working boatmen raised standards of cleanliness and was responsible for the appearance of the almost flamboyant decoration which is synonymous with canal boats.

There is a parallel here with the profusion of decoration which is traditionally found on Gipsy living waggons. This is a comparable example of women rearing their offspring and tending the family unit within a cramped and mobile environment. The instinctive need to embellish the home and to cherish the personal effects (which were limited to a bare minimum due to lack of space) gave rise to the painted buckets, coal skuttles, plant troughs, kettles and jugs. Apart from the excessively bright colours, the painting of landscapes, usually depicting a lake, a castle and a range of mountains became a part of the traditional livery of the narrow boat.

Todays 'restorations' which glide majestically along the trade routes of yesteryear, duplicate the wreaths of flowers and the 'castle in a landscape 'portraits down to the last detail. The decoration of the top plank and the tiller with large and brightly painted hearts, diamonds clubs and crescents and the obligatory roses is carried on today by the proud boat owner for almost the same reasons as the bargees of 150 years ago. It has been suggested that the original working bargees were largely comprised of Gipsy or Romany people as so many parallels exists between the two live styles. A rather colourful theory as to the origin of the somewhat abstract landscape paintings has recently been suggested. The castles, which bare a striking resemblance to the architecture of mountains central and eastern Europe, are said to be derived from the visual memory of the original traveling Romany folk.

Back on the canal, the towpath bank is continuously lined with stone whereas the far bank is completely unlined and is a veritable jungle of Rosebay Willow Herb and Bracken. The meadows which stretch away eastwards towards Crocker Hill are actually creating a false horizon which serves to conceal what really lies between the canal and Crocker Hill; Bosley Reservoir. Less than one mile distant, this picturesque sheet of water remains tantalisingly out of sight from the canal which it feeds. Today, it is difficult to comprehend that this splendid lake, nestling majestically at the foot of the Peak District hills is little more than a holding device for the 402 million gallons which are calculated to be equivalent to 11,000 locks full of water. If the construction of the canal itself was a masterpiece of engineering, the building of the reservoir and feeder were no mean feat. Thousands of tons of stone needed to be transported from Stonyfold and Gawsworth Common Quarries to build the vast dam which would contain the waters of the three streams which Thomas Telford described as "violent mountain torrents" to transform the valley into an 86 acre lake.

Looking back, in retrospect, the construction of the canal at such a late date in the timescale of national canal engineering was a commercial folly as was proved by it's relatively short working life, but what a rich legacy it has left behind to the benefit of the leisure and conservation conscious public of the late 20th century. The amenity value which is provided by the canal itself is blatantly obvious but, added to this, the wildlife habitat which is created by both Bosley and Sutton reservoirs make this part of Cheshire an infinitely richer place as a result. Bosley alone is credited with almost 140 species of plants within the reservoir valley and decades of dedicated ornithological cataloguing now confirms a bird list of sightings covering 50 years and 141 species.

Approximately halfway along the widened watercourse between locks 6 and 7, the presence of a wide hole or winding hole further adds to the impression of spaciousness and to the total volume of water in the pound. Immediately prior to the lock, the bypass weir links the pound with the side pond. Overlooking the side pond from the towpath is the weathered remains of a side paddle gear which originally let water in and out of the lock chamber and side pond prior to the original use of the ponds being abandoned.. No sooner has the towpath dropped to the next level, than the bypass weir of lock No. 8 is upon us.

Once alongside the 8th lock, bridge No. 56 stands directly beyond the bottom gates. Unlike it's two predecessors, the modest arch of bridge No. 56 carries nothing more than a pasture field, an accommodation bridge linking the two halves of a formerly extensive pasture. The towpath plunges from the lock to pass directly beneath the bridge. No. 56 is one of the very few bridges to have no pedestrian link between the towpath and what lies above. Directly beyond the bridge, the waterway widens out into a pound which is almost reminiscent of an extensive mill pool.

From the short pound which lies between bridge No. 56 and lock No. 9, a view either to east or west is obscured. A continuing hedgerow is responsible on the one side but now, beyond the sedge marsh, a mixed broadleaf woodland of mature Oaks and Beeches stretches away eastward. This woodland is actually a stream valley or clough and brings one more wildlife rich habitat within touching distance of the lock flight.

As a consequence of the mixture of marsh, woodland and open meadowland, the symphony of bird song is particularly exquisite. Here you can find the tiny Wren with its loud forceful song full of complex phrases and trills. Willow Warbler s can also be heard singing in or around , the dense sedges,their song blending in melody with the Garden Warbler which is concealed within the cool, shady woodland. From the depths of the wooded clough comes the unmistakeable call of the Chiffchaff, a common woodland inhabitant which, at first glance is indistinguishable from the strikingly similar Willow Warbler and Wood Warbler. All are greenish-olive-brown and shades of white or palest cream-yellow beneath.

The bypass weir immediately prior to lock No. 9 roars into action as the paddle gears which form part of lock No. 8's bottom gates are opened to drain the lock chamber. The lock full of water emptying into the diminutive pound between Nos. 8 and 9, swells it alarmingly. The roaring torrent of water gushes over the bypass sill and into the side pond which accompanies lock No. 9. To the left of the lock chamber, an area of tall, seeded grasses and broad leaved Willow Herb eventually merges with the outer fringes of the deciduous woodland.The towpath area between the lock chamber and the side pond is, as ever, beautifully mown and it is here that the next milestone stands, overlooking the side pond.

A low, squat stone, it is indeed a peculiar example. It is an original stone which has been defaced in the most complete way possible. Most of the information which it formerly carried has been neatly but completely chiselled off and thus far, has not been restored. The one face which should read, "From Marple 17 Miles" now reads, quite simply, "From —— miles". To make matters worse, the opposite face which originally read "From Hall Green 9 1/4 Miles" now reads " —— miles" which is indispensable for the modern day traveller who wishes to calculate the length of his journey! Beyond lock No. 9, the gates of which were replaced in 1980, the towpath leads steeply down to the canal's new level.

Once beside the next pound, an underwater bubbling and gushing which seems to stem from beside the towpath, marks the arrival of the excess water from the side pond. With the passage down through the flight of locks, it is more difficult than usual to relate to the canal's twisting and turning route. It is only now,

VIEW DOWN THE FLIGHT - BOSLEY LOCKS

between locks 9 and 10, that the reality of the canal's complicated directional progress is illustrated perfectly. The massive bulk of Cloud End which once totally dominated the view directly ahead or south now looms ever larger due west! The short pound which lies between locks 9 and 10, unlike it's predecessors is stone lined to either bank as the whole of the pound is transported briefly across a deep valley. Beyond the stone lined water's edge, across the pound, the view is of tree tops! the crowns of Oaks, Beeches and Willows. Beyond the towpath, the ground falls away accordingly into a rough grassy valley where the impoverished nature of the ground is betrayed by the dotted clumps of Gorse bushes and stunted, solitary Hawthorn trees. Beyond the valley, the waterway opens out in width with greater confidence. Away to the west, the marked ridge which indicates the position of the dismantled Churnet Valley line is suddenly visible, moving closer to the canal all the time.

The stone lining of the far bank is replaced by the now familiar sedge marsh. Wet land such as this has a tendency to spread and to reclaim open water at a considerable pace. Beside these excessively wide canal pounds, what must have been an unlined canal bank, growing a few sedges is becoming a separate, semi-aquatic habitat of rush and sedge beds, allowing Willow saplings to gain a foothold where, until quite recently, boats could lie, waiting to use the lock. The waterway narrows right down to pass into the chamber of lock No. 10. Beyond the side pond, a steep embankment once carried the now dismantled railway towards the canal.

The top and bottom gates of lock No. 10 date from 1973. Below the chamber, the towpath is delivered steeply down to the next level where it finds itself alongside a sheet of water which, upon widening out immediately beyond the confines of the lock chamber, closely resembles a reed fringed mill pool. Directly beyond this placid pool which bears not the slightest resemblance to a length of canal, lies lock No. 11.

The further down the Bosley lock flight one progresses, the locks are positioned ever closer together, thus, through necessity, the pound which lies between each lock needs to be wider than it's predecessor to be able to absorb the influx of extra water from the lock. Higher up the flight this water would have been absorbed into a more substantial length of canal. The reed margins which line this quiet backwater give way to a back drop of typical wet woodland, dense tangles of Willows, Osiers and Alders. The scene is more reminiscent of a broad in Norfolk or Suffolk than an old industrial canal in deepest Cheshire.

Because of the short distance between locks 10 and 11, it is possible to detect the curving of the waterway. The deviation could never be discerned purely by looking at the sheet of water which lies between them but, No. 11 is most definitely off-set, quite sharply so, in relation to No. 10, indicating that the canal is indeed veering quite determinedly to the right. The pound narrows so drastically to enter the top gates of lock No. 11 that it briefly resembles a canal once more.

To the left of the mill grit chamber, the far bank is an impenetrable jungle of Docks, Cow Parsley, Sedges and Bull Rushes or Great Reed Mace. To the right of the towpath, the side pond is surrounded by the unmistakeable remains of long lost buildings. The extensive footings, long overgrown with meadow grasses, were almost certainly once part of a cottage which, like the one which stands above the side pond at lock No. 1, formerly housed a lock-keeper whose responsibility would be the locks on this lower end of the flight. At the lower end of the pond, the brick remnants to be seen today are the remains of stables.

Stables were customarily positioned alongside lock flights as exhausted horses which had often towed a laden boat for many miles could be exchanged for an animal which had fed and rested. Just beyond the site of the long demolished stables, the high embankment which formerly carried the Churnet Valley railway meets the waterway at a railway bridge which once carried the track over the canal immediately beyond lock No. 11. Once past the bottom gates of lock No. 11, the towpath drops steeply down to arrive alongside the final wide pound.

This sheet of water is, by far, the most extensive in surface area. Were it not for the presence of lock No. 11, it would be difficult to imagine that this was a canal at all as lock No. 12 is totally hidden from view. The dark water is fringed by Sedges and Rushes and overhung by Willows and Alders. Across the water, the far bank is most indistinct for the lagoon must surely be well in excess of 100 feet wide. It is difficult to determine where the canal ends and the Sedge beds which disguise the far bank actually begin. Incredibly, this most tranquil of bays was once a hive of industry. The excessive width of water here owes it's existence to the fact that up until the late 1950's, a warehouse of ample proportions formerly occupied the site. Actually standing in the water, it enabled cargoes to be off-loaded or loaded onto boats directly in a similar fashion to the warehouse which still stands beside bridge No. 1 at Marple.

Unlike the stone building at Marple, the Bosley warehouse was almost certainly of timber construction and failed to survive the attentions of the weather and the passage of time. Not only was the warehouse strategically positioned from the point of view of the locks and also the Macclesfield - Leek railway but it was also served by it's own narrow gauge railway which ran steeply through the woods to Bosley Mills, further up the valley. Standing alongside the pound, the impression is that the waterway is continuing to curve sharply to the right as the old railway bridge is sharply offset in relation to the position of lock No. 11 and lock No. 12 is completely out of sight around the bend. The canal pound narrows only slightly to allow the railway bridge to span it. In no way does it attempt to squeeze itself down to the seven or eight feet width at which it passes beneath a normal canal bridge arch. The unspectacular bridge is of classic railway design, a stone support on either bank but the canal is actually spanned by a metal, box section bridge which, after decades of neglect, is beginning to show visible signs of rust and decay.

The stone upright of the bridge beside the towpath bares deep rope cuts which paint a vivid picture of noisy steam locomotives clattering along above the canal while the virtually silent narrowboats glide beneath powered by the awesome strength of the draught horse. Beneath the bridge, instead of the familiar arch of dressed stone blocks, fitting like pieces in some huge jigsaw, slabs of concrete and huge iron girders carried the railway aloft. Still in the shadows of the bridge, the canal begins to narrow to enter the bottom lock, No. 12. Standing alongside the top gates of lock No. 12, upon glancing back, the railway bridge which, from this side is heavily festooned with Ivy, is fully visible but, beyond it, lock No. 11 and most of the pound is lost from view, illustrating perfectly the extent by which the waterway has curved. Beyond the free standing paddle ratchets, one on either bank, a set of stop planks overlook the bottom lock from the far bank. Beside this final lock, the side pond spews its excess water into a stone culvert which delivers the resulting torrent back to the canal and it's final level.

Beyond the lock chamber and bottom gates, the towpath plunges steeply downward to arrive beside the canal as it reaches 400 feet above sea level. Directly as the canal leaves the confines of the lock chamber, a short overflow sill is situated on the far bank to help to lessen the dramatic effect of the lock full of water

BOTTOM LOCK - BOSLEY

entering the bottom level for here, of course, there is no regulating pound but simply the remainder of the canal between here and the Trent and Mersey. The flood of water which escapes over the overflow sill is directed into a brook course below.

The length of canal which lies ahead, which rapidly attains it's normal width, is a hive of activity the whole year round as, winter and summer alike, boats will be found moored along the towpath bank. A popular overnight mooring, many cruisers will make this stop the convenient end of the travelling day, looking forward with anticipation (or trepidation) to the journey up through the lock flight the following day. Alternatively, the sheer relief or sense of achievement on having descended the flight often prompts and overnight stop.

One way or another, the towpath walker, on leaving Bosley locks behind, will often need to pick his way through a veritable minefield of taut tethering lines, purposely positioned at ankle height for the benefit of the walker who is out of the habit of looking where he is putting his feet! Numerous picnic tables spread with a staggering array of gourmet delights and chilled wine, the occupants of deck chairs perusing the Ordnance Survey map or some suitable canal guide publication! all clutter the teeming towpath. The customary scents of the countryside give way to the lusty aroma of the barbecue.

The waterway assumes a generous width, allowing boats to pass one another with ease while overtaking stationary craft which are moored to the towpath bank. Beside the towpath, a disused drain off paddle is set in the hedgerow line. The derelict state of this particular paddle gear is accentuated by the fact that the actual ratchet gear has been chained up to prevent its operation. During it's occupational life, the excess water from the paddle was channelled away across the meadow to the west, along a stone lined course which eventually discharged into a natural stream Mooring rings, set in blocks of concrete at intervals of less than 10 yards are a feature of this wide, grassy towpath which in common with the journeydown the flight, is kept immaculately mown and tended.

The meadow land which lies down to the west is remarkably flat, almost artifially level . This isdue to the fact that it is a water meadow or flood plain to the River Dane. This is the river which is also responsible for the dramatic valley across which the canal is about to be transported. Mixed flocks of sheep and cattle graze the lush pasture which grows richly upon it's bed of river silt.

The sudden feeling of openness and spaciousness as the canal strides out across what must surely be it's most dramatic valley crossing is in stark contrast to the intimacy of the lock flight. In the distant east, across the river valley, the strange and unfamiliar shapes of Bosley's massive wood treatment plant tower above the tall trees which mark the river's progress along it's valley. Bosley works was originally built by Charles Roe as a copper rolling and hammering works, together with 19 cottages for the workers. With the help of James Brindley, he harnessed the power of the river Dane. The works went on to become two cotton mills but from the 1920's, the wood flour treatment business which still thrives today was instigated. The size of today's operation can be judged by the fact that over 100 people are employed at any one time.

An embankment of monumental proportions carries the Macclesfield Canal across the valley. In keeping with embanked passages, the canal's banks are lined throughout, firstly with stone then with sheet metal. The sheer volume of soil which would originally have been transported to and mounded across a valley of this size to create a level passage for the canal is absolutely staggering. The "cut and fill" principle by which the canal was constructed was responsible for generating the thousands of tons of soil which was the raw material for these great embankments. When one considers that the canal was actually dug out to a width of 36 feet by 7 1/2 feet deep by 27 3/4 miles in length, it is probably a blessing in disguise that, every so often, a sizeable valley needed to be spanned by embankment, otherwise, disposal of the surplus soil would have presented Crossley the engineer and his team with a problem of mountainous proportions.

The excavation width of 36 feet would eventually end up at a finished canal width of 30 feet (approx) as either bank needed to be lined with a 3 feet thickness of puddling material. Likewise, the basic depth of 7 1/2 feet would finish at 6 feet when an 18 inch puddled bed had been laid. In addition to the soil which was dug out of the basic canal section, vast quantities sometimes needed to be excavated when the canal had to pass through a cutting. The sum total removed over the whole 27 3/4 miles defies calculation but it is a fair bet that, with all of the embankments and half embankments built, a massive surplus would still be on hand to offer to adjoining landowners for land levelling purposes or for the filling of pit holes. In the case of the Bosley embankment, not only does the waterway maintain an above average width during it's valley crossing but it curves gracefully in a beautiful crescent across it's span.

Looking across to the distant east, a perfect example of ancient and modern can be seen. Directly in front of the strange and unfamiliar outline of the wood treatment plant, an ancient stone bridge transports a tiny lane over the river Dane. The rushing torrent, or the musical babbling of the river, depending upon the volume of water which it is carrying, can be heard long before it actually comes into view. In the distant west, the view is now dominated by the massive railway viaduct which, like the canal, needed to cross the valley of the river Dane to travel between Congleton and Macclesfield. The electrified Inter-City express of today fairly hurtles across the 1300 feet span of the twenty majestic brick arches whereas, the first steam locomotive to make the crossing in July of 1848 probably allowed it's passengers time to gaze in awe down into the lush valley and at the silver thread of water almost 100 feet below. The fleeting commuter travelling between Stoke on Trent and Manchester may catch the briefest glimpse of the massive wall of earth which was laid across the valley to carry the canal, whereas, the traveller who crosses the valley by water or by towpath may experience the windswept experience of open space and can also gaze at length upon the skill of the Victorian railway engineer, Thomas Brassey who transformed hundreds of thousands of bricks into the magnificent twenty arches. These twenty arches had taken two years to build by an army of over 2000 men who lived in a shanty town of shacks by the river.

Quite abruptly, the trim hedgerow which has, thus far, accompanied the towpath across the embankment is replaced by the sturdy wrought iron railings, painted out in black, red and gold, which announce the canal's arrival at the magnificent river Dane aqueduct. The fine, stone built, single arch aqueduct carries the canal far above the river which rushes and tumbles along it's rock strewn bed. The splendid, ornate railings are replaced by a tall stone wall as the canal and towpath are actually transported over the river. A glance over the bridge wall to the river far below is sufficient to inflict an attack of vertigo upon the susceptible and will serve to illustrate perfectly the need for the high wall!

Much credit has already been heaped upon the technical brilliance of the design and execution of the Macclesfield Canal as a whole and the majestic proportions of this fine aqueduct is certainly no disappointment. It must be said, however, that aqueducts were definitely not engineer William Crossley's strongest subject. His first attempt at a major aqueduct appears much further along the southward journey and was an unmitigated disaster. The aqueduct which we see here today was Crossley's second and, although the canal was successfully opened for business with the bridge in it's original form, problems soon developed. Several years into the canal's working life, Crossley's aqueduct began to split in two with the weight of water, the western side beginning to move outwards.

The famous railway and canal engineer, G W Buck was commissioned to build two great buttresses to support the western side of the structure which effectively solved the problem. This was not however the end of the story of Crossley's problematical Bosley aqueduct. The original shift which had been halted by the timely addition of G W Buck's buttress had left hairline cracks in the masonry. The clay bed of the canal proved far too thick to allow a leak to occur. It was over a century later in 1961 that the canal 'sprung a leak' for only the second recorded instance. The burrowing activities of a worm or even a rat in the puddling material was responsible for a leak to be sprung via the century old cracks in the stone work. Luckily, the leak was noted and repaired before major damage was incurred by the main structure.

This is a suitable moment to contemplate the incredible impact which the arrival of the Macclesfield Canal must have had on the tiny agricultural settlement of Bosley. From a geographical point of view, Bosley was of paramount importance to the canal. The creation of the 86 acre reservoir in a formerly remote stream vall ey forming the principle water supply for the 28 mile long waterway. The need to drop the canal by in excess of 100 feet at this point via the 12 locks. The cutting of the canal through the parish and the dissection of the river valley by this massive embankment coupled with the bridging of the river itself by this ambitious, towering aqueduct all centered upon this small and scattered village.

Bosley, mentioned in the Domesday survey as Boselega was nothing more than a fragmented sheep and diary farming settlement lying in the shadow of the penultimate peak of the Pennine chain, the Cloud. Of the army of men who ascended upon Bosley, some would be skilled craftsmen, masons, brick layers and carpenters, but the vast majority were labourers and a high percentage of these would be the 'professional' navigators; the legendary 'navvies'.

Top: GOYT MILL at Marple. Bridge Nº 3 (see page 4)
Bottom: ADELPHI MILL at Bollington (see page 64)

DETAIL OF INTRICATE STONEWORK. SKEW BRIDGE Nº 26 at
Sugar Lane, Bollington. (see page 57)

CLARENCE MILL at Bollington. (see page 59)

HOVIS MILL and MACCLESFIELD MARINA. *(see page 87)*

THE OAKGROVE BRIDGES. (see page 112)

Top: BOSLEY LOCK FLIGHT.
Bottom: LOCK Nº 5 and SIDE POND from Bridge Nº 55 (see page 135)

CROSSLEY HALL FARM *(see page 155)*

Top: CONGLETON WHARF *(see page 188)*
Bottom: LAMBERT LANE BRIDGE Nº 77 *(see page 189)*
Both photographs courtesy of David Harrop.

CHAPTER EIGHT
THE DANE TO DANE-IN-SHAW

Beneath William Crossley's aqueduct, the waters of Cheshire's most picturesque of rivers, the Dane, forges onward, deeper into the county. This splendid river begins its life as an imperceptible trickle high on the lonely and desolate Axe Edge Moor which overlooks the Peak District town of Buxton.

Axe Edge is an inhospitable and eerie place in any weather. It is a high, bleak expanse of cold, peaty ground, thinly covered by Cotton Grass, rushes and alpine Heathers. The abundance of sheep bones bleached by biting frosts, and the occasional shepherds dew pond, circular and deep and filled with black peaty water, all add to the stark emptiness. The infant river is little more than a rain filled gutter which can be stepped over and passed by unnoticed. The weird call of the Curlew is often the only recognisable sign of animal or bird life in the inhospitable place which is reputed to enjoy "nine months of winter and three months of bad weather!".

The river Dane or Back Dane as it is known in its youth, begins to cascade downward towards Gradbach where it is joined by Black Brook which immediately doubles it in size. Here the Dipper will be seen in arrow-like flight, low over the water. This Wren-like bird takes the place of the Kingfisher in the high reaches of these mountain torrents. What sets the Dipper apart from all other birds is it's unique ability to actually walk along the bed of the torrent, feeding underwater on nymphs and crustaceans.

The Dane rushes onward through the Dane Valley where it is joined by Clough Brook, a stream which is often measurably more robust than the river which it joins on it's passage through Wildboarclough. The Dane reaches Wincle where it's flow over stony shingle is punctuated by deep, quiet pools where exquisite Brown Trout lurk, away from the main current. From Wincle and Dane Bridge, the river flows onward to Bosley to pass beneath the canal and railway. Here, the darting water bird is the magnificent Kingfisher and the Trout begin to compete with the first Dace and Minnows for the available insects.

Beyond Bosley, the river passes through North Rode, Eaton, Havannah and Buglawton before reaching Congleton. Below Congleton, it's character begins to change, the river slows and widens for it's passage across the Cheshire Plain through Radnor, Somerford, Swettenham, Twemlow, Holmes Chapel, Middlewich and Bostock before joining the river Weaver at Northwich. The towpath across the Dane aqueduct remains wide. The graceful curve which has carried the canal and, indeed, the great embankment right from the foot of the bottom lock ends as the aqueduct is crossed for, ahead now, a straight length of canal and towpath lead to the next canal bridge, Number 57.

For the first time in several miles, the canal's far bank is made up of a broad colony of Yellow Flag Iris, a welcome return to normality after the complicated descent of the locks and the lengthy embankment .Beyond the Iris bed, a hummocky area of pasture land leads up to a cattle track which passes over bridge Number 57.This ancient livestock highway, linking the meadows to the east and west of the bridge probably played a more significant role in the past and, in doing so determined the position of bridge No. 57 as the bridge was originally known as "Old Driving Lane Bridge".The trampled cattle track of today is unrecognisable as a thoroughfare but is still a public footpath.

Directly ahead, the wide grassy towpath is replaced by the first open overflow still to be positioned, thus far, on the towpath bank. The uneven stone setts which form the overflows catchment and run off, temporarily make walking hazardous when any volume of water is escaping from the canal over the sill. Unless wellingtons are being worn, the highest standing stones must serve as stepping stones.Although, as previously described, the whole of the canal's remaining length is responsible for soaking up the influx of extra water which results from lock No. 12 being used, this overflow is strategically positioned to remove any dangerous fluctuation in level. The waters level and edge is marked by a long stone curb or sill which lies at exact normal water level. The resulting excess water crosses what would normally be the towpath then is gradually channelled into an artificial stream course which tumbled down the side of the valley to discharge into the Dane, far below. As a consequence, the overflow is capable of diverting a considerable amount of water safely away, should the need arise.

Immediately beyond the overflow, the canal begins to narrow between stone lined banks to arrive at bridge No. 57.The modest stone arch was obviously built as an accommodation bridge. It was not within the powers of the Macclesfield Canal Company to divert the course of an established route, even this ancient driving lane which had degenerated into a cattle track. On closer inspection, the bridge is built slightly on the skew to allow the old lane to cross the newly arrived canal by means of its own chosen angle.

Having crossed the valley of the Dane, pausing to glance back to reflect, the whole scene is overshadowed by the looming bulk of Crocker Hill and the telecommunications tower. The overpowering feeling of great space accentuated by distant views is about to be extinguished by the entering of a more intimate sheltered passage. Another more subtle but significant change which may not be instantly apparent has also taken place. The length of towpath which has benefitted from the work which was done by by the far-sighted Macclesfield Borough and their Towpath Improvement Scheme of the early 1980's is now behind us. The superb towpath condition which has prevailed from the journeys start at Marple does not extend beyond Bosley. This is not necessarily indicative that the remaining footway is derelict or decrepit but, the changeover is noticeable, as is the total absence of pathside seats! Subtle details such as these make walking within the area of Macclesfield's responsibility a more pleasant experience.

Having passed beneath the arch of bridge No. 57, the waterway enters a shady passage, where the canal's eastern bank is lined by Oak trees which shade the water. Their deeply fissured bark provides a perfect feeding ground for the drab and diminutive Tree Creeper which perpetually performs its acrobatic trunk scaling act in search of insect morsels. Just out from the bridge wall, a set of stop planks stand beside the towpath. The familiar stop plank stands provide the only pathside seating facilities between Bosley and Congleton and one needs to be fairly sprite and nimble to spring up onto the perch which they provide.

The towpath which lies ahead is distinguishable from that which has gone before by the fact that it has not been resurfaced for many years and has a soil or turf surface as opposed to the miles of white limestone surfacing. The wide, dark canal curves up ahead, overhung from the far bank by Oaks and Silver Birch, offering only an occasional glimpse of the meadow land which lies away to the east. .By comparison, the towpath is overhung by large bushes of prickly Gorse which blaze with a vivid golden radiance.

Twining through the Gorse are brambles which reach down to the towpath, laden in late summer and early autumn with huge masses of juicy Blackberries. Occasionally, the towpath traveller may choose to arm himself with plastic bag and infinite patience to spend an hour or two in the therapeutic gathering of nature's bountiful hedgerow harvest. This harvesting of fruits from the hedge is surely an instinctive reaction to a deeply seated race memory. For centuries our ancestors gathered fruits and seeds and roots to survive before the advent of actively hunting game or before the dawn of animal and crop husbandry. The sheer pleasure which many derive from this painstaking cropping of Blackberries and Rosehips or Elderberries is only surpassed by the unique flavours of the wines and preserves produced from ancient farmhouse recipes and the great satisfaction in the knowledge

BLACKBERRY

that the glowing wine or the mouthwatering jam is the delicious end product of one's own labours in scouring the pathside hedgerows for their abundant treasures.

The hedgerow bramble is actually a sophisticated plant which is represented in the British Isles by literally hundreds of varieties, each with fruits of slightly different sizes and, ultimately flavours but, more importantly, different ripening times. Consequently the Bramble can present the passer by with luscious ripe fruit from mid-summer right through to the frosts.

The view of the canal is occasionally obscured from the towpath as the pathside margin has become colonised by tall Willow Herb, Gorse and Brambles. Across the canal, the bank begins to drop away to reveal a gently sloping meadow. The massive bulk of Cloud End rears dramatically upwards from the surrounding agricultural land. The craggy black silhouette totally dominates the view to the east. The Hawthorn bushes on the far bank frequently throng with Long Tail Tits which flit across the canal in the irdistinctive jerky, fluttering flight.

Rounding a long and gradual curve in the waterway, the next bridge comes into view some distance ahead. On the approach to Bridge No. 58, a small stone arch, the bank to the right of the towpath is a jungle of tangled Brambles and Hawthorn trees. The mellow stone of the bridge merges perfectly with it's surroundings. It seems, not at all out of place. Hawthorn trees, twisted and contorted as solitary specimens often are, crowd in around the bridge, seeming to protect and shelter it. Agricultural accommodation bridges such as this were not victims of scrimping or penny pinching as they could so easily have been. The bridge ahead, although it only carries a cattle track, is every bit as substantial and of equal architectural merit as any of it's contempories which need to withstand the constant passage of motor traffic.

Passing beneath the arch of No. 58, the same meadow to the east continues to slope gently away towards The Cloud. Still within the shadow of the bridge, the canal is briefly transported across the wooded course of a tiny stream which is neatly culverted beneath. The miniscule torrent springs from the ground just below Peover Farm which nestles directly below Cloud End. Within half a mile of emerging from the ground, it passes beneath the canal. Less than a quarter of a mile to the west, it joins the River Dane.

Emerging from the shelter of the mature trees which inhabit the stream clough, extensive pasture land stretches away and upward to the east. Quite suddenly, on the horizon which is created by the rising meadows, a singularly isolated building of exquisite beauty comes into view. The unexpected appearance of this building in so lonely a spot makes the appreciation of its historic architecture all the more fulfilling. It must be remembered that the last building to be seen was way back at bridge No. 55, half way down the lock flight.

Big Fenton Farm epitomises the black and white timber frame building style so very typical of Cheshire. It is only this tantalisingly distant view which we can enjoy; we shall draw no nearer to it. Big Fenton's extremely isolated position; a considerable distance from a very minor lane, has tended to protect and cushion it from the glare of attention which would, doubtless, have been forced upon it otherwise. The sizeable farmhouse is of sixteenth century origin and, at one time formed part of the enormous agricultural empire of the landed Antrobus family. The house contains a small chapel which is believed to have been used for Catholic worship. Beneath part of the house is a small room which is known as the "Priest's hiding place".The way in which the house is viewed from the canal, across two extensive and otherwise featureless pastures, seems to add an aura of mystery. The distant view westward is across the river valley where the clusters of farms and smallholdings are actually in North Rode.Glancing eastwards, Big Fenton Farm disappears from view, hidden by the rising ground, but, in it's place, the extensive range of farmyard buildings which accompany it can be seen clearly instead.

As a constant backdrop to the house and now the farm buildings, The Cloud looms to a height of 1190 feet at the summit. Thomas Telford's "adjacent mountain" probably derives it's strange name from "clud" which means rock. Another distinct possibility is that the name is a corruption of "clawd" meaning fort,as part of the hill top is widely believed to have been occupied by an Iron Age hill fort. Although no hard and fast evidence has survived to substantiate this latter statement, almost every old deed, document, plan and map of the hill shows the position of the abandoned Iron Age settlement.

What is beyond any question of doubt is that Neolithic man did indeed inhabit the Cloud and surrounding areas between 2750 and 2250 BC. Somewhere around 2500 BC our Neolithic ancestors constructed a chambered tomb of monumental proportions to inter their dead on the southern slopes of the hill.The Cloud is dissected by the modern day county boundary between Cheshire and Staffordshire and just within Staffordshire, close to the present day Congleton-Leek road lies the remains of the Bridestones.

Only a very small portion of this formerly extensive Megalithic structure remain visible. There are traces of the semicircular forecourt area at the east and almost 20 feet of the long gallery is still intact. Originally the barrow is believed to have exceeded 300 feet in length.The type of gallery grave identified at the Bridestones site is classified as a Clyde-Carlingford sub-group of which the finest examples are to be found in Ulster and Galloway which adds a further touch of mystery to the proceedings.

Travelling onward, a further half or quarter mile marker stone is almost concealed in the grass and herbage beside the towpath.With Bridge No. 58 still visible behind, No. 59 comes into view ahead . The meadows to the left slope gently upwards to Big Fenton Farm but now, the featureless line of the field is broken by a sizeable depression which is both surrounded by mature trees and is, more than likely, a long abandoned sand hole or clay pit. As bridge No. 59 draws nearer, it becomes clear that this is another agricultural accommodation bridge, simply built to create a link between the two halves of a meadow which was once a whole.

It is so quiet and tranquil here, so remote and completely rural that it would be a gross intrusion if so much as a single track lane trespassed into this peaceful haven of rolling pastures and quiet water by daring to cross the bridge which lies ahead. Arriving at the rustic stone arch, one cannot fail to be impressed by the consistency of the Macclesfield Canal's architecture linked, of course, in part to the equally consistent availability of superior building stone. From the bridge, the waterway begins to curve quite determinedly to the left which, upon glancing eastward, unites a view of the brilliantly black and white gable end of Big Fenton Farm with the view of its considerable collection of attendant buildings.

Once again, we are treated to a perfect example of how the canal twists and turns and deviates as the view to the west is now taken up by the reasonably close proximity of the 20 arch railway viaduct. As the canal crossed the river Dane, the prevailing view was of the viaduct straddling the far end of the valley. We now discover that the canal has followed the edge of the valley around to position us almost directly alongside the arches. The pastures to the west which mark the edge of the river valley are grazed by flocks of sheep during late summer, autumn and winter but grow lush crops of grass during Spring which are cut early for silage. Dense colonies of Cow Parsley and Willow Herb which tend to flower at almost head height during the summer months colonise the area between the water's edge and the towpath occasionally obscuring the view of the water.

The next milestone stands beside the towpath, which reads "From Hall Green - Miles" which should of course read eight and a quarter miles. By comparison, the opposite face reads "From Marple 18 miles" with perfect clarity. Beneath the encrusting lichen this could well be another example of a stone which has been refaced with concrete render and the message recarved but, if this is the case, why only one face? The customary Hawthorn hedgerow is temporarily replaced by a thicket of Snowberry bushes.

As previously described, the exotic Snowberry is a garden escapee which is rarely found singly. It much prefers, as here, to form a tangled thicket. The spongy white berries which decorate the thick tangle of branches during the late autumn and winter are quite inedible and are totally ignored by birds which is often the case with alien species. Across to the west a huge embankment comes into view, carrying the mainline railway from its passage across the arches of brick towards the canal.

Across to the east, the overall view of the Cloud is now altering imperceptibly. Previously, the view has been square on to Cloud End. But now, the wooded Cloudside and the Cloud plantation, an extensive area of Scots Pine woodland, can be seen. The views from Cloud End are legendary. With the naked eye, from the summit, the lock flight at Bosley and the Dane aqueduct can be seen and with binoculars, the canal can be followed almost into Staffordshire.

In these enlightened times, public access to the hill is totally unrestricted, particularly since 1962 when 135 acres comprising the highest ground, the pine woodland, the rocky outcrops at the summit and the Giant's Footprint (a depression in solid gritstone which bears an uncanny resemblance to a shoeprint some 3-4 feet in length) was acquired through National Land Fund procedures by the National Trust. Thirty years prior to this date, the situation was very different. Prior to the enclosure acts of 1802 and 1810, the hill had been a common with Lord Egerton of the Tatton estate as the land owner. By the early decades of this century, those who flocked to Cheshire's wild and remote places at the spearhead of the great "Open Air Movement" found all pathways across the Cloud obstructed by barbed wire fences and padlocked gates. Massive local opposition was mounted by an action group which formed in Congleton, against Lord Egerton who was eventually forced to give way to popular opinion.

Up ahead, the railway line crosses the canal for the first time having accompanied it more or less continuously from Macclesfield. The huge embankment arrives beside the towpath directly ahead and crosses the waterway by means of three tall brick arches which are extra to the twenty which span the river valley further along the embankment to the west. The canal passes beneath the middle arch of the three. The waterway makes no attempt to narrow to pass beneath the railway. The arch to the left provides sheltered parking for an interesting assortment of agricultural implements from balers and muckspreaders to hay trailers and harrows. This vast example of Victorian railway architecture can hardly be described as blending into the landscape as the unassuming canal bridge does. The sombre shades of mellow stone illustrate once more how mill grit is very much an integral part of this landscape and how brick is not, no matter how tastefully or masterfully laid and assembled.

The sweet smell of cattle permanently hangs in the air as the towpath traveller passes beneath the railway. They obviously take shelter beneath the lofty arch when inclement weather takes them by surprise. As they pass along their muddy highway between fields, they relentlessly trample their rich manure into the mud beneath the arch.

The viaduct as a whole is constructed from extremely hard and weather resistant blue brick. Although it loses points for not blending into the surroundings as completely as its canal counterpart, it must be stressed that the arches which span the canal and towpath are superbly built at an oblique angle to the waterway and consequently qualify as skew bridges. Like the skew canal bridge of stone, epitomised by Sugar Lane bridge just north of Bollington, the angled brickwork of the high arch has been exquisitely designed and executed.

Probably the most obvious feature upon emerging from the viaduct arch is that the next stone canal bridge, No. 60, lies little more than 100 yards ahead. The other overwhelming feature of the short length of canal which lies between the railway arch and bridge No. 60 is the enormous Willow tree which grows from the canal's bank This colossal tree with a trunk of tremendous girth for its species leans alarmingly across the canal as from the day it first germinated from the seed, it has grown vigorously away from the towering railway viaduct and towards clear sunlight. The acute angle of inclination means that major branches overhang the canal and the towpath and, in fact, extend beyond even the towpath and the hedgerow beside it to overhang into the field!

The grassy areas to left and right of the towpath are host to inhospitable colonies of stinging nettles, an annoyance to the passer-by but vital as a nursery environment for the eggs and caterpillars of numerous Butterflies and Moths. From the canal's far bank, an uneven pasture rises steeply away eastwards. The canal curves slightly even along this short length as the stone bridge, No. 60 is noticeably off-set in relation to the viaduct Three or four meadows distant to the west lies the extensive range of out buildings which accompany a large farm. This unlikely setting is, in fact, the site of an ancient moated manor house called Crossley.

The only visible remains which survive to betray the presence of the formerly fortified dwelling are traces of the partly filled-in moat to the immediate west of the present farmhouse. Documentary evidence exists which indicates that the family bearing the name Crossley and inhabiting this site were long established by the 12th century. In 1190, Agnes, daughter and co-heiress of Gilbert de Crossley of Crossley in Buglawton was married. This marriage forged a link between the Crossley's and a somewhat more powerful family who held extensive lands south of Congleton, whose ancient seat (if existent today) would also lie beside the Macclesfield Canal, the De Moretons of Great Moreton.

Crossley, with it's moated dwelling formed a small subordinate manor within the larger manorship and township of Buglawton. The circumstances surrounding the decay and disappearance of the house, leaving no more than a dry ditch and a "site of antiquity" mention on the ordnance survey map, are vague George Ormarod in his definitive "History of Cheshire" quotes a document dated 1819 which states "it is a ruinous farm called Crossley which once gave it's name to an ancient family". The position of the moat and mound, directly overlooking the river Dane indicates that the dwelling within the moat once commanded a fine view across the river valley.

The Hawthorn hedgerow gradually rises up to meet bridge No. 60, obscuring the view westward towards Crossley .No. 60 is a further example of an accommodation bridge, a modest stone arch carrying nothing more pretentious than a field across the canal. This particular bridge appears somewhat laid bare or unprotected as it lacks the towering sentries which shade so many of it's predecessors, the spreading Ash or the clustering Hawthorn. Passing beneath the bridge, the view ahead is of farm buildings which suddenly abound on the far bank.

Beyond the bridge, the ground drops away into a busy farmyard which lies considerably lower than the canal's level to the east. The range of outbuildings of many styles and greatly differing ages initially obscure the view of the house around which they crowd. The modern breezeblock loose boxes and barn with tin sheet roof, crammed to overflowing with hay and straw, stand alongside brick built cattle enclosures with slate roofs where scores of domestic pigeons perch along the ridge. A shippon of weathered old brick displays the traditional circular opening into the hayloft above and intricate ventilation inlets in the form of crosses in the brickwork. The view westward is now unhindered by a low, neat hedgerow which affords uninterrupted views down towards Crossley.

The canal is suddenly on a full embankment once more as it passes the farm buildings almost at roof level and the ground to the west drops even more steeply away. From behind the hay barn, the first view of the farmhouse on the far bank is of the massive chimney breast and stack which ascends the gable end of the magnificent house. A truly huge chimney built from rough hewn blocks of stone which starkly contrasts with the main fabric of the house.

Crossley Hall Farm, like Big Fenton is the classic epitome of rural Cheshire, the stark white of whattle and daub panels and the jet black of the painted oak of the timber framing. The large house stands, in all its glory, aloof from the maze of outbuildings which jostle around it. From the elevated position on the canal towpath, a fine view of this beautiful house with its blue tiled roof fairly takes the breath away.

The house dates from the 16th century. The question now arises, did the 12th century house within the moat decay and crumble to be replaced by this house in the 16th century or did the moated house survive beyond the 16th century and was this building its "Hall Farm" as it's present day name suggests? To further confuse the issue, the document dated 1819 and quoted by Mr Ormarod distinctly states "it is a ruinous farm called Crossley". Does this statement refer to the remains of the moated 12th century building or was this house in pitifully poor repair at that time as this building is most definitely a farm? Such are the delights of local history (the answers to the numerous questions are only rarely to be found written down!) The final twist in the tail is that, even in these enlightened times, Crossley Hall Farm is more often than not referred to as Crossley Hall!

The ground to the right continues to fall sharply away westwards while, across the water, the ground to the east now drops to a small, walled paddock or croft which lies in front of the farmhouse. Frequently, during the early years of the century, this sheltered paddock would provide the perfect venue for the annual Sunday School trip organised by the Methodist Sunday School in Congleton. A narrow boat would be laid on for the occasion, cleaned, scrubbed down, and fitted out with wooden forms for seating the children. Trestle tables, food, tablecloths and a huge brass tea urn would be put on board ready to be set up in the paddock or some freshly mown hay field, courtesy of the genial Mr Abraham Swindells. The Sunday School scholars would play games of cricket or racing while the mammoth picnic was prepared. This may seem somewhat antiquated and naive in this day and age but serves to illustrate the dawning of the Macclesfield Canal as an amenity commodity. Today, the enclosed croft provides sheltered grazing for young calves. The further along the embankment one progresses, the better the view of the black and white farmhouse. The building is actually in a "H" shaped plan, i.e. two gable ends project forward from two wings running north to south. These are linked by a central section which runs from east to west, forming the cross-bar of the "H".

Sycamore, Ash and Elder trees overhang the towpath as the embankment slices through a stream clough. A similar mix of deciduous trees reaches down to the canal's far bank as the tiny stream is culverted beneath the embankment. The same brook is similarly culverted beneath the Congleton to Buxton road to flow eventually into the River Dane downstream of Crossley and Colley Mill. As the canal passes over the culverted stream, the pathside hedgerow gives way to an indistinct boundary of Bracken, interspersed by Ash and Elder trees, as the ground falls steeply away into the clough valley where the predominate tree is the multi-trunked Hazel.

The Hazel, although abundantly common in woodland and hedgerows, is rarely encountered along the canal. The most instantly recognisable form of the Hazel is when the tree has been coppiced, i.e. regularly cut back to ground level to produce a multitude of slender, pliant stems, traditionally used in the making of numerous items, from baskets and walking sticks to boats and even houses. .However, when left to it's own devices, the Hazel seems to do a reasonable job of coppicing itself, usually appearing as a dense, multi-stemmed shrub. The long, yellow, male catkins which shed their pollen during February decorate the hedgerows and clough valleys just as winter begins to slacken it's icy grip. The clusters of brown nuts, each surrounded by deeply toothed green bracts provide an extra autumnal harvest for bird and mammal alike.

Beside the towpath stands a redundant drain off paddle beyond which, the stone lined course of it's artificial stream bed runs away, into the clough valley to join the natural stream. Running almost parallel to the canal now on the far bank is another neat Hawthorn hedgerow which marks the course of the narrow "Peover Lane" which links Crossley Hall Farm with the main Congleton - Buxton road. Peover Lane climbs steeply on it's winding route beyond Crossley to provide a roadway link for Big Fenton Farm before arriving directly below Cloud End, thus providing one of several links between Buglawton and the Cloud.

The canal curves quite dramatically to reveal bridge No. 61 directly ahead. The bridge is only slightly more robust in proportions than the foregoing accommodation bridges but this particular bridge carries an almost constant barrage of traffic as the busy A54, Congleton - Buxton road crosses the canal for the second time. The crossing of the road serves as a further illustration of the extent by which the canal actually curves and twists when one considers that, back at bridge No. 55, half way down the flight of locks, the same road crossed running (from Congleton) right to left or west to east, it now runs (again from Congleton) left to right or east to west!

From the arch of No. 61, it is easily possible to gaze through the arch of No. 62 as the two bridges are closer together than any so far encountered. In fact, the distance between the two is a little over fifty yards, which hardly gives the canal a fighting chance to widen out before having to narrow again.

Emerging from bridge No. 61, with the Congleton - Buxton road thundering above, a high bank with a hedgerow running along the top accompanies the wide grassy towpath. The modest parcel of ground which forms the far bank between bridges 61 and 62 is an uneven paddock or croft which is sandwiched between the main road and a farm track overshadowed by brick built outbuildings. The farm track which crosses bridge No. 62 directly ahead is totally shaded by the towering presence of stout Lime trees which were planted long ago to fulfil the role which they perform so admirably today. As long as man has built roadways or trackways, streets or lanes, he has planted Lime trees alongside them.

The 'common' native Lime is a full bodied and stately tree of majestic proportions. It is capable of reaching 130 feet in height during a life time which can span five centuries or more. It is probably the tallest broad leaf tree in the British isles. The characteristic bushy mass of side shoots which more often than not totally hide the trunk, start from ground level, adding to the general bulky appearance of the tree and making it appear as a mass of foliage. It is ironic that this most perfect of native giants is normally synonymous with urban streets and parks where the copious amounts of honeydew, dropped by the greenfly and aphids which infest the Lime's heart shaped leaves in countless millions, wreaks havoc with the paintwork of cars which are forced to park in Lime-shaded avenues. The leafy giants look at their best, as here, shadowing a quiet farm track and shading mellow brick shippons.

The canal narrows to pass beneath bridge No. 62, a delightful stone arch which, upon it's south facing side is covered in blanketing ivy. Emerging from the low arch, hung with ivy, a high stone wall which begins from the very fabric of the bridge, runs alongside the canal's eastern margin. Beyond the wall, the brick farm buildings cluster in its shade. The bridge and the wall are as one. There is no join and as they share the same stone and, doubtless shared the same stone mason, they both wear the thick clothing of ivy which cascades down the wall towards the water. Topped by a half round copeing stone, the wall towers 12-14 feet above the canal and extends for some considerable distance ahead.

When the pathside bank eventually lowers, the view is of expansive pasture land falling away westward towards North Rode. Glancing back over the right shoulder, the twenty railway arches, spanning the valley of the Dane, are clearly visible and, incredibly, beyond the railway, the view is dominated by Crocker Hill which tends to suggest that the canal is progressing in great arching loops instead of any semblance of a straight course.

Down to the west lie two flooded marl pits, surrounded by tall Elders and Hawthorn. The extensive fertile meadows which lie between the canal and the river Dane are occasionally ploughed and planted with potatoes on an annual crop rotation basis. Certain strips and corners of the fields however, have not felt the bite of the plough for many decades. An indication as to which areas are permanently under grass is evident from late summer into early autumn by the amazing size and quality of wild mushrooms which will follow a season that has seen above average rainfall. As if to compliment the acres of potatoes and the field mushrooms, the canal's margin on the towpath bank is an unusual mixture of Flowering Rush, Willow Herb and a sizeable colony of garden mint! The mint which has arrived here by accident has rapidly established a foothold along the water's edge, a habit for which it is notorious in the garden. It's invasive habit is legendary and it can prove difficult to eradicate.

On the approach to bridge No. 63, the ground rises considerably to both east and west giving the impression of having entered a cutting. The bridge is yet another example of an agricultural accommodation bridge, so frequently encountered along this length. If it were not for the close proximity of the Cloud as a source of building stone, these bridges would doubtless have originally been constructed as wooden swing bridges and as a result, would probably be non-existent by now. Unlike the long lost swing bridges of the Hurdsfield lengths, the stone bridges of Crossley and Buglawton survive to link the dissected grazing pastures of old.

Emerging from the arch of No. 63, the waterway begins to curve decisively to the left where, between the towpath and the hedgerow, sizeable clumps of Garlic Mustard will be encountered in flower from April to June. There is no way that even the most poetic of imaginative naturalist could describe the Garlic Mustard as being 'spectacular' or even, for that matter, pretty. Its large triangular leaves are hairy on the underside and are not unlike those of the stinging nettle as are it's white flowers. It is one of those plants which was awarded a variety of common or local names by country folk down the ages. "Jack by the Hedge" or "Poor Mans Mustard" commonly describe this wood margin or hedgerow native which will be found, thinly and irregularly distributed all along the Macclesfield Canal's course. The whole plant, but particularly the leaves give off a strong smell of garlic when crushed.

Rounding a gradual curve, a considerable length of straight canal stretches away, increasingly overhung from the far bank by tree cover. In addition to the screen of Elders to the east, a bank rises up beside the towpath, creating a sheltered passage. The already broad canal suddenly widens out into a wide bay or winding hole which is lined, on the far bank, by a sedge margin. From the tall sedges, a ghostly grey Heron will often drag it's ungainly bulk dramatically into the air, disturbed by the approaching human, not realising that it was totally camouflaged by the whispering sedges.

The canal is briefly sheet metal lined as it is transported across a stream clough which reaches down to the canal's far bank from the east. The tiny trickle of a stream springs from the ground just one fields' width away to the east and enters the river Dane almost the identical distance away to the west. This brief existence above ground, between the emerging from the turf to entering the rushing river, calls for a full culvert beneath the canal and provides Cheshire's landscape with one more clough habitat.

The bank is topped by tall Ash trees which tower skyward, dwarfing the towpath and canal. Among the Ashes high above the towpath, the presence of a wild Crab Apple tree is betrayed by the carpet of spilled fruit which covers the towpath in autumn and, for that matter floats in considerable numbers in the water. Looking as these hard, bitter little fruits which rain down onto the towpath when an autumn breeze shakes the tree, it is hard to believe that they are the ancestor of the Cox's Orange Pippin and the Bramleys Seedling. Our comprehensive range of delicious apples are the result of centuries of selective breeding and improvement which started with the native hedgerow Crab. The humble Crab still plays a vital role in the rearing of orchard apples as all of todays select strains are grafted onto its vigorous rootstock.

The first real sign of towpath erosion or disintegration becomes evident in this deep cutting, large sections have actually slid away into the canal making walking somewhat more challenging. In fading light or poor visibility, it can be positively dangerous. Bridge No. 64 comes into view ahead, a straight length of wide, dark water stretches away to meet it .Quite suddenly, another stream clough is dissected by the canal. Another miniscule torrent babbles along it's course, soon to be consumed without trace by the nearby river which imperceptibly gains momentum with each minor addition to it's volume.

The next milestone appears beside the towpath, partially hidden by tall, unruly brambles and grasses. This short, stumpy original stone reads on one face, "From Hall Green - 1/4 miles", the erased figure should read 7 1/4. The opposite face reads "From Marple 19 miles" quite clearly which is unusual because the undamaged message is obviously original, not restored, so here is one which escaped the chisel The waterway continues to be heavily overhung by foliage on the final approach to bridge No. 64 and as the canal narrows, the trees and bushes from both banks reach right up to the stonework of the bridge walls.

Passing beneath the arch of one more agricultural accommodation bridge, it is interesting to note that, at the time of the canal's completion and opening in 1831, these accommodation bridges were customarily given the name of the owner or the tenant of field or pasture being dissected by the newly arrived waterway - at least he had the accolade of having a bridge named after him to compensate for having his valuable field cut into two halves!

Needles to say, many of these obscure names have failed to endure the passage of time. Few people today would refer to the bridge, No. 64 as Pearson Bridge. Luckily, there are written records in existence of the majority of the named bridges. For example:-

    64   Pearson's
    63   Staniers 2
    62   Staniers 1
    61   Congleton - Buxton Road at Crossley

As comprehensive list as possible will appear at the end of the book running Marple - Kidsgrove.

Bridge No. 64 has a most noticeable pink pigmentation in it's stone, reminiscent of the bridges throughout the Macclesfield town lengths where the pink tinge is the hallmark of stone from the Tegg's Nose quarries. It is just possible that the stone which built No. 64, for some unexplained reason, was brought in from Macclesfield in place of the stone from the nearby Cloud quarries.

To the east, the tree cover falls away from the far bank to provide a view of pastures climbing steadily away in the direction of Cloud End, the vision of which is as commanding now as when it first appeared, half way down the lock flight. Both of the canal's banks are briefly lined by sheet metal as the waterway crosses another stream clough. Yet another trickle, which over many centuries has eroded it's way into the landscape, is born in the pasture to the east by a spring, passes beneath the canal and joins the river immediately to the west. For the duration of it's fleetingly brief existence, it has, by it's own action, created a fertile little valley which provides a habitat for Oaks, Sycamores, Hawthorns and Elderberry, for Brambles, Bluebells and Wood Sorrell and all the insects, mammals and birds which would normally be found in mixed woodland. Once the canal has passed over the actual stream course, the belt of mixed Elder and Ash trees returns to the far bank.

A pretty and unusual flower which will be found growing right at the waters edge along these Buglawton lengths, is the Orange or wild Balsam. It can actually be encountered, in patches all along the canal. On a national basis, its distribution is equally scattered. The further south one travels along the canal the more frequently Balsam will occur. Its flowers are quite exquisite and closely resemble those of an oriental Orchid. The five petals of purest orange form a tapering spotted throat which evolve into a curled spur at the rear of the flower. A native of North America, the Balsam has become naturalized in watery places since the

19th century.

The patchy distribution along the canal may be largely due to the fact that unlike the common and native waterside herbs and plants, the Balsam is an annual which is dependant upon the germination of its seed for survival. Its the dispersal of this valuable seed is particularly interesting. The Balsams as a family distribute their seeds by forcibly expelling them from an exploding seed capsule. The Orange Balsam is less spectacular in this department than its close cousin, the giant Himalayan Balsam which is widely naturalized on the nearby river Dane. This monster of a Plant showers its surroundings with seeds as big as ball bearings from exploding capsules which actually go bang.

Looking eastward, beyond the belt of trees, meadows climb gently upward. It is here, on the horizon which is created by the meadows that a distant view is obtained of a large building in a singularly isolated position, the roof of which is hidden by battlemented castellations. Viewed at this considerable distance, with the perfectly positioned dramatic backdrop of the Cloud, this is a somewhat romantic and glorified vision of Buglawton Hall which, in truth is a rather uninspiring late 18th century "Gentlemen's Residence". In it's defence, the building does incorporate fragments of an earlier building and probably occupies the site of the original manor house of Buglawton.

The 18th century house was enlarged in the 19th century while in the ownership of the Pearson family. During the period of rebuilding and enlargement at Buglawton hall, an intense battle over land ownership rights raged between the family at Buglawton and the powerful Antrobus family at Eaton Hall. Whereas Buglawton Hall is some 1/2 mile east of the river, Eaton lies approximately 3/4 mile west but, the two estates shared a disputed boundary in the bottom of the valley. After much ado, it was agreed that the river should form a boundary between the two townships and the Antrobus family had a massive iron post set upright in the dead centre of the river as a marker, in case the river chose to alter it's natural course, as rivers often do, in favour of the Pearson's at Buglawton.

As a direct consequence of this conflict, the river Dane forms the modern day parish boundary between Congleton and Eaton and places the Macclesfield Canal just within Buglawton . The hall at Buglawton was eventually sold to the Moseley family who were the family firm behind the world famous Dunlop Tyres. Mrs Moseley, a keen horticulturist, was largely responsible for the gardens and landscaped park such as they exist today . Early in the 1930's, the hall passed into the ownership of the Johnson family, industrialists in the Staffordshire Potteries.

The three Johnson brothers each acquired a country seat away from the comparative squalor of the Staffordshire "Pot-Bank" which was their fortune ; namely Buglawton Hall, Boden Hall (between Smallwood and Rode Heath)and Henshall Hall at Congleton . Mrs Johnson suffered permanent injury following a riding accident at Buglawton and eventually moved to London, leaving her husband to live a solitary existence at Buglawton for many years. Following a dispersal sale, the hall was acquired by Manchester City Council in 1953 and converted for use as a special school, a function which it still fulfils today.

Beside the towpath, the ground continues to fall away into the overgrown valley for, immediately having crossed the first clough valley, a second is crossed. This second valley is infinitely deeper and considerably wider than the first as it reaches down to the canal's course from the east but, to the west, the two cloughs merge and the two streams unite to join the river as one. The canal is actually embanked in grand style across this second valley as it rivals a modest river valley in span. Ash, Willows, Elders, Hazels, Sycamores and Whitebeams greatly enhance the wide range of wildlife which can exist within this mini-woodland. The constant cooing of Wood Pigeons and the manic screeching of Jays temporarily transport the passer-by into deep woodland. Immediately beyond the embankments, a redundant and derelict drain off paddle gear is situated beside the towpath which would formerly have released excess water down into the stream course below. The canal ahead is shadowed from both sides by high banks and largely overhung by dense tree cover, as it passes along the equivalent of a shallow cutting

The high bank beside the towpath is densely clothed with Broom. The Broom is arguably the most handsome of our native shrubs while in flower. It's normal flowering period is May to early June, but it is so free flowering that it will often blossom repeatedly, if less profusely, several times during the season to as late as October. The Broom is far from prolific along the canal, preferring open grassland on sandy soil, typically on heathland or open areas in woodland. The brilliantly yellow flowers, butterfly like in form, borne singly or in pairs, rival the Gorse in profusion and sheer brightness and clarity of colour. Often mistaken for an exotic garden escapee when encountered in it's wild state, the Broom in it's multitudes of hybridised colour variants is a horticultural success story second to none. Considering that the first garden hybrid was produced by cross-pollination at Kew, London in 1900, surely there is no other garden shrub which can no be obtained in so many colour variations? The Broom will also be brought to the attention of the passer by in a simular way as the previously described Orange Balsam. During the hottest of weather Broom gives off loud cracks as

BROOM

its seed pods split and burst- jettisoning their contents over a considerable area.

Through the arch of the approaching bridge, No. 65, the canal can be seen to be curving acutely to the left beyond. The high bank of the cutting continues right up to the bridge wall on the far bank although the thick tree cover begins to thin out, leaving the bank a mass of Dog Roses which, in autumn are festooned with scarlet hips. Likewise, the bank beside the towpath continues right up to the stone of the bridge, never permitting a view to either east or west.

Bridge No. 65 is another example of an accommodation bridge which, even when newly built was know by several names including Pointon's and Stanley Bridge. Immediately beyond the bridge, a set of stop planks are perched precariously almost at the water's edge on the far bank, a feature which was last encountered during the descent of the lock flight. After the crowding, overhanging closeness of the cutting, the ground to both east and west now opens out to a sudden spaciousness.

From the unlined eastern bank, a pasture which begins at the water's edge rises ever so gently away. The margin is very indistinct where, over the years, it has been trampled into the canal by cattle. To the more distant east, rearing ever more dramatically out of the landscape, is a vivid view of Cloud End and Cloud Side. To the west, beyond the river Dane, the ground rises gently upward into the township of Eaton. In the distant west, a strange apparition is of mountains of bright, clean sand which, from this considerable distance, resemble far away sand dunes.

On closer inspection, the exposed banks of sand prove to be a fleeting glimpse of the massive sand quarrying operation at Eaton Hall. The whole of the Congleton area has the dubious honour of sitting fairly and squarely upon the nation's only plentiful supply of fine silica sand, so vital to the foundry industry. Dubious in that the actual quarrying process ravages considerable tracts of land. When the quarry is eventually exhausted, it does inevitably become a valuable addition to the environment as a large, deep lagoon or lake. Indeed, Congleton is already well on the way to becoming the "new Lake District" as within the immediate area, 10 or more such quarries are or have recently been operational.

Some thirty years ago, sand surveys revealed massive quantities of sand beneath the Eaton Hall estate. Eventually, some 300 acres of land were purchased along with the grand Victorian brick mansion. This house was the latest to occupy the general area being the seat of the formerly powerful Antrobus family for many centuries. Some twenty years after the purchase of the estate and the subsequent commencement of quarrying, the interior of this grand old house was removed and every item of any value was sold. For example, the grand staircase was taken out and shipped to the USA, having been bought for almost the identical sum which had been paid for the whole estate some 20 years previously! The annihilation of the hall was total and absolute and the spot where it stood until quite recently is now a yawning hole in the ground. Strangely, the "estate" such as it is, still exists. Apart from a considerable acreage of land, several buildings are still held including the village smithy and the converted village school which is now the home of the Antrobus family.

As an important postscript to this story, the tall brick building which can just be made out from the canal, standing quite isolated among the mountains of sand is actually the hall's stable wing and, nearby, the ice house has also survived. Ironically, these two sad remnants of this once great house are subject to the protection that should have saved the house to which they once belonged. By a twist of fate, the council saw fit (at the 11th hour) to save these fragments the indignity which befell the hall; (at the risk of becoming political) because they came to regret their decision to allow the demolition of the house. The towpath remains wide and grassy as it accompanies the canal around this sweeping bend. The curve is such that the view of bridge No. 65 is soon lost behind. The grassy pastures to the east rise more steeply away now so that just the uppermost tip of Cloud End remains visible above the horizon

As the curve continues, the housing of Buglawton crowds towards the canal, presenting the traveller with the first urban infringement to be encountered since Macclesfield was left behind so many miles back. The curve has been so acute that the waterway must have, temporarily at least, changed direction entirely . As the deviation comes to an end, bridge No. 66 lies ahead.

On the approach to bridge No. 66, the canal widens out into a wide bay or winding hole. Where the canal's far bank skirts the outline of the wide bay, a thick belt of sedge is interspersed with clumps of yellow Flag Iris The hedgerow which has separated the towpath from the lush valley pasture grazed by horses and ponies, now forms the 'back hedge' to gardens as modern housing backs onto the towpath. Bridge No. 66 or Town Field Bridge continues the seemingly endless procession of agricultural accommodation bridges. From beneath the arch, the canal can be seen to be stretching away ahead in an absolutely perfect straight line as beyond No. 66, No.s 67, 68 and 69 are all within sight. The scene beyond the bridge is radically different from the idyllic rural situation to which the towpath traveller has become accustomed since leaving Macclesfield.

As the canal stretches away, the towpath is actually a narrow, well worn footway which runs along a wide area which is immaculately mown by the householders whose gardens reach to the pathside hedge. As each individual plot of garden reaches the towpath, a gateway set it the hedge gives immediate access to the householder. The rather odd aspect of the scene is that the houses are built well below the canal's level because the waterway has continued half embanked beyond the bridge. The dwellings, of which the majority are bungalows, are built at the foot of the embankment and their gardens are, in reality built into the embankment itself. The view to the west tends to be across roofs or, where bungalows have been converted, directly into upper rooms via dormer roof windows. The increasing demand for housing which has seen Buglawton cease to exist as a separate township during the last half century and become part and parcel of the outskirts of Congleton has, thankfully, not yet managed to cross the canal as a meadow continues to climb away from the eastern bank. It was somewhere here, near to Town Field Bridge that a branch canal was originally proposed in 1838 to run through Congleton to Biddulph Forge over the county boundary into Staffordshire, to serve the numerous coal mines in the Biddulph area. A considerable number of rail links were also proposed to join the branch canal to all the collieries throughout the Biddulph and Gillow Heath valleys. This was one more scheme which never progressed beyond the drawing board.

Beside the towpath, the canal's own Hawthorn boundary hedge has frequently been grubbed out to be replaced by the almost obligatory screen of green Leylandii conifers or a neat wooden fence. Beyond the boundary line, engineer William Crossley's original embankment has been planted with ornamental trees and shrubs and has been flagged and terraced. As far as the eye can see now to the west the residential sprawl of Buglawton stretches away to merge with Congleton. The waterway narrows to pass beneath bridge No. 67, a former accommodation bridge which originally linked the land of a tenant or land owner farmer named Foden. The land to the east of the stone arch is still pasture but, to the west, gardens extend up to it's very stonework.

Beyond Foden's Bridge, No's 68 and 69 are plainly visible ahead. In complete contrast to the situation prior to bridge No. 67, the houses to the west are slightly above canal level so their access from the garden gate to the towpath is invariably by means of steps. Within a further twenty yards, the situation reverts, the ground falling away leaving the houses below canal level once more which serves to illustrate how accurately the canal needed to be engineered to cross ground which was so freely undulating.

Looking ahead toward bridge No. 68, the continous flow of traffic the A54 Congleton - Buxton road crosses for the third time!. Incredibly, this time, Congleton is off to the right of the bridge and Bosley to the left. This illustrates perfectly the way in which the canal has twisted and turned since it's passage through the lock flight. Way back at bridge No. 54, the road ran in this same direction yet, by the time the A54 crossed again at Crossley Hall Farm, Congleton lay off to the left and Bosley down to the right!

Immediately prior to bridge No. 68, which occupies an area within Buglawton known as Tall Ash, the remains of a stone line wharf mark the far bank. The level ground beyond which formed the jetty or loading area marks the position of Myatt's Wharf. James Myatt was the owner of this parcel of land at Tall Ash and, with the arrival of the canal, was quick to cash in by building his own wharf to handle goods for the whole of Buglawton upon which he charged a levy. It has been recorded that during the construction of the canal and later the nearby railway line, a rail track formerly ran from the stone quarries on the Cloud to the point where Myatt's Wharf lay beside the Congleton - Buxton road to facilitate the easy transportation for the colossal quantity of stone needed for the abundance of bridges which typify this particular area.

The final approach to bridge No. 68, is spoiled somewhat by the condition of the towpath as it degenerates into an uneven mess where the surface has broken away and disappeared, leaving behind a quagmire during the wetter months. The sheet metal lining of the towpath bank continues virtually up to the bridge and is the only thing which prevents the whole walkway from disappearing into the canal. The bridge itself is rather more substantial in construction than the preceding accommodation bridges. The volume of traffic which streams over it today was certainly never anticipated when it's design was conceived by Telford or Crossley. Tall Ash it may be by name but, ironically, the bridge is overshadowed by 5 or 6 enormous Lombardy Poplars!

Emerging from bridge No. 68, a set of concrete flag steps lead steeply up to the A54 above which now seems strange after the profusion of accommodation bridges which have so dominated the previous few miles. These invariably have no legitimate footway between the towpath and the bridge top, as so few of them carry a public right of way. The wide canal, absolutely dead straight, provides an unimpeded view of bridge No. 69 which lies directly ahead along a sheltered cutting. The remarkably straight length of canal which runs through Buglawton is actually a little over one mile in duration and is strikingly uncharacteristic of the Macclesfield Canal. What makes it all the more noticeable is that within that distance, no less than seven bridges are encountered, most of which can be seen from one another.

Ever since the canal left High Lane, some 17 miles back, before it even entered Cheshire, it has assumed the pleasing line of a natural stream as it has turned into and out of the mouths of the minor and major valleys which have lain in it's path but now, all of that is abandoned as the waterway forges relentlessly ahead in a route so straight. The canal's passage between bridges No. 68 and 69 is by unlined margins and between high banks, wildly overgrown with rampant vegetation. Halfway between the two bridges, the next milestone is encountered beside the towpath. This original stone imparts the mileage, "Hall Green 6 1/4 miles" with perfect clarity. "From Marple 20 miles" is equally readable. Sheltered cuttings such as this provide a suitable habitat for a relatively wide spread native flower which is conspicuously patchy in it's distribution throughout Cheshire.

Ragged Robin suggests an unkempt or unsightly weed but this is far removed from the truth. This delightful, exceptionally pretty plant is recognisable by the long finger lobed petals of a lovely pale red which, try as they might, cannot be described as pink. These flowers, which appear during May and June, are more delicate than ragged. As the flowers are borne on slender flowering stems high above the narrow, shiny leaves, Ragged Robin presents a pretty picture, peeping out from among the tall grasses beside the towpath.

Looking ahead towards Bridge No.69, although it represents a return to the agricultural accommodation bridge, in design, it is a real odd-ball. In truth, if even the most seasoned authority on the Macclesfield Canal was shown a series of photographs of a random selection of stone bridges with their waterways board number plate erased, the differences between them are so subtle as to make identification very difficult. Having said this, as was stressed at the beginning of this account, no two are exactly alike. Bridge No. 69, however is instantly recognisable having an exceptionally low arch but then being topped by a ridiculously high parapet or wall. The Macclesfield Canal's legendary architecture, acclaimed throughout the national canal network, falls flat on it's face here as this strange bridge is most closely likened to the entrance of a railway tunnel. From the arch itself, an excessive 12 courses of stone tower upwards to the field which passes above. Because no view to either east or west has been available through the cutting, the fact that the cattle crossing the bridge are doing so from field to field indicates that, as far as residential development is concerned, Buglawton is behind us.

RAGGED ROBIN

Passing beneath the low arch, the canal stretches away to bridge No. 70 which lies some distance ahead. The waterway continues to be unlined to either bank, a situation which allows a more varied, interesting and indistinct margin of Reeds, Rushes and sedges to exist. Likewise, the overgrown bank beside the towpath, an impenetrable sea of Dog Roses and Blackberry Brambles, provides a splendid habitat for all kinds of wildlife. The high bank across the water is a mass of Hawthorns, stunted and bush-like which, in turn, provide a habitat for the woodland type of birds, the Long Tailed Tits, Chaffinches, Blue Tits, Tree Sparrows and Thrushes.

The hundreds of thousands of Hawthorns which accompany the canal's journey both as hedgerow components or as specimen trees provide the population of smaller birds with literally hundreds of tons of food in the form of succulent berries from early autumn through to the depths of winter. Aesthetically, the humble Hawthorn is transformed in autumn, it is resplendent when smothered in blood red berries. Particularly if the tree manages to drop some of it's old leaves in November while still laden with fruit, it glows a crimson red which, when viewed in mass, is a stirring sight among the coppers and browns of late autumn. During this same late season, White Flowering Dead Nettles continue to flower in the margins, among the rushes and sedge. These same margins, earlier in the year, are host to a plant which will be found almost from Marple right through to Kidsgrove, a real coloniser of damp places which has been part of Britain's flora since the last ice age. The beautiful Meadow Sweet is prolific along the canal; the water's margins and pathside banks are far richer places as a result. A flower with such a pretty name cannot fail to please. The Meadow Sweet smells delicious and, when seen in drifts along the canal bank in June and July, it looks magnificent. During medieval and Tudor times, the flowers, which smell distinctly of vanilla, were strewn among the Rushes on the floors of houses to sweeten the air. The dense clusters of blossom sprout like creamy-yellow foam from the end of tall, branching stems. Meadow Sweet; although it describes the flower to perfection, is reputed to be a corruption of the saxon, "mede-sweete" as these ancient Britons used the flower to flavour their mead.

MEADOW SWEET

As bridge No. 70 draws nearer, a further bridge is visible through it's arch. This time however, it is not a distant stone arch which is framed in the arch of No. 70 but an unfamiliar shape which will remain a mystery until No. 70 is reached.

The most spectacular and colourful bird to grace the British Isles is, without doubt, the glorious Kingfisher. Although this sparkling jewel of a creature is synonymous with water and is relatively common in Cheshire, it is rarely encountered along the canal. The casual visitor or holiday cruiser would be uncommonly lucky to be treated to the classic flash of brilliant metallic blue blazing fast and low along the water. In truth, a canal is not a suitable habitat for this denizen of clear, flowing water. The regular and consistent depth of water and the frequently turbid condition caused by sediment disturbance by boat traffic make spotting fish virtually impossible, even to the eagle-eyed Kingfisher. In addition to the unsuitability of the water for feeding, the canal bank does not offer the terrain which the bird requires for nesting. The Kingfisher makes use of the soft soil or sandy banks standing well above the water to avoid accidental flooding in the event of the water level rising and in soft ground so that the tunnel can be "quarried" into the bank.

Having said all of this, in certain areas, the regular canal user will be able to see Kingfishers virtually every day of the year. When these areas are studied (and the Buglawton length is the favourite) it becomes clear that the Kingfisher uses the canal as a commuter would use a motorway; as a straight thoroughfare, uncomplicated, wide and usable at speed between stopping-off points. The stopping-off points for the Kingfishers are the stream and brook cloughs which are so numerous and frequently encountered in this area. The babbling stream is a perfect hunting ground with crystal clear water which alternates between cascading rapids and quiet, slack pools which teem with Minnows and Sticklebacks; classic Kingfisher fodder. The Kingfisher will travel up or down his chosen stream, feeding as he goes and when he has exhausted one venue, he will join the dual carriageway where it is culverted across his stream and will hurtle along the wide, straight canal which is infinitely preferable to a lengthy journey flying over land, until the next clough is reached. Another favourite area is Bosley as the Kingfisher is extremely prolific along the river Dane. Under certain circumstances the Kingfisher will feed from the canal. In early summer, during a favourable season, the resident Roach will breed to excess. During these bountiful years, literally hundreds of thousands of tiny Roach will shoal and throng the surface layers of the water providing an irresistible bonanza for the Kingfisher, which, when perched on an overhanging canal side Alder, resembles and exotic escapee from the steamy tropical rain forest.

On the approach to Bridge No 70, the canal's banks are suddenly metal lined as the cutting which has sheltered the waterway since Tall Ash is abruptly replaced by a valley and embankment as the ground to both east and west falls steeply away into a major clough valley. From the edge of the towpath, the hedgerow ceases to exist and the ground simply drops off into the yawning expanse of the clough Looking across the canal, the view is into the upper crowns of tall, mature broadleaf trees. A valley of this magnitude, logically, belongs to a brook of considerable proportions, namely Timbers Brook.

Timbersbrook, the hamlet, which nestles directly below the 1,190 foot bulk of the Cloud derives it's name from "the brook in the wood". The water has always been the life force of the community, providing power and enabling industry to exist within it's boundaries. The water which feeds Timbers Brook originates from springs below "Cat Stones", an unusual landmark on Cloud side. This odd name has several possible explanations. Cracks and fissures in the rock are said to resemble a cat which is about to pounce. More romantic however, it the suggestion that the "Catstones" is an ancient site of religious importance where a pagan cat goddess was worshipped some 1,500 to 2,000 years ago.

At the beginning of the 20th century, the waters of the Timbers Brook were used to power the silk mill which eventually evolved to become the Silver Springs bleaching and dyeing company. The "works" provided vital employment for decades within this otherwise entirely rural area, employing 230 people at it's height. The factory closed in 1961 and, following it's demolition, the site was converted into a recreational area. As the valley comes to an end, meadows briefly rise away from the canal's far bank towards the hamlet of Timbersbrook and the most dramatic view yet of the Cloud in profile. The canal narrows to pass beneath bridge No. 70 which represents a return to the small, unassuming agricultural accommodation bridge.

Just prior to the towpath actually passing beneath the arch, an unusual and unfamiliar plant flowers profusely in brilliant golden yellow as it grows from between the blocks of stone which line the water's edge through the bridge arch. The effect of the rich yellow flowers against the grey stone and dark water is most pleasing as this example of Square Stemmed St John's Wort has chosen an unusual niche to colonise. Normally this member of the extensive Hypericum family chooses to grow in more traditional marshy and damp grassy areas but here it greatly enriches the scene by its presence.

Emerging from Bridge No. 70, it becomes clear that the strange bridge which was framed in the arch of No. 70 on the approach was actually the Stoke - Manchester railway crossing the canal for the second time ahead. In addition to the railway bridge, a pedestrian footbridge is clearly visible beyond. Looking back through the stone arch of No. 70, at least 3 of the previous bridges are visible, stretching away as far as the eye can see.

To the right of the towpath stands a set of stop planks but never before has a set stood in so wide open a situation because the towpath and it's attendant hedgerow are separated by a wide plot of waste ground which grows a luxuriant sward of meadow grasses, Nettles and Cow Parsley, some twenty yards in width. Thankfully, this oasis of vegetation escapes being mown so, it exists as a fragment of natural grassland providing a habitat for scores of grassland species of animal and insect. Across the canal, a steep grass bank climbs away into a pasture. In places the bank is clothed by dense clumps of Gorse and Brambles. During hot summer days, the vegetation to both right and left of the canal is alive with the chirping of Grasshoppers, a sound which is synonymous with the hottest of weather.

One of the less common plants to colonise the grassland area beside the path is Henbit, an attractive member of the Dead Nettle group. Unlike the more common White Flowering Dead Nettle, Henbit flowers are a most delicate pink. Another characteristic of Henbit are its stalkless upper leaves which, fused together, form a disc or frill below each whorl of flowers. The Henbit will be encountered in full flower right through to October and November so it will appear bright and fresh as the rampant grasses around it begin to wither and die.

Approaching the point where the main line railway crosses the canal, one is again aware of the way in which the canal has wandered and woven it's way along, particularly since leaving Bosley Locks . The fact that the railway has needed to cross the canal twice in a distance of two miles says it all, bearing in mind that railways were and are customarily built in monotonously straight lines. The towpath degenerates into a diabolical series of hummocks and deep pot holes which fill with liquid mud during the wetter seasons and resemble an assault course. As was the the case at Crossley, the canal passes beneath the railway at it's full width because, it must be remembered, the canal was already here when the railway arrived to compete with it for the available business.

The canal could never hope to represent a serious competition to the speed and efficiency of the the North Staffordshire Railway so it was no coincidence that fifteen short years after it's grand opening, the canal and the Macclesfield Canal Company were bought out by the arrogant newcomer, the railway.At this crossing, the actual bridge is supported by brick pillars, one on either canal bank, instead of the elegant brick arches which typified the crossing at Crossley. The bridge itself is of massive girder construction and simply spans between the two pillars..

Looking ahead along the canal, the view is dominated by the pedestrian footbridge which crosses directly ahead, as if attempting to compete with the railway which has just done the same. In this remote, rural situation, the rapidly approaching footbridge presents a very peculiar picture. It passes over the water at what appears to be an excessively generous height and sits upon two sturdy stone built supports or "legs" which outwardly appear unnecessarily robust and heavy.The bridge spans the waterway at its normal width, as did the railway. The bridge itself is largely of girder construction with high railings for the protection of the user and is similar to Haggs Foot Pedestrian Bridge (No. 16) between Higher Poynton and Adlington .The well worn footpath it carries leads from Bath Vale up to Timbersbrook and Cloud Side. .

The footbridge is actually numbered bridge No. 71, unlike the railway bridges which were not numbered by the British Waterways Board .On the metal work of the bridge, a small name plate reveals that the metal sections as seen today were built by British Waterways Board at Newark in Nottinghamshire in 1979. Looking ahead along a length of absolutely straight waterway, the distant view is of a large house of great character which, from this distance, seems to rear up from the water itself. The expansive valley land to the east is a breathtaking set piece of broadleaf woodland where the commonly encountered species are interspersed by giant Beeches of monumental proportions .As an ideal back drop to the lush sylvan valley, the Cloud is now viewed perfectly "side on" with Cloud End in dramatic profile. In addition to Cloud Side, the next hill along, which is actually a continuation of Cloud Side, comes into view for the first time; Rainow Hill . The tiny settlement beneath Rainow Hill, a dozen or so houses, is also visible, the aptly named hamlet of Under Rainow. White flowering Dead Nettle colonises the area between the footpath and the canal's sheet metal lined bank.

The imposing house, The Limes, towers above the canal as it stands upon rising ground, it's massive stone chimney stacks and white painted ornate gables captivating the view ahead

Pasture land stretches eastward in the direction of the Cloud as the waterway widens out into a bay or winding hole. This expansive sheet of water is in the process of being reclaimed by nature as thick sedge beds with dramatic purple-brown flower plumes swaying in the breeze, colonise ever further into the wide bay. A bank rises up beside the towpath, draped in Brambles and Dog Roses while across the water, a tree covered bank rises sharply up to the gardens which surround "The Limes". Further back, behind "The Limes" a very similar building "Brook House' also displays high ornate gables and architectural stone chimney stacks. These two houses, in so isolated a situation, display tremendous character and grace of style.

On the sheltered, almost claustrophobic approach to bridge No. 72, massive Sycamores tower above a dense undergrowth of Snowberry bushes on the far bank, half concealing "The Limes". The Snowberry has more than colonised, it has overpowered the 100 yard length of wooded bank up to the bridge having initially escaped from the garden above. The final approach is a dramatic affair in late autumn and winter when the jungle of Snowberry is adorned with masses of waxy white berries.

Bridge No. 72, Brook House Lane Bridge, which was originally known as Porters Farm Bridge is a handsome if unusual structure. The stone arch is exceedingly low to the water and slightly "on the skew" whereas, the remainder of the bridge wall is exceptionally tall; 11 courses of stone plus the copeing. The most unusual feature, however, is the fact that the aforementioned bridge wall is much lower on the right than on the left. In other words, the whole thing slopes from left to right! Given that the actual archway is in perfect equilibrium, the whole thing gives a most unbalanced appearance. Having done and said all this, bridge No. 72, heavily hung with ivy, is a most attractive structure. The bridge carries Brook House Lane which begins below Rainow Hill to the east and runs past Hoofridge Farm and to Brook House or Brook House Farm as it is now known and on to the "The Limes".

Beyond the bridge, to the west, the lane ceases to have a tarmac surface and degenerates into a track which passes the main line railway to become nothing more than a footpath into Congleton. A set of stop planks on the towpath bank stands beside a stone sett ramp which leads up to Brook House Lane. A high, overgrown bank beside the uneven towpath means that the waterway briefly continues it's sheltered passage. The old trackway which gradually descends the far bank was originally a vehicular access from Brook House Lane to a busy wharf which lies just ahead.

The waterway abruptly and dramatically widens out. Sheltered within it's own leafy dell, a short, stone lined canal arm branches off the main waterway to the east. This is the third and last canal arm or branch and the only one to be situated on the eastern or uphill bank of the canal. At 43 yards in length, it is, by far, the shortest of the three arms which exist today. The whole of the arm has banks of massive mill grit block construction which indicates that it was, in reality, a glorified wharf unlike the High Lane arm which is, technically, a branch canal. Today, in it's redundancy, it is one of the most tranquil and unspoiled of the canal's original features. It has not been converted or spoiled by modern commercialism but rests silently amid tall, shady trees, providing a peaceful overnight mooring for an odd narrow boat. The original need for any kind of landing stage to be situated here was that a central loading/unloading point for stone from the prolific Over Rainow and Cloud quarries was necessary, due to the numerous canal and railway bridges which had to be constructed with in a stone's throw from here (no pun intended!).

Beyond the arm, the banks of the canal itself are suddenly lined with blocks of Rainow mill grit of a similar magnitude. Within yards of the expansive sheet of water which lies at the mouth of the canal arm, the waterway narrows down to barely 10 feet to be carried over the disused Biddulph Valley Railway via a stone aqueduct. The stone bridge walls of the aqueduct spring up on either bank. Immediately prior to the aqueduct, strange and unfamiliar metal work can be seen set in the mill grit blocks which comprise the canal banks.

Closer inspection reveals that timber work is attached to the heavy metal components. The device is actually an ingenious system of flood control. Just beyond the Biddulph Valley Railway aqueduct, the canal will strike out onto, arguably it's most ambitious embankment. A breach in the canal's bank here would be catastrophic as water would be lost for miles in either direction. The strange device which we see here is actually a set of flood gates which would be activated by the sudden flow of water should disaster threaten. In the event of the flood gates activating, all of the water between here and Bosley Locks would be saved.

The Biddulph Valley Railway line originally ran between Congleton's Brunswick Wharf and the Staffordshire potteries via Biddulph, including the picturesque passage through the Whitemoor Valley between Biddulph and Congleton. It's purpose was to convey coal between the vast North Staffordshire coal field and Congleton. Instead of travelling back to Staffordshire unladen, Congleton's speciality export, sand, was transported back into the potteries. In it's early years as a mineral line, it was owned by the North Staffordshire Railway Company. Later, working in conjunction with the canal, it's cargo carrying role escalated and diversified. The canal arm which had been established to handle the stone from Rainow and the Cloud became a thriving merchants wharf.

The wharf began to handle huge quantities of silk from Vaudreys Mill at Bath Vale, but, in conjunction with the railway, directly below, goods transferred here between the two transport systems were as diverse as cheese, timber, stone, wine coal, sugar, ore bricks, sand, silk, cotton and pottery. After passing from the North Staffordshire Railway to the LMS, the line was closed by British Rail in 1963. After standing in limbo with track and sleepers in place for several years, the line gradually became a valuable and very pleasant public amenity area fulfilling as important a role between Congleton and the potteries as the Middlewood Way does between Marple and Macclesfield. It provides an easy footpath and bridleway as well as cycle track and a line between other major walking routes such as the canal. Today, instead of sharing merchandise and trade, the canal arm and the Biddulph Valley Line share a common tranquillity. Passing the embankment flood gates, moving onto the railway aqueduct, a glance over the bridge wall reveals by how much nature can soften a former railway line in less than three decades.

From the railway aqueduct, bridge No. 72 at Brook House Lane is almost out of sight as the waterways deviates once more .Immediately beyond the aqueduct bridge, a wooden stile beside the towpath links the two old transport systems; the canal, running North/South and the Biddulph Valley Way running East/West.

The canal is suddenly sheet metal lined to both banks as the ground to both east and west falls away. The canal is dramatically delivered onto an embankment which rivals any along the journey, a hugely ambitious mountain of soil piled high across a yawning valley. This colossal embankment is easily a match for that at Bollington or the river Dane valley and bears a striking resemblance to the latter. As the railway is left behind, a sense of familiarity pervades the scene. The deep valley and the precipitous embankment wall is separated from the towpath by a stone fence identical to the one which was employed along the major embankment at Pott Shrigley. Stone slabs, not unlike graveyard headstones, stand about a yard high, eight feet apart and with two holes, circular, one at the top and one towards the bottom. Like Pott Shrigley, the holes in the posts were to pass a steel winding rope through which completed the "fence". Again, like Pott Shrigley, the steel rope is long gone. The line of stone posts serves to mark, quite simply, the point where the wide grassy towpath plunges away into the valley. Glancing westward, down into the valley, one could be forgiven for mistaking the scene for that of some distance back at Bosley where the river Dane was crossed by the canal. Again, a river of deceptively similar proportions is crossed but this time it is not a river.

The Dane-in-Shaw Brook here is almost identical in size to the Dane as it was crossed..This brook however never becomes larger and is a tributary of the Dane which it joins in Congleton's public park along with the previously described Timbers Brook. The two come together to form Tommy's Brook before becoming one with the river. The Dane-in-Shaw Brook assumes a sinuous, snaking course along it's valley as it makes it's way, as did the Dane previously, towards a fine railway viaduct. The scene as a whole is so similar, it is almost uncanny. Like Bosley, the western end of the valley is dominated by the towering railway viaduct, this time of ten arches as opposed to the twenty at Bosley. The view across the canal and away to the east, is of the tiny settlement of Dane-in-Shaw.

Upstream of Dane-in-Shaw, the brook which passes beneath the embankment is known as Biddulph Brook. It comes into being by the merging of numerous streams and rivulets in and around Gillow Heath and Biddulph in Staffordshire before flowing through Whitemoor and Mossley and into Dane-in-Shaw. The power of the Biddulph Brook was harnessed in Dane-in-Shaw to power a mill for many years.

The hamlet with such a strange name lies just outside Mossley on the Congleton - Leek road and has been known by many names over the centuries. The Anglo-Saxons knew it as Dangingshealh. By 1407 it was Danehynchill. By 1593 it was know as Dane-Ynsale and as Dane-Henshaw in 1825. Today, the accepted spelling is Dane-in-Shaw, but the correct pronunciation is Dane-enshaw As to the derivation of the name Dane-in-Shaw, the most likely explanation is that it is a corruption of "Dannings";which means "connecting with the Dane". The "Healh" part of the Saxon name is appropiate as Haslh" means "twisting valley"..It is only beyond Dane-in-Shaw that the Biddulph Brook assumes the name Dane-in-Shaw which it carries to Congleton.

From the canal's embankment, Dane-in-Shaw mill is very briefly visible to the east .Where the brook zig-zags it's way westwards to the 10 arches, it is spanned by a substantial wooden footbridge which, from our elevated position on the embankment, appear minute; like a child's toy.

The railway commuter probably enjoys a slightly better view of the canal across the Dane-in-Shaw valley than across the Dane valley. The Dane valley is invariably crossed at great speed being roughly half way between Macclesfield and Congleton railway stations. A train, having stopped at Congleton, will still be straining to move away and gain momentum as it reaches the Dane-in-Shaw valley.

This huge embankment was responsible for a three month delay in the official opening of the Macclesfield Canal. The original date for the ceremony had been planned for 30 August 1831 but had to be postponed as the Dane-in-Shaw embankment was considered not to be completely safe. Almost three months further work needed to be done on the consolidation of the vast earth bank before 9 November was decided upon. As a result of the delay, women were not invited to the opening ceremony. November was considered to be far too advanced in the year for the fairer sex! The advice reads "....... thought inadvisable to include ladies in the participation in the ceremony, on account of the advanced period of the season and a very natural anxiety for the preservation of their health which might have been engendered by exposure to the cold and damp atmosphere."

No matter how meticulously the eastern horizon is scrutinised, the Cloud, which first came into view part way down the lock flight, is now nowhere to be seen. It's place is taken by the continuation of Rainow Hill and the more distant Over Overton. As the dead straight passage over the embankment draws to a close, the view ahead is, once more complicated by modern housing.

Chapter 9
HIGHTOWN TO ASTBURY

With a panoramic view of the 10 arches to the west, the canal narrows down between stone lined banks as the metal lining of the embankment comes to an end. The magnitude of these blocks of mill grit and the extreme narrowing of the waterway give every indication that this was the site of some long lost swing bridge although there is no hard and fast evidence and no 'foundations' as such in the banks. Upon widening out, the far bank is unlined but the towpath bank, and, for that matter, the towpath itself, becomes the second of two overflow sills or weirs to be situated on this bank The first was in the identical situation at the completion of the great embankment of the river Dane at Bosley.

The second overflow sill is thirty one yards long. For that distance, the canal's bank is made up of a concrete sill at normal water level. Where the towpath should be behind the sill, the stone setts of the overflow weir slope gently away westward into the valley where they come together to form a stone lined brook course by which, the excess water from the canal is eventually delivered to the Dane-in-Shaw Brook far below. Beyond the thirty one yards of overflow, the stone setts climb back up to a normal gravel towpath.

As the canal moves away from the embankment and the overflow, the eastern bank is dominated by modern housing. This is housing which has arrived during the last decade. It has crept to the very edge of the yawning Dane-in-Shaw valley. Let us hope that the valley is too wide and deep for it to somehow make its way across. Congleton already merges with Buglawton further to the west without it having to do so here at the expense of this breathtaking valley. The irony of this particular situation is that this housing estate was, 15 years ago, an 'estate' of a very different kind.

Where the neat little avenues and cul-de-sacs lined with pretty brick boxes extend eastwards away from the canal, the Henshall Hall Estate, up until 1976, meant, quite literally, the estate surrounding Henshall Hall. Agricultural land formerly reached to the canal's far bank and, in fact, occupied the area beyond the towpath bank to the west until Henshall Hall was demolished. Quite how this was ever allowed to happen is a mystery, why Henshall Hall was not protected is not clear and maybe not relevant to this account. What cannot go unrecorded is that the great house now demolished, although built as recently as 1877, was not a run of the mill gentlemen's residence but an exceptionally fine and large brick built house on a very grand scale. It's architectural style defied classification and, to be fair was rather haphazard with very little symmetry. However, it was a beautiful building of immense character. Formerly known as Moss House, this massive house which took four years to build was given its most recent name by one of its previous owners, John Henshall Williamson.

To the right of the towpath, the next milestone is situated. Beneath a thick incrustation of lichen, it is just possible to make out "From Hall Green, 5 1/4 miles" and "From Marple 21 Miles". Beyond the milestone, the traveller moves on into a shallow cutting. A tall bank of rough overgrown vegetation towers above the towpath. Across the water, a grassy bank leads steeply up to the modern housing. The impeccable formal gardens which were laid out around Henshall Hall are now fading memories on equally fading brown photographs. Henshall Hall served as a military hospital during the first world war, its terraced lawns and geometrically perfect flower beds suffering their first taste of neglect.

Ahead, bridge No. 73 is plainly visible along this sheltered passage. Beyond the high bank to the right of the towpath, the Henshall Hall development has successfully crossed the canal and is currently spreading over the ground to the west, sickeningly ever closer to the unspoiled valley of the Dane-in-Shaw Brook. Henshall Hall's last owners were Mr and Mrs Stuart Johnson; one of the previously described Johnson brothers of the Staffordshire potteries empire. During the 1920' and 1930's, the Johnson's acquired considerable 'chunks' of land in the Congleton area, Henshall Hall and Buglawton alone represented an admirable family holding As bridge No. 73 draws nearer, it is obvious that it has undergone major alterations, in fact, total reconstruction would be a more accurate description.

When the development of the Henshall lands first threatened to cross the canal in the early 1980's, the developers would dearly loved to have been able to demolish and replace bridge No. 73. Unexpectedly, the loud voice of protest from various local factions and conservation bodies raised to a crescendo in defence of the Macclesfield Canal's original architecture. After a bitter battle, the developers were pressured into transforming the original agricultural accommodation bridge into a double carriageway road bridge, capable of transporting traffic between the two separate halves of the housing scheme. The most significant aspect of this planning decision was that the extension of the bridge was to be executed in a manner which both complimented and blended with the original architecture. Consequently, as the waterway narrows, we arrive at a bridge which has been more than doubled in width.

Beneath the arch, the concrete towpath is an extension of the original stone block footway. The 'new' arch now spans a 34 foot length of canal. An old and decrepit set of stop planks situated on the far bank contrast with brightly painted 'extra safety' hand rails which were installed above the bridge walls as the 1980's became the 1990's. The guard rails represent far more than embellishment or decoration as the bridge links the two component parts of this ambitious housing scheme for pedestrians as well as vehicles. On a modern housing estate which is enclosed and isolated from a main road, the majority of the pedestrians tend to be 'free range' children who are naturally attracted to the canal and bridge like so many moths to the flame.

The next bridge is in view immediately upon leaving No. 73, lying at the end of a long, somewhat sheltered length of waterway. Considering the massive refurbishment of the previous bridge, the length of towpath which leads from it is in a diabolical condition; reminiscent of a minefield. A huge, towering bank of grossly overgrown vegetation overshadows this assault course of a footway. At the top of this impenetrable jungle of a bank, a Hawthorn hedgerow which is massively overgrown in its own right, totally conceals the housing beyond. As the far bank also rises steeply up from an unlined sedge margin, the canal lies, well and truly within a deep cutting.

Among the thorny mass which is the path side bank, tightly curved sprays of pinkish flowers rise boldly, three to four feet aloft, above bristly stems and leaves on warm sunny days . This is the first sighting since leaving Marple of Common Comfrey. This tall, handsome plant, when viewed aesthetically appears to be almost all foliage although the nodding, bell shaped pink or white flowers in coiled sprays have an unquestionable beauty. It is this excess of coarse, hairy foliage however which holds the key to its bygone popularity for it held the accolade of having the power to cure a staggering range of wildly varying ills.

COMFREY

Not all of this 'miracle herbal cure' stuff is 'hocus pocus'. The author can testify that comfrey does indeed possess remarkable qualities which, in a fermentation, rapidly and dramatically reduces the painful swelling associated with sprains and fractures. Originating from a background of very straightforward and uncomplicated country folk, the said author was brought up to accept comfrey as the poor mans aspirin or paracetamol! For those who still maintain that drinking gallons of the fermentation will cure all internal ailments; you have my blessing but no guarantee!

Beyond the next bridge which is, as yet, some distance away, arguably the most offensive 'blot on the landscape' to overlook this most pleasing of waterways rears its ugly head for the first time. The looming bulk of Hightown's gaunt corn mill does for Congleton's architectural credibility what the now removed Berlin Wall did for Germany!

Nearing bridge No. 74, the towering bank beside the towpath is a dense thicket of Snowberry. Across the canal, a similarly overgrown bank leads up to the neat and orderly estate housing. The appreciation of this particular length of canal may often be diminished by the encroachment of modern housing and by the threat of the looming spectre of the corn mill. By way of compensation, the ground to the immediate right and left of the towpath is, during May and June, host to bold drifts of the tiny white flowers of Wavy Bittercress. The summer snow drifts of Bittercress briefly rival any summer bedding scheme of garden Alyssum.

As bridge No. 74 is neared, at least two more bridges can be seen through its arch. Several bridges which have been encountered since Buglawton have represented subtle departures form the 'normal' architectural style: No. 74 leaves it all together! Bridge No. 74 towers above the waterway. We have encountered bridges before which were of above average height; No. 74 stands a full 24 feet above the canal which is almost twice the overall height of the majority.

Incredibly, almost all of this excessive height is arch. There is often a temptation for an adult of average stature to stoop very slightly while passing beneath the canal's normal bridges. Here, the arch itself rises 19 to 20 feet above the water. The bridge caries Morley Drive, a single track carriageway which links the busy A527 Congleton - Leek road with Morleys, the large dried fruit processing plant which lies (largely hidden) beyond the towering bank and hedgerow to the right.

This substantial bridge carries a considerable volume of commercial traffic serving the extensive works. Through the lofty arch, the next two bridges are clearly visible. In fact, the next bridge is so vast and out of context that, not only is it visible through the arch of No. 74, but the traffic which passes over it can be seen, equally clearly, over the top of No. 74. Gazing up to the large, prominent key stone of the arch of bridge No. 74, some 18 to 20 feet above the water, the circumstances which dictated the need for this exceptional structure to be built in this way can only have been governed by the depth of the cutting within which it stands. As the canal narrows to pass beneath Morleys Bridge, a set of 23 steep stone steps link the towpath to Morley Drive . Like something out of a nightmare, a huge and grotesque concrete flyover dramatically transports the A527 Congleton - Leek road high above the canal.

This is a carbon copy of the archetypal 1950's - 1960's motorway flyover. It would certainly seem more at home spanning the M6 or M1 than the Macclesfield Canal. Even from this considerable distance, the original road bridge, built at the time of the canal's completion, can be seen, condemned to live out its days in the permanent shadow of its brash and ambitious replacement. Through the arch of the original road bridge, a metal railway bridge is plainly visible. Towering directly above this mottley assortment of bridges is the huge corn mill. This 'darkest corner' of an otherwise near perfect waterway journey is reached by an unlined length of canal which lies between towering banks.

An unknown element among Congleton's population seemed to be labouring under the misgiving that this unfortunate stretch of waterway is either an extension of, or a substitute for, the towns refuse disposal facility. At the beginning of our journey, travelling through the heart of the council housing estates which sprawl between Marple and Hawk Green - despite once spotting a supermarket trolley lying on the bed of the canal - litter is not an obvious problem. Likewise, some few miles further on, through less than scenic and densely populated High Lane, the canal is almost the focal point of the community as the duck feeding ritual graphically portrays, Similarly, through the very centre of industrialised Macclesfield, the waterway, although not always a place of great beauty, remained neat, clean and, above all, obviously appreciated. Why then, here, in this supposedly select neighbourhood of this reasonable opulent and proud town does this wonderful waterway fairly reek of abuse and neglect!

Here, instead of the gregarious mallards, Coca cola tins and empty beer cans jostle for position on the water's surface. The canal's unlined margins are colonised by empty potato crisp packets and cardboard drinks cartons. A bobbing wine bottle completes this cordon bleu of filth. This is not an off chance observation resulting from a single visit; it is a sad realisation by a native of the Congleton area.

The rough bank beside the towpath leads to a wildly unkempt hedgerow beyond which lies extensive car parking which is attached to the fruit processing works. Like some malignant disease, the revolting tide of garbage even flows down the bank towards the towpath. All kinds of indescribable household effects protrude from the sea of nettles and brambles. The car parking is replaced by a pleasant red brick house of some character with tall chimney stacks which may have formerly belonged to the North Staffordshire Railway. As yet unseen from the towpath the house is sandwiched between the waterway and the main line railway.

Above the bank on the eastern side of the canal, modern housing borders Morley Drive as it swings round to join the A527 which thunders across the flyover directly ahead. Crossing the canal at something of a strange angle and supported by towering concrete struts, the buzzing carriageway passes over the canal at a height of 35 or maybe 40 feet. The stream of traffic is actually hidden from view from the canal by red brick walls which go some small way towards breaking up the otherwise monotonous mountain of concrete which typifies the uninspiring, motorway overpass type bridge.

From this distance, it becomes clear that the old road bridge was actually engulfed by the new bridge which was so dramatically slung over it. It crosses the canal at precisely the same skewed angle as the flyover and if in fact, the old bridge has been physically incorporated into the lower portion of the new one. The huge ramps of concrete embrace the mellow old stone of what is actually bridge No. 75. Throughout its trauma, the old bridge has even retained its blue and yellow British

Waterways board number plate.

A rough footpath, extremely narrow and steep, leaves the towpath immediately prior to the flyover leading directly to Congleton's railway station which, although almost totally hidden from the sight of the towpath traveller and canal user, lies directly above. Consequently, the ambitious flyover not only 'flies over' the canal, it also 'flies over' the railway which lies directly alongside. In fact, it narrowly misses 'flying over' Congleton's station buildings which stand in its shadow. At the foot of the steep path which leads up to the station, a public footpath sign leans at a crazy angle. Its arms point towards "Bosley 5 miles" and "Peel Lane 1 1/4 miles".

A 40 foot length of stone lined canal lies, in deep shadow, below the flyover where pillars of featureless concrete soar upwards to support the wide, two lane carriageway above. Without ever 'coming out' into the open, the towpath passes beneath the arch of the old road bridge. This too was a large, ambitious structure, superbly skewed across the waterway, heavily built in stone but with its arch lined in blue brick. There is no space or divisional line between the fly over and bridge No. 75 which formerly carried the A527 over the canal and across the railway via a level crossing.

While standing beneath the exquisitely crafted brick arch, looking back beneath the concrete ceiling of the flyover, the towering arch of Morleys Bridge permits a distant view of bridge No. 73 amid the Henshall Hall housing estate. The towpath traveller, cocooned within this jumble of bridges looks under the arches of two, through the arch of a further one to gaze at a perfectly framed miniature of Henshall Hall bridge. Turning to face southward once more, bridge No. 75, because of its skew, shelters a further 47 feet of towpath. Collectively, due to the presence of these two bridges, an 87 foot length of canal never sees direct sunlight. Just as the sunlit towpath sports a multitude of herbs and flowers, this dark, dank passage provides a habitat for delicate ferns and lichens.

When daylight does eventually get a chance to flood in once more, it is stifled yet again by the fact that the fabric of the massive corn mill springs from the very stonework of bridge No 75 and towers upward, in excess of five storey's from the water. Where the mill rears up out of the canal, the lower stories are built from old blue brick, remnants of several former mill buildings which have successively burned down in a number of serious fires. Were it not for the presence of an unlimited supply of water from the canal, the mill would have been burned to the ground on several occasions. This most recent reincarnation of the Pheonix rising from the ashes rises a further 4 or 5 storeys' in modern red brick The central section of the building rises to a height in excess of 100 feet, clad in drab grey sheeting, this gaunt edifice is visible for many miles around. It was from below the water here that, during 1987, an invisible but lethal poison leached from the storage facilities beneath the mill. Molasses in liquid form leaked, over a period of time, deoxygenating the water as it spread, aggravated by hot weather. The eventual result was a total wipeout of the canal's fish population for a distance of some four miles or more southward. Hundreds of thousands of fish perished along with the associated aquatic life forming the complete food chain.

The next four or five miles of waterway has its fishing rights controlled by as many different angling clubs, all of which suffered a total annihilation of their sport. It is only now, some four years on that the recovery operation is reaching completion and after a restocking policy which has been implemented over the last couple of years. The first two years were crucial for the recovery and recolonisation by the multitudes of life forms which constitute the lower rungs of the food ladder. Once the natural aquatic flora and fauna had been allowed to re-establish itself, batches of fish were released at random locations between Congleton station the source of the pollution and Scholar Green. Throughout 1987, 88 and 89, Bream, up to 10 inches in length and Tench, Roach and Carp were introduced in batches numbering from 21,000 to 17,000 fish at each stocking.

At the end of the 20 yard length, the railway bridge is reached. Like the modern flyover, and the original road bridge, it crosses the canal at an oblique or skewed angle. As the North Staffordshire railway crosses the canal for the third time, the corn mill towers above, casting a deep and permanent shadow across both canal and railway and filling the air with incessant noise. The canal makes no attempt to narrow down to pass beneath the heavy sheet metal and girder bridge which is supported by stout red brick pillars. Upon leaving the railway bridge, a tall bank beside the towpath soars steeply up towards the "Queens Head" public house.

Looking ahead along what continues to be a sheltered cutting, the next bridge, No.76, is just a short distance in front. The more distant view through the arch of No. 76 holds a promise of better things to come as the bridge is approached via a waterway that is, more often than not, awash with litter and other floating debris of dubious origins.

This depressing tale of neglect is not solely the opinion of the author; for example, during the winter of 1990, a 14 member strong working party organised by the Macclesfield Canal Society took two hours to complete a clean up of the immediate vicinity of the flyover where 20 bags of garbage and litter were collected. A spokesman for the society on that occasion is quoted by the local press as saying "Congleton is by far the worst area of the Macclesfield Canal - I just don't think that people appreciate what they have got".

A long flight of brick and concrete flag steps have recently been incorporated into the high bank linking the towpath with the Queen's Head, which is hidden from view above, 26 steps lead the footsore traveller up to the delights of the hostelry above. Across the canal, a similar situation prevails where a tree and litter clad bank rises steeply away from the water's edge to a massive and rampantly overgrown Hawthorn hedge. Thankfully, the noise of the corn processing operation begins to subside but, glancing behind, all that can be seen is the mill towering above the railway.

On the approach to bridge No. 76, modern housing once more puts in an appearance behind the huge Hawthorns which surmount both banks of the cutting. The housing which lies to the west has arrived in the last 6 or 7 years whereas that to the east is a complete newcomer being a product of the past 2 or 3. The canal, which has remained within a cutting virtually since leaving the Dane-in-Shaw valley, arrives at Bridge No. 76. It is only as the bridge is reached that what at first seems to be a delightful accommodation type stone bridge is revealed for what is really is, a very fine roving bridge. For the first time since leaving Macclesfield, the towpath is about to be transferred to the eastern bank.

Looking back at the unsavoury jumble of concrete and metal, red brick and steel, it is like a breath of fresh air to witness the welcome return to classic stone architecture; the mellow stone partly clothed in a lush growth of Ivy. Passing beneath the arch of bridge No. 76, or Morris Change Bridge as it was originally know, the towpath, which suddenly becomes cobbled stone, curves and climbs steeply upwards towards the top of the bridge. A gracefully curving wall, topped by round copeing stones accompanies the steeply climbing towpath. It is not difficult to vividly picture the heavily shod hooves of the draught horse slipping and toiling up this precipitous incline, straining against the tow line which would drag up the bridge wall while the laden boat slid silently beneath the arch.

The bridge top carries a track or footway, no more than ten feet in width which rapidly becomes a tarmacced path to both east and west, leading away into the respective housing schemes which lie to either side. These walkways are screened with the customary and almost obsessive interwoven fencing and screen of Leylandii conifers. The land to the east of the bridge is a maze of compact and architecturally identical houses, while the estate to the west does at least display some variation in styles, however subtle .A steep but straight stone sett ramp delivers the towpath to the eastern bank The canal is lined with huge blocks of mill grit and the towpath has been resurfaced with limestone. To the left, the housing virtually reaches to the towpath. Gardens which are a little more mature arrive at the canal's far bank from the slightly longer established housing to the west.

The wide canal stretches determinedly away between sheet metal lined banks. The need for the metal bank lining becomes clear as the roving bridge is left behind and as the housing which occupies the western bank begins to drop away and the waterway becomes half embanked. Beyond the remnants of the towpaths companion hedgerow, the housing to the east stretches away as far as the eye can see. Typically, a flock of semi-tame Mallards and Aylesbury cross ducks swim determinedly towards the approaching towpath traveller in the ardent hope that he is of the bread throwing variety.

Surprisingly, the litter problem only improves slowly considering that the waterway it making its way through the heart of this smart, youthful housing area; empty crisp packets and soft drinks cans seeming to be the most prolific species! .The houses begin to fall away from the towpath side as Derwent Drive, the roadway which links the housing with the main thoroughfare into Congleton now runs alongside. Similarly, across the waterway, Daven Road runs parallel to the canal.

The already wide canal opens out suddenly into a considerable sheet of water as a stone lined wharf occupies the far bank adding its appreciable width to that of the canal. Alongside the wharf, the towpath bank beings to fall steeply away towards Canal Road. This major wharf was one of several which proliferated along the western bank once the towpath had been 'swapped over' by the change bridge.

Just like the 'town length' through Macclesfield, with its profusion of disused wharfs, this can be considered as being Congleton's 'town length', despite the fact that up until the last decade or so, green fields lay to the immediate east and west. This is the nearest that the canal ever gets to Congleton's town centre although, for many miles now it has been skirting its outskirts. Because the heart of Congleton's original town lies within the valley of the river Dane, the canal has, through necessity, needed to keep to the more even passage around the said valley which, in truth, began as Bosley locks were left behind.

It has been suggested that the name 'Congleton' may be derived from 'corner town', and the original settlement may have been established on a bend in the river. Glancing behind, the towering corn mill is, thankfully, hidden by the maze of modern housing. The centre piece in the picture behind is the distant change bridge. However, in the background, Cloud End looms, large as life, seemingly there to perform one last curtain call.

No sooner does the wharf come to an end on the far bank than the waterway narrows right down to one boat's width. This complete contrast is executed to allow the water to pass between the white painted wrought iron railings and stone pillar uprights of one of its most famous aqueducts, Congleton's Canal Road (or formerly) Dog Lane Aqueduct. Initially, Canal Road Aqueduct appears to be an exceedingly handsome stone built bridge. However, venturing out across Canal Road which lies some 14-16 feet below, we find that the canal crosses between the two stone supports by means of a superb example of a cast iron aqueduct. The engineer of the Macclesfield Canal, William Crossley Junior was, as the waterways nationally acclaimed architecture testifies, a brilliant designer of bridges. However, as already mentioned at the Dane Valley bridge at Bosley, he was troubled by his aqueducts.

The one here, at Congleton, was actually his first and rapidly proved to be a complete and total disaster. As already discussed at some considerable length, Thomas Telford actually surveyed the proposed Macclesfield Canal twice but went on to play no further part in its construction. He did actively campaign for the funding of the project and subsequently held shares in the Macclesfield Canal Company. With the total failure of Crossley's first major aqueduct, the canal company pleaded with Telford to build a replacement, which he did, creating the bridge we see today. This stood Crossley in better stead, having witnessed the masters technique first hand. With the 'hiccup' at Bosley aqueduct - rectified by G W Buck - out of the way, Crossley went on to build masterful aqueducts which are as sound today as they were at the canal's opening in 1831.

Traffic plies its way beneath Crossley's waterway and Telford's bridge. To the immediate west lies Congleton and to the east lies Mossley, formerly an isolated settlement within a natural peat moss but now another 'outer flank' of Congleton.

CANAL ROAD AQUEDUCT- CONGLETON

It is only when standing upon the aqueduct that a glimpse of Congleton town becomes fleetingly available with its unusual town hall just in view, a building which has been described as 'like a cross between a 17th century Dutch guild hall and St Mark's Venice'. Like Macclesfield, Congleton retains its medieval street plan. This settlement on the 'bend of the river Dane', possibly dates from the stone age. By the late Saxon period, the area was held by the Saxon thane or lord, Earl Godwin, father of King Harold of Hastings fame. During the 13th century, the manor of Congleton was held as part of the estate of the de Lacy family and it was Henry de Lacy who granted the town charter in 1272 which authorised the right to hold markets and a fair as well as establishing the positions of Mayor, Catchpole (the Sheriffs Officer) and Ale tasters.

By the time of the Tudor period, the town sported a flourishing industry in lace making and leather working. 'Congleton Points', the metal and silver tags put on the ends of shoe and boot laces were another early flag on the towns industrial map. A lasting reminder of this industry can be found just 400 yards west of the Canal Road aqueduct, in the name of a small side road, Silver Street. Also in the town, a bell foundry was built on the river bank, and later several silk mills flourished.

The first silk mill was built, drawing its power from the river Dane in 1751. Silk ribbon weaving and later, cotton spinning led to such an increase in the towns industrial prosperity that eventually Congleton's need for improved communications led to its voice, along with that of Macclesfield being raised in demanding a direct canal link with Manchester and the Staffordshire potteries. Ironically, after the arrival of the canal in 1831 and the railway in 1848, a serious recession in the silk trade set in .Congleton's salvation came with the development of fustion and velvet cutting, an enterprise which mopped up the surplus labour and filled the idle mills. In fact, at the peak, 34 fustion mills were operative in Congleton's town centre. The textile related trades continued to be Congleton's main life line right through to the 20th century.

Looking eastward from the aqueduct, Canal Road, which was formerly know by the less than poetic name of "Dog Lane", rises steeply out of Congleton to pass through the settlement of Astbury Lane Ends, to ascend into Mossley. Where the waterway crosses the aqueduct, it is so constricted that there is a strong compulsion to try to jump or stride across it. By total contrast, immediately upon leaving the confines of the aqueduct, this sliver of waterway widens out into a huge sheet of water. The towpath bank continues sheet metal lined and the surface of the pathway remains impeccable, as the canal opens right out into a scene which is strikingly reminiscent of that at the Hovis Mill at Macclesfield. The superbly surfaced towpath even sports picnic table and bench sets; the first seating of any description to be encountered since leaving Bosley, a luxury which is unheard of along these southern reaches.

Winter and summer alike, boats will be found to be moored against the metal lined towpath on a long term basis, taking advantage of the excessive width of both waterway and towpath and the close proximity of Congleton town, some 7 to 8 minutes walk away. The similarity between this scene and the one some 12 or so miles back at the Hovis Mill at Macclesfield is accentuated by the presence of the large brick building which stands on the far side of the waterway, looking out across this expansive bay.

On closer inspection, it becomes obvious that this building has never been a mill and is currently in a state of lonely dereliction. The water from which it seems to rise, although representing Congleton's 'town moorings', is never crowded with moored craft as Macclesfield Marina so definitely was. In actual fact, the building has more in common with the stone built warehouse, between bridges 1 and 2 at Marple junction. The generous expanse of water points to the buildings original purpose, allowing boats to manoeuvre to load and unload. The stone built, all weather warehouse at Marple served as the canal depot for the northern end of the waterway, likewise, this sad and empty building fulfilled a similar function for this southern end. The stone jetties either side of the warehouse originally thronged with activity as they formed Congleton's principal wharf, explaining the need for the towpath's temporary change of banks.

Macclesfield's Hovis Mill with its central archway enabled boats to actually navigate into the shelter of the building to load or unload in inclement weather. Similarly, the stone warehouse at Marple incorporated a facility for all weather loading. Here, at Congleton, the lengthy stone quays were the only available loading/off loading points so perishable cargoes would need to wait for hospitable weather. The multi-storey warehouse could have originally incorporated office accommodation as it represented the southernmost administrative headquarters for the canal company. The paper work which accompanied the handling of the huge variety of wares must have been staggering. The diverse industries within the valley of Congleton plus the agricultural produce from the rich rural community made this wharf as busy as any along the whole waterway.

Bland modern housing again pushes towards the towpath hedgerow from the eastern bank. The derelict warehouse has somehow 'missed out' over the years. It has not been lucky enough to have benefitted from the presence of modern industry as all of its contemporaries have. The Adelphi and Clarence mills, the Goyt and the Hovis mills and the Marple warehouse have all found a niche in modern society - but not so here. Some of the small outbuildings in its yard have, until recently housed diverse yet low key enterprises but now, all is desolation.

Local heritage pressure groups have campaigned long and hard for the site to be considered at Congleton's much needed and, as yet, non existent heritage centre. Suggestions have been put forward that this might be the perfect venue for the museum which the town has fought for over several decades. At the time of writing, neglect and the extremes of the British weather appear to be having the upper hand.

The strangest thing of all is, while standing facing the warehouse, and looking back along the waterway towards the aqueduct, towering above the maze of modern housing is Crocker Hill and the telecommunications mast! This surely represents a roll call of our best loved and most faithful of travelling companions, particularly as Cloud End which was so plainly visible behind some moments before is now nowhere to be seen. Leaving the warehouse behind, the towpath, still excessively wide, begins to curve to the left.

With the continuing curve comes the view of the next bridge. On the approach, bridge No. 77 appears as a robust stone arch, tall and heavily built. A rough bank begins to rise up beside the towpath, clothed with grasses and brambles, at the top of which, the pathside Hawthorn hedgerow has been skilfully laid in recent years; a process which has promoted vigorous upward growth. On the final approach to bridge No. 77, an open field graces the far bank for the first time in so many miles.

Approaching the bridge from this side, it bares a striking resemblance to No. 43 at Gurnet, between Macclesfield and Sutton where the towpath was restored to the western bank at the end of Macclesfield's 'town length'. Immediately prior to No. 77 or Lamberts Lane Bridge, the high bank to the left of the towpath is replaced by a towering wall of gritstone which rises from towpath to bridge top. At its foot stands a set of stop planks. This substantial bridge is built on the skew. A 28 foot length of canal passes beneath Lamberts Lane Bridge It is only when the towpath traveller passes beneath the arch that the true splendour of this architectural masterpiece is revealed.

The towpath is suddenly and dramatically transported upward and round in a tight, sinuous curve as the British canal systems most celebrated change over bridge is negotiated. The towpath which has become a steeply climbing stone sett footpath twists sharply and steeply up between two low walls, topped by beautifully rounded copeing stones which curve in unison. As the pathway is delivered to the bridge top, one might be forgiven for being puzzled as to why the bridge seemed so substantial on the approach. The footpath proves to be just 7 feet in width whereas the total width of the bridge was a little over 28 feet. However, beyond the 4 feet high wall to the right of the towpath lies the single track Lamberts Lane. In essence, this is two bridges in one. The northern half is a substantial stone arch carrying an unadopted roadway and the southern half is a exquisite turnover bridge which, marking the end of Congleton's town length, returns the towpath to the western or downhill bank. This splendid bridge is widely acclaimed to be the jewel in engineer William Crossley's crown.

Lamberts Lane change or turn over bridge No. 77 has always been know locally as "Snailly Bridge". This has led to Congleton people in general referring to change bridges as a whole as "Snailly Bridges" and the previous Morris Change, No. 76 is often referred to as "Second Snailly". No one can be sure where the reference to snails comes from. It may be that the sinuous twist of the ascending towpath and bridge walls have been likened to the spirals of a snail shell or possibly, in years gone by, the shaded, somewhat damp situation of this bridge may have led to it being collonized by shelled terrestrial snails.

The seven feet wide footpath, enclosed by bridge walls, is separated from Lamberts Lane which runs from Astbury Lane Ends to the east down to either Congleton or, more distantly, Astbury Marsh to the west. Beyond this unsurfaced trackway, a further bridge wall marks the total width of this magnificent bridge. The towpath is delivered back down to waterside on the western bank by means

SCENTLESS MAYWEED

of a steep cobbled ramp. A set of 14 concrete steps with a stout wooden handrail link the towpath with Lamberts Lane above.

Venturing out from bridge No. 77, the towpath seems to have deteriorated in condition once more. Deep pot holes must once again be negotiated at the risk of sprained ankles. During the summer months, one of Britain's boldest of wild daisies, the Scentless Mayweed, grows freely beside the towpath around Lamberts Lane bridge. The big, snow white flowers with centres of golden yellow are universally recognisable as belonging to the daisy type Chamomile flower. A classic wayside and wasteland flower, it is also frequently encountered in arable fields where its large flower heads, often 1 1/2 inches across, form flamboyant drifts of brilliant white.

The canal stretches ahead between unlined banks in an absolutely straight line as far as the eye can see. Across the water, an overgrown bank of Brambles and Hawthorn scrub leads steeply up to red brick housing, which was again, a product of the late 1960's - 1970's housing boom. This intense building activity transformed the confluence of several lanes and roads, one or two farmsteads and a handful of cottages known as Astbury Lane Ends into a new residential area squeezed between Congleton and Mossley.

It is from among this particular scheme that the other physical feature responsible for putting the Astbury Lane Ends area on the map rears alarmingly skyward. Almost qualifying as a canal landmark, the looming form of the Astbury Lane Ends water tower is a massive concrete structure which bristles with radio masts and lightening conductors. It has a capacity of 150,000 gallons of water which represents roughly one days supply for the higher level of Congleton which it supplies. An identical concrete tower to this one, standing alongside a Victorian version to the west of the town completes Congleton's water supply system. The Astbury Lane Ends tower has overshadowed the canal since 1929 but, up until recent years, cattle grazed around it.

The margins of the unlined canal are colonised by beds of Sedge and Flag Iris far into the distance. Glancing back at Snailly Bridge from this distance, a parting glimpse of the old warehouse is briefly available, framed through the magnificent arch. The housing on the eastern bank is now represented by smart bungalows whose gardens terrace down to the water's edge, terminating in a landing stage or waterside patio area. The whole range of shrub and flower gardens reach the water's edge; garden sheds perch precariously on the terraces, bird tables and tiny green houses are situated on the embanked slope as the waterway continues to make its way along a cutting. The next milestone is situated at the foot of the Bramble bank. A tall, erect and original stone, its message is intact save for the distance from Hall Green It should read "From Hall Green 4 1/4 miles" and clearly reads, "From Marple 22 miles".

One of the sloping gardens incorporates a 'built in' duck pen from which, a stream of snow white Muscovy's hurry to inspect the passing towpath traveller. This unusual strain have chosen to shrug off the Muscovy's smart metallic black and white penguin suit in favour of a white as pure as driven snow. The fleshy red 'outlaw' mask around the eyes and the bulbous lump above the beak immediately set them apart from the bland white Mallard who's plumage they have borrowed. The large size, aggressive posture and threatening hiss render them unmistakable.

The pathside bank suddenly drops away entirely and the towpath is bordered by the neatest of Hawthorn hedges which has been laid very recently and with considerable skill. The view over the low hedge, which is as compact as a stone wall, is of Astbury Golf Course. The golf course which literally stretches to the limit of visibility westward is dotted with ancient gnarled Oaks. These trees of great antiquity would, no doubt, have succumbed to the chain saw or felling axe long ago if they were standing in such glorious isolation amid agricultural land. Not only would their presence not be tolerated in a working field but their safety could not even be guaranteed in a hedgerow. Here, however, they are preserved for no other reason than their great beauty. Conversely, it is most rewarding to see brand new plantings of young trees in ambitious spinneys of Scots Pine, Oak, Beech and Whitebeam. All of this wealth of tree planting and management is most commendable and goes some way towards justifying the amount of money which many see fit to invest in their game of golf!

The already wide waterway abruptly opens out into an expansive bay or winding hole. As assorted 'posse' of ducks haunt the winding hole; domesticated and ridiculously tame. Welsh Harlequins, Aylesbury's and Mallards pursue the towpath traveller with manic enthusiasm. As the canal returns to its customary width beyond the winding hole, bungalows again crowd towards the water's edge.

No sooner has its normal width been achieved than the canal is squeezed down to barely one boats width to pass through the mill grit foundations of a long removed swing bridge. This particular bridge has been missing for many years and was absent when British Waterways numbered the existing bridges. From the very stonework of this long lost and nameless bridge springs an unusual and rarely encountered wild flower in prolifically gay abandon.

WOOD SAGE

From July to September, the delicate spikes of

yellow / green flowers throng around the bridge foundations, even from between the blocks of stone. The presence of Wood Sage in such profusion in this particular spot is unusual. It is a prime example of the Macclesfield Canal providing a habitat which is colonized by a staggering array of varied flora and fauna. The delicate flowers are clustered in pairs towards the tip of the upright stems. Wood Sage is not a true sage in the culinary sense but is a valuable wild herb which belongs to the mint family. The wrinkled, toothed leaves which are strongly aromatic when crushed resemble those of the mint kin but smell distinctly of Hops. Each individual flower when viewed closely is quite exquisite in its design. Each is composed of a five lobed lower lip above which the brown stamens are exposed. Glancing back, the concrete water tower looms over the diminutive bungalows and 'Snailly Bridge' still occupies centre stage.

From the swing bridge foundations, the canal widens out between unlined banks yet, within 100 yards, it again narrows right down to where a foot bridge spans the site of yet another removed swing bridge. This swing bridge, unlike the removed one some 100 - 150 yards back has only disappeared during the last 10 or 15 years. Sadly, this fully functional swing bridge fell foul to the extremes of mindless vandalism. It was far too easy to swing it recklessly to and fro - due to its masterful engineering it swung beautifully. Its survival into the latter 20th century had been a matter of some considerable importance as it carried an exceedingly busy footpath across the canal. As narrow boating as a leisure pursuit increased 100 fold in both popularity and in volume, the swing bridge became increasingly busy, catering for boats passing through and feet passing over. It was felt that its condition was deteriorating rapidly through misuse and that it was a potential danger to the vandals who chose to abuse it. Midway through the 1970's it was dismantled. To insure the continuity of the increasingly busy footpath, the present foot bridge was built to replace it. Thus, bridge No. 78 or Billy Tights Swing Bridge as it was originally known disappeared to be replaced by this metal and stone construction. The modern day bridge has been built onto the foundations of the swing bridge which enables it to span a width of just 10 feet of water instead of a full width of canal. From either bank, a stone pillar, each incorporating 13 steep concrete steps, supports the girder and steel plate bridge.

The phenomenally busy footpath of which the bridge is an integral part leads from Astbury Lane Ends to the east, down through the golf course, into Congleton to the west. The footpath to both right and left hugs the uppermost edge of a deep stream clough which the canal neatly intersects just beyond the bridge by means of an incredibly high mini embankment. The densely wooded clough extends into the distance to both east and west. Having returned to a normal width beyond the bridge, the canal becomes metal lined, briefly, to both banks as it crosses the deep clough and its stream which, for a millenium has been known by the odd name of "The Howty". The Howty brook arises from a lacework of tiny rivulets and drains which stem from the remnants of the Mossley Moss and from Astbury Lane Ends to the east. It comes together as a single stream of some character before passing beneath the canal. It flows determindly westward towards Congleton before being culverted beneath much of the town centre - its flooding creating such a nuisance in medieval times - and emptying into the Dane. A laid Hawthorn accompanies the canal across the clough; a valley which hosts many sizeable broad leaf trees of great maturity.

Leaving the wooded valley, the decrepit remains of a drain off paddle which once discharged its water into the Howty brook is slowly disintegrating into the pathside hedgerow. Across the wide canal, the golf course stretches away eastward, extending to 120 acres in total. Its existence ensures that this somewhat unintentional wildlife haven will staunch the potential spread of suburbia from Astbury Lane Ends. The margins of the canal here are home to clumps of yellow Water Lilies. The generous width of the waterway must ensure that the fleshy underwater rhyzome or root of the Water Lily colony remains largely undisturbed by boat traffic which, by and large, restricts itself to the slightly deeper central 'boat channel'. The thick and leathery floating leaves or 'pads' are by far the largest of any British aquatic plant, often 16" x 12". The buttercup yellow flowers which appear during June, July and August add an almost exotic touch to the proceedings as the now much hybridized water lily is normally associated with the 'ornamental lily pond'. The water's edge on the eastern bank is marked by a line of squat, semi-mature Oaks.

WATER LILY

Beside the towpath, the hedgerow has again been tightly laid. The 2-3 years worth of vigorous growth which has fairly shot up from the old wood is a living testimony as to the virtue of this age old craft.

Pressing onwards along the wide towpath with rolling fairways to both right and left, it is not unreasonable to feel a compulsion to duck to avoid flying golf balls. This should not prove to be necessary as the canal is not employed as an obstacle on the course. Having said this, the sudden smack of club against ball from just behind the now lofty pathside hedge only serves to heighten the natural compulsion!

As the next stone bridge draws nearer, the waterway continues to cut an unerringly straight swathe through the golf course. The irregular line of the waterside trees, predominantly Oaks, on the far bank is now replaced by a most impressive line of pollarded Willows; stoutly trunked trees with handsome, deeply fissured bark which have had their boughs cut hard back on numerous occasions. This prevents them from developing the untidy haphazard shape which is so characteristic of the Willow family. Looking further eastwards beyond the fine Willows, the diversity of tree species, planted as individual specimens and dotted around the fairways almost qualifies the golf course as an arboretum. Very clever use has been made of both solitary trees and of spinneys but the end result is an impressive and important collection of species. The laying process has produced an incredibly dense pathside hedgerow, through which the land to the west can only occasionally be seen to be falling steeply away from canal level.

The fine club house comes into view away to the east. This building was erected in 1966 after the previous all wooden structure which had existed since the club was formed in 1922 burned down. This original building was situated just off Lamberts Lane for it was within 22 acres of rented ground bordering the lane that Astbury Golf Club was founded.

Peel Lane bridge dominates the view ahead. This substantial stone arch carries a large volume of traffic between Astbury Lane Ends and Mossley to the east and Astbury village to the west. This should be a fairly remote and tranquil spot but, due to the fact that Peel Lane bridge has survived as a single track or single carriageway span, the peace and quiet which should be broken only by the healthy smack of the golf ball being struck, is constantly disturbed by the frequent sounding of vehicle horns as one line of traffic announces its intention to cross Astbury's famous narrow and hump backed bridge to the inconvenience of oncoming traffic from the other direction. If ever there was a candidate for a bridge to have traffic light control it is here.

To the east, the Club House and associated car parking lies alongside Peel Lane. A different stream of 'traffic' plies its way across Peel Lane Bridge day in and day out. Golfers, laden with their accessories use the bridge as the only link between the two halves of the dissected course.

The waterway opens up once more, having passed beneath the arch of No. 79 and the attention is drawn towards the sharp deviation in the waterway ahead. .Beyond the low and beautifully neat pathside hedgerow, the golf course has vanished. In its place, lush pasture rolls away towards Peel Farm. By comparison, to the east, the golf course has successfully crossed Peel Lane and continues to occupy the eastern bank.The ground which lies to the east makes up the practice fields as opposed to being another fragmented section of the main course. The practice fields slope gently upwards away from the canal but the eastern horizon is now dominated by another outcrop of high ground. The place most recently vacated by The Cloud and Rainow Hill is now taken by Congleton Edge.

The Edge is another dramatic example of the almost continous mill grit outcrop, so typified by Kerridge Ridge, Marple Ridge, Crocker Hill etc. Like so many of its contemporaries, Congleton Edge has periodically been quarried for its mill grit, if to a slightly lesser extent. As the waterway and towpath begins to sweep to the left, the rich pastures which lie beyond the hedgerow are grazed by the Peel Farm herd of pedigree Friesian cattle, sleek coated thoroughbreds whose sweet aroma permeates the hedgerow.

The name 'Peel', relating to Peel Lane and farm, recalls part of the history of Astbury or Newbold Astbury, to give it its correct name; one of Cheshire's oldest and most historically important settlements. The Peel was originally the Peel Tower of the Peel and Motte or Motte and Baily Manor House which formerly occupied the area where Peel Farm stands today. The Newbold Manor was probably built in late Anglo Saxon times because the name "Newbold" which is Saxon for 'new buildings' is thought to refer to the fortified dwelling with its associated outbuildings.

In the depths of winter, from canalside Alders such as those which now line the eastern bank, can be heard the liquid, twittering song of Goldfinches as they dance from tree to tree. These exquisite little birds with their bright red faces, white heads with jet black cap and bright yellow bar on black wings, once made popular cage birds. Like the winter flocks of Long Tailed Tits and Great Tits, the Goldfinch flocks are drawn in from the open areas which are their normal habitat where their preferred food is thistle seed.

As the curve in the waterway is rounded, a long 'straight' stretches away towards the next bridge which is just visible in the distance. The ground which lies between the canal and Peel Farm undulates with unnatural vigour. These sweeping undulations are not the result of any naturally occuring forces, they are, in fact, the remnants of the massive earth works and ambitious moat which, for centuries defended the ancient seat of Newbold.

The Manors of Newbold and Astbury were given together as one holding to the newly created Earl of Chester by the conquering William of Normandy. The first Earl, Hugh Lupus, awarded the lands of Newbold Astbury to Baron Gislebertus Venator or Venator Abilis meaning Gilbert Venator. 'Venator' translates as hunter and Abilis means ability; a picture emerges of a hunter of exceptional ability, named Gilbert. The Venator name eventually was corrupted into Vanables; a fine Cheshire name which is represented throughout the county including the parish of Astbury in the twentieth century. The original fortification, inhabited by the descents of Gilbert the Hunter and dating from the late Saxon period was demolished in the early sixteenth century and replaced by a new manor house which incorporated "A small, aggressive square tower called a Peel".

The ground which now fairly plummets away from the canal only to rise steeply back up to the site of the present Peel Farm is the only surviving evidence of this once powerful seat. The golf practice fields come to an end on the far bank and are replaced by a pasture meadow. On closer scrutiny, the banky little pasture which climbs away eastwards to its own horizon, obscuring the view of Congleton Edge, bears a striking similarity to the uneven pasture to the west with dips and hummocks of its own. It becomes clear from the condition of the field to the east, that William Crossley's watercourse cut straight through these ancient earthworks.

Moving along the straight length of canal, a clearer view reveals Peel Farm standing on a mound of raised ground with the grassed over and much disturbed expanse of the fortification banks and moat around it. No sooner does the golf practise area come to an end and the 'hummocky' field begin, than the first of a solid line of moored boats is encountered against the far bank. This orderly line of assorted cruising craft extends far into the distance reaching the next bridge which is at the utmost limit of the view ahead. Somewhat haphazard, 'home made' mooring jetties or landing stages accompany the moored craft which otherwise would be simply tethered at the edge of a sheep field.

A second large farm stead comes into view in the rolling western vista. South of Peel Farm and beyond the extremes of the old eathworks stands Bank Farm. Whereas Peel Farm stood beside Peel Lane, Bank Farm stands beside Dodds Lane. The two lanes come together a little further westwards and run, united, into the heart of Astbury village. Between the two farms and rearing up cathedral like out of the Cheshire countryside, is the most photographed and painted, sketched and admired of the counties churches, the unique and unmistakable spire of St Mary's Astbury. Much has been written over the years in reverence of this fabulous building,.It is the very epicentre of this formerly massive rural parish which ironically, once included the tiny and nondescript sttlement of Congleton. It is not possible, in this context to do literary justice to the historic church of St Mary's.

To condense the mass of available information, the first church to occcupy the site was built entirely of wood by its Saxon patrons and was long established when the Norman invaders compiled their Domesday survey in 1086. Norman stone masons eventually replaced the Saxon church around 1150. This original Norman building was rebuilt less than 100 years later in 1240 and is now visible as the older section of the present northaisle. The new section of the north aisle (with a higher string course) dates from the 1300's. From 1430 to 1485 the main church was built alongside the north aisle. The architectural feature which sets St Mary's apart is the fact that the tower and spire stand isolated and detached from the main fabric of the church. The reason for the famous detached spire is ridiculously simple; the existing walls in 1450 were quite incapable of supporting it, consequently, building it apart avoided rebuilding the whole church.

Not surprisingly, an ecclesiastical edifice of such antiquity contains many internal memorial of great interest and age. As a matter of interest, the second oldest of the church's surviving memorials is a magnificent stone effigy and epitaph to Lady Jane Grey Egerton of Ridley whose family seat was Newbold Manor House. She is said to have died "Full of years and in the year of the incarnate word 1599".

As bridge No. 80 draws nearer, the improvised landing jetties accompany the moored boats, virtually to the bridge. Looking down to the immediate west, Dodds Lane comes into view, linking Bank Farm to bridge No. 80 which is Dodds Lane Bridge. A third farm stead comes into view, this time to the immediate east of the bridge, Upper Hulme Farm, to whom the boat moorings belong.

Upper Hulme Farm has recently undergone a total and extremely skillful rebuilding. What was formerly a centuries old stone farm house or holding has been extended in beautiful reclaimed Cheshire brick. Its neat and orderly yard and outbuildings reach almost to the waters edge on the approach to Dodds Lane Bridge. Dodds Lane is markedly different in character to Peel Lane, being a single carriageway also twisting and turning by nature. Correspondingly, bridge No. 80 is noticeably less robust in its construction than its predecessor.

It is a bare trickle of traffic which uses Dodds Lane Bridge compared to the veritable torrent using Peel Lane. This is largely because Dodds Lane leads up from the village, serving the most isolated farm steads and travels eastward into Newbold. The foregoing statement deserves some slight elaboration. As previously described, this ancient parish was known, from the advent of recorded history as Newbold or Newbold Astbury. The village with its unmistakeable church and group of historic houses and cottages is known simply as Astbury. It is the remote open land and farm steads which lie east of the village, towards the mill grit outcrop of Congleton Edge which, for some unknown reason maintains the ancient parish name of Newbold.

Just prior to the bridge, Dodds Lane arrives directly alongside the towpath. Looking westward down the lane towards Bank Farm, the eye is invariably drawn by a tangible, living link with Astbury's most ancient past. Incredibly, two living entities within the parish are possibly just old enough to have witnessed the overthrow of Astbury's Saxon thane or lord - Ulviet, by the onward march of William's conquering army.

Just yards from the canal, in the hedgerow beside the lane stands a most ancient oak. It is calculated to be anywhere between 600 and 1000 years old. The kindest description for its appearance today would be something like 'weather beaten' or 'seasoned'. The huge trunk has been long deprived of its upper growth by numerous storms and lightening strikes. This decapitated giant valiantly puts forth lush new growth before its long lost crown.

Astbury's second and most famous 'living fossil' is its incredible church yard Yew. A written account of the tree, dated 1915, is worded thus:

"On the north side of the church stands a remarkable Yew tree. It leans over the church yard path in so threatening a manner that numerous props have been recently placed to support it. The trunk is completely hollow, a large hole in the thin outer shell allows several people at a time to shelter within. In spite of this deficiency, the upper branches are quite vigorous and appear in perfect health. It has been computed that the tree is at least 1000 years old, hence, it was well established when the act of Edward III required the planting of yews in church yards to supply the tough bows necessary to the English long bow men."

In 1991, the tree appears no different from the preceding account of some 70 odd years before.

The line of moored craft comes to an end just prior to the bridge, giving way to a tiny paddock or croft where lambs graze or gangly legged calves pick at their first green stuff. The pathside Hawthorn gives way to a five bar gate which provides an access to a modest roadside parking area and also the perfect opportunity for the canal traveller to visit the fascinating village of Astbury with its cathedral-like church and welcoming Inn, the Egerton Arms.

CHAPTER TEN
ASTBURY TO HALL GREEN

Before passing beneath bridge No. 80, 14 haphazard steps link the towpath with Dodds Lane above. Unlike Peel Lane before it, Dodds Lane executes an acute 'z' to cross the bridge: if ever a skew bridge was needed but never built, it was here! Just yards out from the bridge, the far bank becomes sheet metal lined as the ground beyond falls precipitously away into a stream valley which is so deep and steeply sided as to resemble a ravine. The modest water course has cut so deeply into the alluvial ground that it appears lost in a fissure. The canal crosses the brief and narrow clough by means of an embankment which is ridiculously high. On its approach to the canal, the clough is revealed as a perfectly miniature river valley, liberally filled with mature trees of Ash, Alder and Oak.

The stream rises away to the east where Congleton Edge rolls down into Newbold. The Dairy Brook, after flowing through Astbury, joins Loach Brook at West Heath to the west of Congleton where it flows on to eventually join the river Dane at Somerford. The ground which plummets away into the valley to the west has become terraced over the centuries by cattle carefully making their way down the precipitous incline. Gorse has gained a foothold on these terraces and it blazes brilliantly yellow for much of the year. Because of the oblique angle at which the clough lies in relation to the canal, the majority of the valley has disappeared from the east almost before it manifests itself to the west. Looking eastward, back up the valley, mounds of freshly excavated sandy soil on the clough's steep sides betray the presence of a thriving rabbit warren. Closer inspection reveals a veritable epidemic of tunnel entrances, pock marking the steep slopes.

The canal begins to curve quite sharply to the right while actually being embanked across the clough. In the normal course of events, a brook or steam will be culverted beneath the canal then it is gone, flowing determinedly on to its destination but here, Dairy Brook and its expansive, wooded valley accompany the canal well into the distance. The sheet metal lining of the far bank is no longer necessary and is replaced by a margin which, over the decades, has been relentlessly trampled by cattle.

Beyond the wide, grassy towpath and the now rather sparse Hawthorn, the floor of the clough woodland is, from May through to August, clothed by drifts of Wood Sorrel. The leaves of Wood Sorrel look very like and are frequently mistaken for those of Clover although the plants are totally unrelated. The prolific yet delicate flowers are cup shaped and of the purest white veined with lilac. The path is briefly overshadowed by a fine Larch tree of commendable proportions which spreads its branches outward from the upper edge of the steep clough. Larch is a tree which is not indigenous to the alluvial Cheshire Plain and is rarely seen as a lone or specimen tree as here. It is normally planted 'en mass' on some Cumbrian or Scottish valley side, purely for its timber. As a specimen tree it reaches handsome proportions and its intriguing position as the only deciduous member of an otherwise exclusively evergreen order (conifers) makes it all the more interesting. This particular tree is as big a Larch as one is likely to encounter anywhere, given its isolated aspect and considerable age. It strews the towpath with it's curious little cones. One of the next trees to cast its shade upon the towpath is a towering Scots Pine, another 'exotic' to Cheshire. Other than these few aliens, the clough continues to be populated by the more normal Alders, Hollies and Oaks.

The meadows which rise gently away from the canal's far bank are frequently subdivided by hedgerows which run from the eastern horizon down to the water's edge. The numerous bobbing white tails which dash for cover to these hedgerows when disturbed indicate that the areas' healthy rabbit population uses the traditional 'hedge cop' for the siting of their warren as well as the nearby clough. Compared to the journey along Congleton's abused waterway and through the densely populated Astbury Lane Ends and the unnatural neatness of the golf course, the canal now lies amid remote tranquillity as blissful as any to be encountered so far along the journey. As the clough comes to an end, the next milestone stands beside the towpath. A tall original stone, its message can be read with perfect clarity; "From Hall Green, 3 1/4 miles" and, "From Marple, 23 Miles".

Beyond the clough, a dense, low hedgerow reveals meadow land rolling gently away towards Astbury. The wooded clough of Dairy Brook accompanies the edge of the meadow land far into the distant west. The water margin at the towpath bank is, throughout the late summer, prolifically colonized by Scullcap, an unobtrusive and less than flamboyant member of the mint family. Scullcap is one of those flowers which, frequently overlooked, is a component part of the typical flush of summer flowering waterside herbage. When studied closely, its tiny pale blue flowers which are grouped in pairs, are found to be exquisitely beautiful. Scullcap is another example of a plant, like the previously described Ivy leaved Toadflax, whose flowers exhibit a spreading lower lip like that of the garden snap dragon. The plants' common name is derived from the calyx or sheath from which the flower arises which is thought to resemble the leather skull helmet worn by Roman soldiers.

The view to the west is a perfectly rural, picture postcard scene of the noble spire of Astbury

SCULLCAP

church - the only man made edifice in a seemingly endless tapestry of greens and golds, meadows and hedgerows. During the later months of summer, the towpath traveller may be startled by considerable numbers of Small Tortoiseshell butterflies taking off from the wide, grassy towpath ahead of each foot fall . Surely the most common of British butterflies, the Small Tortoiseshell is totally synonymous with an English summer. Its every need is catered for along the canal. Its food plants which are Thistles and Nettles and the host plant for its eggs and its black and yellow caterpillars which is the common Stinging Nettle grows abundantly in the hedgerow bottom. The brightly speckled wings of the adult insect, gaily patterned in orange, black and white flutter delicately over the pathside hedgerow or alight gently among the waterside vegetation.

The canal is so blissfully remote from any appreciable habitation that the only sounds which dare to violate the tranquillity are sharp plops as feeding fish break the canal's surface and the ever changing symphony of bird song. Looking westward, an isolated farmstead intrudes into the sea of endless green. Although Mill House Farm appears to enjoy a position of total isolation, it actually forms part of the tiny hamlet of Ciss Green. 'Hamlet' is a gross overstatement. Ciss Green is a minuscule settlement yet proudly independent; a tiny island within the huge rural parish of Astbury. The wooded brook course of the Dairy Brook can be seen meandering westwards through Ciss Green and onward into Astbury. Even though Ciss Green amounts to just 10-12 buildings, it has provided Astbury with a tangible link with its most distant past.

In 1923, the remains of a dug out canoe were discovered in the bed of the Dairy Brook by a farmer. The canoe was carefully excavated and was eventually dated to around 500 BC. At face value, this would seem to be an odd find but it is beyond doubt that the early Saxon settlement of Astbury which was situated around the present site of the church evolved because the little mound upon which the village now stands, once stood proud above a great marsh. The area which lies between Astbury and Congleton is known to this day as Astbury Marsh - this area has obviously existed as swamp land within the time scale of recorded history. This 'Astbury Marsh' could have extended around the village to link up with the great marsh at Ciss Green and Moreton where the Saxon inhabitants lived by fishing and trapping wild fowl.

Where the wide waterway is constricted by encroaching Sedge colonies, Branched Bur Reed briefly rears high out of the sedge bed. It is a dramatic plant whose globe-like flowerheads eventually swell to become bur-like long beaked fruits. These fruits usually survive intact - if withered and brown - through the hardest of winters, adding interest and diversity of form to the windswept winter waterside. Glancing to the distant east the first section of the hill of Congleton Edge comes to an abrupt end. A distinct and clearly visible dip or indentation, visible from many miles away, separates it from the second part of the escarpment.

This 'dip' has been known for centuries by the poetically appropriate name of "Nick O' Th Hill". The view down to the west at this particular point provides a dramatic example of ancient and modern. The colossal bowl of the Jodrell Bank (Grade 2 listed) radio telescope which has been visible intermittently for many miles suddenly appears to be immediately adjacent to the cathedral like form of Astbury Church. In reality, a distance of at least ten miles separate the two landmarks yet, from here, they almost appear as one.

Looking ahead to both the right and left of the canal, it is obvious that a lane, running from Astbury and through Ciss Green, is about to pass beneath the waterway, making its way steeply up into Newbold. Its route can be followed through the patchwork of meadows by its hedgerows for it is an ancient rural thoroughfare which has escaped being either widened or straightened and it runs, for much of its length, between high banks - a classic example of a sunken lane. Its towering hedgerows contain many fine, mature trees and represent a rich and varied hedgerow habitat. Its single track carriageway represents something of a challenge for the modern motorist and its breathtaking hair pin bends were much safer when negotiated at horse drawn pace. For such an insignificant and remote carriageway, Watery Lane is delivered beneath the canal by means of a most impressive aqueduct. From the point of view of the canal user the only obvious indication that the canal is crossing anything at all, never mind a major aqueduct, it the sudden metal lining of both banks. So many trees cluster around the entrance and exit of the tunnel - for that is what it actually is - that the less observant could pass across it and never realize that the lane lies some thirty feet below.

This is not a major aqueduct in the Dane Bridge at Bosley or Town Aqueduct at Bollington sense of the word. This bridge does not soar to dizzy heights, dwarfing all around it . Having said this, to encounter the bridge unexpectedly while travelling Watery Lane is reminiscent of being swallowed by an opening in the ground. The already narrow lane is squeezed down to enter the tunnel which has a bare 8 feet 6 inch head room in the total darkness. The tunnel spans a 90 foot length of lane which adds to the claustrophobia. The dark, dank tunnel has dripped water from its roof since before living memory and Ivy hangs down, over both entrance and exit alike, further reducing the 'visual' headroom. All of these combine to help Dripping Bridge and Watery Lane to live up to their

BRANCHED BUR REED

names. Water lies permanently in the darkness beneath the bridge, the halfway point of which happens to represent the lowest point along Watery Lane as the roadway slopes down to the tunnel from either side.

Alongside a stile in the pathside hedgerow, a squat 1/2 or 1/4 mile marker stone has survived intact from the canal's working life, its confusing message having no relevance to the modern day, having nothing whatsoever to do with the fractions between the milestones proper.

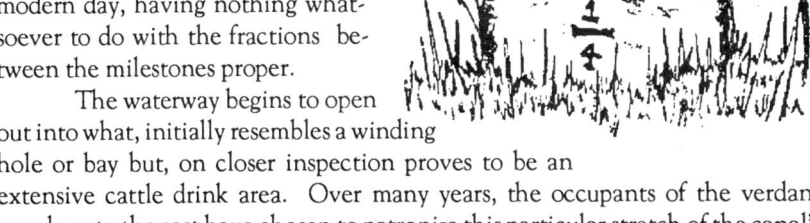

The waterway begins to open out into what, initially resembles a winding hole or bay but, on closer inspection proves to be an extensive cattle drink area. Over many years, the occupants of the verdant meadows to the east have chosen to patronize this particular stretch of the canal's bank to drink and to stand in the water in hot weather. It is not unusual during oppressively hot summer afternoons to find scores of cows standing placidly, knee deep in the water, enjoying the simple, sensual pleasure of cooling their cloven hooves and their lower legs.

The ground drops increasingly steeply away from the pathside hedgerow, down into the seemingly endless ocean of pastures and tree dotted meadows which roll away towards Astbury. In the most distant east, the hill of Congleton Edge has come to an end and the ground which now rises upward does so towards the next major mill grit outcrop. This massive hill will eventually dominate the remainder of our journey, Mow Cop.

Having returned to something like a normal width beyond the cattle drink, the waterway opens out into a huge sheet of water as extensive as any to be encountered since the wide hole at Higher Poynton. Whether this huge sheet of water began as a winding hole, provided by the canal engineers for the purpose of turning the long narrow cargo boats ,or if it came about by natural means may never be determined as it now exists as a huge sedge bed which is also host to the canal's most extensive beds of Bullrush or Great Reed Mace. This is a favourite spot for the lone pleasure angler (as the well worn patches on the metal lined towpath bank testify). He is able to cast his bait across the deep central boat channel and beyond, where the far margin would normally be, and up to the edge of the sedges and rushes. This is an impenetrable semi-aquatic jungle where the fish population can escape the incessant boat traffic and bask undisturbed save for the lightening fast dagger bill of the ghostly grey Heron. The art is to tempt the fish out of the weed to feed freely at its edge by showering the area with samples of the hook bait.

This huge colony of aquatic vegetation must measure some 300 to 400 feet in length. The width of the waterway, from the metal bank lining, across the navigable canal, plus the width of the sedge bed, must amount to a generous 150 to 200 feet across. On hot August evenings, the whole bed seethes with pied wagtails, flittering, almost hovering, brushing the swaying flowerheads of the rushes and sedges, mopping up the clouds of gnats and midges which swarm among the vegetation.

By complete contrast, in the heart of deepest winter, when the canal has been frozen solid for days or even weeks, a dusting of light snow lying on the ice may betray the presence of another predator, more ominous than the Heron. The small, cat-like footprints leading across the canal into the heart of the now gaunt and frost blasted sedges may spell Mink! It was here, along this tree lined bank in the depths of the 1988 winter that the author first spotted a Mink first hand. Traveling northwards along the towpath, the younger family members and assorted dogs (a noisy tribe at the best of times) startled what, at first glance looked, for all the world, like a black/chocolate brown cat from amongst the roots of the Hawthorns and Hollies across the canal. It was only as the animal scurried up the bank to gain access to the field above that we realised that the legs were far too short and the sinuous, almost liquid movement was comparable to that of the Weasle/Stoat/Ferret family . This left no doubt in our minds that we were witnessing the hurried escape of a mink, the 'polecat in a fur coat'.

Beyond the extensive sedge bed, the waterway begins to swing to the left revealing Oak Farm Bridge, No. 81 ahead, and beyond that, perfectly framed in its arch lies the next, No. 82. Down to the west, through the pathside Hawthorn, Oak Farm comes into view, surrounded by an impressive range of traditional outbuildings in mellow brick and standing alongside the tiny Oak Lane. On the final approach to the bridge, the far bank is host to a huge Dog Rose bush, which, in season, is a profusion of flowers,whilst late autumn and early winter sees the Rose decorated with an absolute abundance of rich red hips. Its now leafless stems are laden with fruits, resembling a Christmas tree decked out in masses of shiny red baubles. This glut of hedgerow produce makes the towpath an absolute paradise for the devotees of country wine.

From the immediate vicinity of the towpath it is possible to make well in excess of a dozen good quality wines of excellent flavour and considerable alcoholic merit!

Spring time provides huge quantities of Hawthorn blossom for a delicious light"flowery" white wine. This is followed by Elder flower which can be made into a creditable champagne. Continuing the flower theme, Dandelion flowers make a delightful wine which should be ready to accompany Christmas dinner the same year, but if kept as long again, does do a fair impersonation of a fine pale cream sherry. The canalside Gorse bushes provide another delicious source of spring time flower wine before early Summer turns the attention of the connoisseur away from flowers.

As the humble Bramble begins to grow at frantic pace through the canalside undergrowth, the fleshy 'growing tip' can be nipped off between thumb and finger to produce Bramble Tip wine, a little known and under-exploited delicacy.

Another frequently encountered hedgerow twiner, the Honeysuckle, produces a summer flower wine, the flavour of which is beyond description - to be surpassed only by Meadow Sweet, another common canalside flower whose name, it will be remembered, was derived from the Saxon "Mead Sweet"- to sweeten mead. Rose petal rounds off the seasons flower harvest as thoughts turn to the classic Elderberry and the equally prolific and flavoursome Blackberry. September sees the search area widen as Sloes are gathered both to flavour Gin and to produce a rich red wine which is comparable to both Elderberry and Blackberry. Throughout Autumn and well into the frosts, Rose Hips and Hawthorn berries are secured in bulk to make wine "fresh" and also to commit to the deep freeze in quantity to ensure year round production!

An unassuming 'scramble' footpath links the towpath with Oak Lane, up the side of the bridge, - no elaborate steps or ramp here. When compared to Oak Lane, the previously described Watery Lane assumes dual carriageway proportions. It is every bit as narrow as its bridleway origins would suggest, definitely not designed for modern transport. It travels between Newbold to the east and Ciss Green to the west. The bridge in no way resembles an arch which carries a roadway. In fact, on the the approach, it appears little more substantial than an accommodation bridge.

The total distance between bridges 81 and 82 is only 170 yards of which, the first 100 spans a wide, deep and well wooded stream valley. Unlike its predecessors, this major valley with its winding brook is too expansive to fit into the classification of a clough, in fact, beyond the embankment to the east, ponies graze the damp grassland in the valley bottom. The stream which passes beneath the canal exists as a result of many scores of tiny rivulets and drains over an extensive area below Congleton Edge, Nick O'th Hill and Newbold coming together. The resulting appreciable waterway flows, not into Astbury but into Moreton, another separate entity within the great mother parish of Astbury. The stream goes on to form one of the two principal water supplies for the ancient manorial lake at Moreton.

The passage across the embankment is enriched by the presence of aromatic clumps of Garden Mint with flowers of the palest powder blue, growing between the towpath and metal bank lining. Not a yard away from the Mint, the welcoming blue of Myosotis flowers brighten the summer months. Any gardener worth his salt will recognize the name Myosotis as being the family name of that much beloved garden favourite, the Forget-Me-Not. This pretty example growing alongside the towpath could, however, be a representative of numerous varieties. Although it is positioned just 12 inches or less from the water it is definitely not the most obvious variety the water Forget-Me-Not. The towpath is a far cry from its chosen habitat. My own method of identifying water Forget-Me-Not is that, to pick a sample, large enough to identify, one needs to first sink to the knees in mud to do so! This particular one is either the wood Forget-Me-Not, the common or field Forget-Me-Not or even an escapee of the garden variety.

GARDEN MINT

Beyond the metal lining of the far bank, all that is visible while crossing the stream valley is the tops of Alder and Ash trees. A briefly available glimpse down to the distant west prior to bridge No. 82 reveals farmsteads and cottages which are in the scattered township of Moreton. The waterway narrows to pass beneath the arch of bridge No.82, a modest stone arch which represents a return to the simple agricultural accommodation bridge. No linking pathway exists between the towpath and the bridge top where no public right of way exists. Looking along the straight length of canal which stretches away ahead, the next bridge, No, 83 or Wharf Lane Bridge is clearly visible.

The waterway once more opens out into a wide bay which initially resembles a winding hole but proves to be another cattle drink. The meadow which slopes steeply down to the canal's far bank obviously consists of an extremely sandy loam as it has very easily and cleanly eroded into the canal to form the wide, shallow lagoon where generations of cattle have come to drink. Chunks or slices of pasture have crumbled into the water, revealing clay land drain pipes which once transported sub-surface water down to the canal but now lie uselessly at the waters edge. The towpath is now accompanied by a neat, low Hawthorn which was laid by British Waterways 5 or 6 years ago after decades of neglect. This gives an unimpeded view westwards across an expansive grass field which rolls away towards Home Farm, Moreton.

Down to the west, beyond the expansive grass field and standing among tall mature trees of Scots Pine and evergreen or Holm Oak, is Great Moreton Hall's East Lodge. The high Gothic gables and tall ornate chimneys of this stone gate house stand proud among the crowding trees. The lodge acts as a gate house standing sentry over Great Moreton's east or tradesman's drive.

The unlined margin of the towpath bank is colonised by Branched Bur Reed and where Lady's Smock grows in spring, White Flowering Dead Nettle thrives throughout the summer and into the Autumn. The barley field to the east comes to an end and is replaced by a field of sugar root beet which provides rich winter feed for cattle. During mid summer, long before the beet is harvested, the regimented rows or drills are hidden by great, brilliant white drifts of the daisy like flowers of Scentless Mayweed. Beyond the beet field, the adjoining pasture meadow is interrupted by what initially seems to be a large pit hole. The extensive hole which is surrounded by scrubby Hawthorns and banks of Gorse proves to be dry (not flooded) and covers a much larger area than the average marl pit. Old parish maps name this hole as "Old Gravel Pit" and, at the time of the canal's completion in 1831, bridge No. 83 which lies just ahead was originally known as Gravel Pit Bridge. In the distant east, beyond the beet field and the worked out gravel pit and over the Manchester - Stoke railway which lies beyond the brow of the hill, Lime Kiln Wood and Hanging Wood rise steeply up through Roe Park, the ancient hunting grounds of the Lords of Great Moreton.

Wharf Lane comes into view - leading westward, down towards Great Moreton Hall and eastwards, up into Newbold. The grass beside the towpath is decorated by the whorls of the long, claret coloured flowers of Hedge Woundwort. The flowers appear in loose spikes on the top of purplish stems during July and August. This widespread plant has been used medicinally by man since the days of the ancient Greeks although the offensive smell of its crushed leaves ought to be sufficient to ensure that it is left to grow and flower in peace. It is fairly common if patchy in its distribution along the whole of the canal, appearing in some numbers around Kerridge and Hurdsfield and again at Sutton. The hairy, heart shaped leaves were used as a poultice to treat wounds and to stem bleeding.

On the final approach to bridge No. 83, the water again opens out in width as the far bank is occupied by a stone lined wharf. This particular wharf came into being almost exactly a decade after the canal's completion. In 1840, work began on the building of the present Great Moreton Hall, replacing the ageing timber framed Moreton Magna manor house which had stood since 1602. This wharf was established on the nearest access point on the canal to the hall initially, to receive materials appertaining to the building of the flamboyant new house which were being imported from overseas. Caen stone from Normandy and marble from various regions of mainland Europe for internal decoration were shipped across, eventually finding their way onto the internal canal system via the Manchester Ship Canal. Ultimately they were hauled the final 1/4 of a mile or so to the Hall by horse drawn wagons from this wharf.

After Great Moreton Hall's completion (1843-5) the estate wharf was retained for receiving bulk cargoes, consequently, Gravel Pit Bridge became Wharf Lane Bridge as the tiny lane became Wharf Lane. Great Moreton retained the ownership of the wharf up until 1930 but actually continued to use it up until the late 1970's. Great Moreton ceased to be a private house in 1930 and became a young ladies college. In 1954, it became a boys school, operated by Manchester Education Committee. Around this time Great Moreton Hall School acquired an old narrow boat, in need of restoration. It was duly moored in the old estate wharf awaiting refurbishment as a school project - where it lay, virtually untouched until the end of 1970's, a victim of repeated vandalism and total neglect. It became something of a landmark as the canal became a part of the great new inland tourist boom until finally being set of fire and sinking as a result. The old boat (ironically named Freedom) became a yardstick in measuring the lack of or amount of interest being generated by the waterway system as a whole. During the 1950's as the canal an idle and neglected part of a dying industrial trade route, the old boat followed suit. The 1960's saw the turning point as the waterway was rediscovered as an amenity area and as the opulent 1970's became the high-tech luxury 1980's, the skeleton of the old boat was rescued and 'magicked' away to become a luxurious water-borne holiday home. With the dawn of the 1990's, the old wharf has been taken over and cleaned up for use as private moorings.

The water's edge on the approach to Wharf Lane Bridge is home to a delightful native plant which is capable of living either on land or actually in the water. It is not unusual to find both water and land growing varieties of aquatic or Amphibious Bistort in the same colony or clump. There are subtle vegetative features which enable it to live a complete aquatic existence. Between June and August the small but distinctive spikes of pink flowers rise above straight branchless stems making a striking display among the lush waterside herbage. The leaves of Bistort differ between its two chosen habitats but the pretty cylindrical terminal spikes of the flower are unmistakeable in either form.

Beyond the wharf, the canal narrows down between stone lined banks to pass beneath the arch of the bridge where a rough, 'scramble' path links the towpath with Wharf Lane above. Wharf Lane Bridge represents a rather more substantial affair than the preceding accommodation bridge - somewhat on a par with Oak Lane Bridge. From beneath Wharf Lane Bridge, the next, No. 84 is clearly in view some distance ahead.

BISTORT

Behind the sturdy towpath Hawthorn a 'hummocky' field slopes away, along with Wharf Lane, down to New Road, Moreton. To the west, several large and well appointed red brick houses come into view which were built as estate workers houses during the early 1920's by Great Moreton Hall's second gentleman owner, Robert G Peel, industrial magnate and philantropist. The brick houses stand across the road from the older

East Lodge which, along with Home Farm, represent buildings which date from the first generation of estate building i.e. those which were built along with the hall.

Less than 200 feet out from the bridge, the reason for the metal bank lining becomes apparent as the waterway is, once more embanked across a wooded stream clough. This one is more typical of the classic clough, a deep yet narrow ravine whose steep sides have become colonised with dense tree cover. As the canal is actually being transported across the embankment, the decaying remains of a drain-off paddle is set in the hedgerow. This represents a point where excess water from the canal could be diverted into an artificially created, stone built stream course which flows into the natural stream just as it is culverted through the embankment.

The uneven nature of the field which lies between the canal and New Road is once more due to mans activities - this time it is a result of the extraction of sand in considerable quantities during the building of Great Moreton Hall. The sand had, in turn been deposited by the action of the stream over many centuries. This particular torrent is the culmination of several rivulets which rise from the high ground on Roe Park to the east. It passes beneath the canal and down to Great Moreton where it is harnessed to become the principal water supply for the ancient manorial lake and for the hall's ornamental pool. Having served Great Moreton's various water features, it comes together once more and is joined by reinforcements to become the infant river Wheelock. After flowing westwards through Rode Heath and Hassal Green, Wheelock, Middlewich and Bostock, the river Wheelock joins the river Weaver near to Northwich. An extensive pasture field stretches away eastward to the Manchester - Stoke mainline railway beyond which, Lime Kiln Wood, Roe Park Wood and Quarry Wood climb steeply up to Mow Cop.

Through the pathside hedgerow a traditional mixture of hay meadows and arable fields can be seen to be falling ever more steeply away towards Great Moreton Hall. In late summer, the grassy towpaths between Moreton and Kent Green blaze with the golden daisy-like flowers of Hawkweed. The large flower heads of brilliant yellow petals surrounding an orange yellow centre close in the afternoon. The plant stands up to 4 feet towering above the pathside grasses.

Away to the west, New Hall Farm comes into view, a handsome brick house built during

HAWKWEED

Great Moreton's second generation of building as a model farm, once the home of Robert Peel's pedigree herd of Great Moreton large white pigs. The backdrop to this fine brick house and its attendant outbuildings is the dense woodland which surrounds the Hall from which the strange and alien shapes of Chilean Pines, Coast Redwoods, Swamp Cypress and Wellingtonia's rear up from an underplanting of Himalayan Rhododendrons. Towering above the trees is the uppermost castellated tower of the magnificent Gothic revival mansion.

The old manor house and estate had been purchased in 1814 by brothers George and James Ackers, cotton and textile giants from Lancashire. James chose to live in Gloucestershire and George died in 1836 leaving his only son George Holland Ackers his business empire and vast estate at the tender age of 24 years. Acker's fortunes flourished and in 1840 he approached Edward Blore, special architect to King William IV and Queen Victoria, about the erection of this magnificently proportioned stone built house. When Acker's boundless wealth and Blore's skill, imagination and great sense of the Gothic style combined, the result was a living fantasy; a huge stone pile of fortress proportions.

The wide, unlined waterway stretches away towards bridge No. 84. The final approach to the bridge is greatly overshadowed by towering Alders from the far bank ,but the huge tree which totally swamps this modest agricultural accommodation bridge is actually an exceptional example of a wild flowering Cherry. When in full blossom in late April, early May, the bridge is completely engulfed in the foaming mass of flowers. The huge plants which grow tall and erect against the stonework of the bridge are Great Burdock. This giant among the family of composite or, 'thistle like' plants, has large broadly heart shaped leaves and purple thistle like flower heads. The flowers appear from July - September. After evolving to become fruiting bodies they eventually die and become dry burs (hence Bur-dock),which tenaciously stick to clothing and to animal fur. The stout stems of Burdock survive the winter in a dried state to ensure the safe disposal of the adhesive burs.

Emerging from No. 84, the waterway continues to be overhung by trees from the far bank. Likewise, the towpath continues to be shadowed by a high bank as the waterway continues to follow an exceptionally straight course. The wide canal lies between unlined banks which are home to the delicate Lady's Smock and Speedwells in Spring before the vigorous Branched Bur Reed accelerates into growth as the summer days lengthen. Flowering Rush squeezes in among the reed, its dead and brittle flower stems surviving intact through the winter months. To the east, a grassy bank rises up to meet the expansive pasture which separates the canal from the railway. Beyond, high meadows, which have been carved out of the ancient woodland, stretch upwards through Roe Park. To the east, Roe Park represents the most southerly surviving fragment of the once extensive forest of Macclesfield which formerly covered much of Cheshire.

During the Saxon period Roe Park was one of the last strong holds of the native Roe deer. There is evidence that it was here, sometime around 1100 that Alexander De Moreton, first lord of Great Moreton built his heavily fortified stronghold along the prevailing Norman "Peel and Motte" lines. The extensive Roe Park, remained an integral part of the Great Moreton estate until 1930 when the lands were split up and sold off.

The next milestone stands beside the towpath, it is a defaced original which reads "From Hall Green —— Miles". This figures should read 2 1/4. The opposite face reads, quite clearly "From Marple 24 Miles". On the approach to bridge No. 85, the canal's banks become metal lined once more and beyond the pathside Hawthorn, the ground drops sharply away into a narrow strip of woodland which is all that now separates the canal from New Road. Looking ahead, buildings surround bridge No. 85. This is Ackers Crossing - neither a village nor a hamlet in the true sense but an estate settlement. Ackers Crossing is sometimes referred to as Great Moreton and a short terrace of cottages are "Great Moreton Terrace".

Ackers Crossing is not even an estate village which grew up around the great house, it evolved around a railway stop. George Holland Ackers, the lord of the manor, traveled frequently by train either to his business empire in Lancashire or to his exclusive London address. Exserting his privileged position to the full, he created his own stop or halt at which to meet his train at the nearest point to the Hall (less than a quarter of a mile down the line from the nearest station!) During the 1840's, in its heyday, Ackers Crossing consisted of an ornate little 'railway house' beside the track, marking "Ackers Crossing Point", the terrace of cottages, and "Kingspool", a larger estate house in the classic pattern of rough faced stone, with high gables and architectural chimney stacks, built alongside bridge No. 85, Ackers Crossing Bridge. When the canal was cut, some 11 or so years prior to the building of Great Moreton Hall and before Ackers created his new road to the railway, the bridge had been built as an accommodation bridge and was originally know by the name of the tenant of the field which had been dissected, Simpsons Bridge.

The mixed woodland beyond the towpath of Sycamore, Alders, Holly and Hazel is totally blanketed by Bluebells in spring. The grassy valley to the east is grazed by rowdy flocks of fat geese and domestic ducks. Goats bleat plaintively at their honking and quacking compatriots. As time went by, Ackers Crossing was added to; a dozen or so private houses and bungalows arrived and even a group of council houses before the green belt planning restrictions prevented its further expansion.. It is some of these more modern homes whose gardens reach down to the canal's far bank prior to the bridge.

The narrow plot of woodland to the right of the towpath peters out all together as New Road arrives alongside the towpath, separated by just the hedgerow as it climbs to cross the canal via the bridge. Out of necessity, the road is forced to execute a savage 'z' to cross the bridge, bearing in mind, the bridge was never designed to carry a roadway at all. Where the spacious gardens terrace down to the canal on the far bank, the obligatory jetties or landing stages line the water's edge. A set of stop planks stands amongst a sea of Speedwell and Cow Parsley beside the towpath and eleven well worn stone steps lead up the side of the bridge to New Road. Emerging from Ackers Crossing Bridge, the towpath and canal are totally overshadowed by Kingspool, a fine house which is unmistakeably an estate house, despite having been in private ownership for many decades. In addition to the house, both of the canal's banks are overhung by tall trees which add to the overall impression of being in the deepest recesses of a shadowy cutting. The far bank is unlined and trees grow, almost from the water's edge, stretching determinedly across towards the towpath bank. One of these, a large crab apple, drops the majority of its fruit into the water where they bob around for months on end. Just one house and its garden inhabit the eastern bank beyond the bridge after which, Ackers Crossing is lost without trace.

A brief view is momentarily available, due to a break in the thick, screening tree cover, of Great Moreton Hall's south or garden front which is softened by smooth faced stone work, rolling terraced lawns and formal flower beds. Beyond the waterside Alders the eastern bank is occupied by a potato field which stretches towards Mow Cop. As the towpath and waterway continue to curve, another insignificant stream course is culverted beneath the canal. Arising from springs and wells in Quarry Wood on Roe Park, the water, flows on down to Great Moreton via the Round Plantation and the Long Plantation to join up with the head waters of the newly born river Wheelock directly to the west of Great Moreton's mansion grounds. To the more distant east, beyond and above Quarry Wood the next significant landmark, literally, rears its ugly head. This is the so called "Old Man of Mow".

Like Lyme Cage, White Nancy, the telecommunications tower on Crocker Hill and so on, The Old Man of Mow is widely believed to be a product of mans activities. The Old Man is actually a pillar of rock which stands around 65 feet high and measuring about the same at its widest girth. Some believed that its bizarre size, shape and isolated situation were due to its being deposited by retreating glaciers and its reputed similarity to a wizened old man both gave it its name and attributed supernatural powers to it on occasions. The rock is suitably unique to now be owned and preserved by the National Trust. The point where 'The Old Man' stands is roughly the centre of an old stone quarry. Before quarrying on the site, during the early seventeenth century, the top of the hill was the highest point on Mow Cop (1,100 feet above sea level). At this point was a cairn or marker stone which denoted the boundary line between the feudal manors of Moreton and Odd Rode. The cairn was removed by the quarriers and the rock where it had stood was marked and the quarrying continued around it to a depth of 65 feet, leaving the pillar of rock standing as the highest point on Mow Cop and replacing the cairn as the manorial boundary. The precise boundary line was subsequently marked on the face of the rock marking the parishes of Astbury and Odd Rode, the two counties of Cheshire and Staffordshire; the two diocese of Lichfield and Chester and the two provinces of Canterbury and York.

Smooth Hawksbeard, a common flower in grassy places is one of the familiar yet rarely named or recognised yellow wayside plants of mid-late summer. It is frequently encountered growing freely in the pathside grasses between Moreton and Hall Green. The plant has the smallest flowers of all the Hawksbeards at a half inch across and is best described as resembling a tiny thistle flower but of purest golden yellow. The leaves, usually lost from sight among the pathside grasses are dandelion shaped forming a rosette at the base.

The view to the west through the dense pathside Hawthorn is no longer into the great parish of Astbury but into the neighbouring parish of Odd Rode. The meadows which slope endlessly away westward are now noticeably lower than the canal and towpath level which explains the need for the metal bank lining which has persisted from Ackers Crossing Bridge. Lapwings wheel and tumble above the lush meadows which lie between the canal and Mow Cop, uttering their haunting cry as they cartwheel through the air.

To the east, between the canal and the railway, the roadside trees and hedgerow can be seen, running parallel, accompanying the roadway which ceased to be New Road, Moreton at Ackers Crossing and became Station Road, Kent Green. The canal is briefly overhung from the far bank by an Ash tree of monumental proportions. It is almost possible to touch the tips of the foliage from the towpath bank. Although the ground which lies down to the west is now within the parish of Odd Rode, it is still in the continuing township of Moreton. Whereas Great Moreton lay within the parish of Astbury, the ancient township of Moreton covered such an extensive area that it actually lay within two parishes. As a consequence, two ancient families were able to hold lands within the same township and were both able to assume the name of the township, the De Moretons of Great Moreton or Magna Moreton and the Moreton family of Little Moreton in Odd Rode.

Three quarters of a mile down to the west lies the manor house of the Moreton family, the nationally famous and instantly recognizable black and white Little Moreton Hall. This house is, without doubt, one of the most well known sights in Cheshire. Completely surrounded by its own moat, it is a superb example of English half timbered architecture It is totally medieval in style and fairly 'oozes' history. Even from a distance its great antiquity is obvious from the way in which its walls and roofs lean and incline at precarious angles. The renowned architectural historian Nikolaus Pevsner's description of Little Moreton "happily reeling and somewhat disorderly" is probably the most endearing yet accurate to date. The special charm of Little Moreton is that it has survived almost completely unchanged since the mid sixteenth century, untouched by the excesses of later generations and thankfully unspoiled by the Victorian passion for rebuilding, remodeling or restoring.

The Moreton family held the manorial lands for over six centuries and it was Ralph Moreton who began the present house in about 1480. A house in the 'H' plan, it consisted of two wings on either side of a great hall. A second stage of building was begun by William Moreton in 1559. This was completed and formed by his son, by about 1580 the east and the south range with its projecting gatehouse and long gallery. By this date, Little Moreton Hall must have looked exactly as it does today. The house ceased to be a family home at the beginning of the eighteenth century and was tenanted by farmers for two hundred years before being passed to the National Trust in 1937. It draws many thousands of visitors every year and remains among the most popular of the Trust's properties.

Looking ahead, bridge No. 86 lies a short distance away. An isolated almost desolate field bridge or accommodation bridge. A modest, rustic affair, overhung by an Ash tree, it is almost unique in that it stands amid a totally flat landscape. As the ground to the east and west fails to rise up to greet it, it looks almost as if it had been dropped across the waterway as an afterthought. A worn cattle track leads up to and over the arch, linking the two halves of what would once have been a larger pasture. The grassy towpath margins rejoice with the presence of one of the Macclesfield Canal's commonest grassland flowers of summer. From June through to September from Hall Green almost to Marple it will be encountered anywhere and almost everywhere. Hardheads is not a pretty enough name for this tall, handsome plant like a thistle with no prickles. It gets is name from its knob-like flower heads of reddish-purple. It is also known as Common Knapweed or Black Knapweed, neither of which do it justice. The heads owe their hardness to the rows of overlapping blackish scales which surround the flower heads.

On the final approach to bridge No. 86, or Lowndes Bridge, a large farm occupies the site known as Old House Green at the top of the meadow which rises gently away from the canal, beside Station Road. It is Old House Green which farms the majority of the land between the canal and Little Moreton. On the stonework of bridge No. 86, a National Trust plaque depicting the unmistakeable Oak twig emblem points towards "Little Moreton Hall". Emerging from the arch, a corresponding plaque and a neat wooden stile and

HARDHEADS

directional wooden pointer leave no doubt as to the destination of the footpath which leads its threadbare route westward down into Odd Rode. To the distant east, above the railway and above Close Farm which lies in a green island of grassland amid the extensive, dark ocean of Quarry Wood, the "Old Man of Mow" seems to jut aggressively from the uppermost edge of the woodland. The softly wooded if steeply rising Cheshire side of Mow Cop is a far cry from the bleak, windswept and much quarried upper ridge and the densely built up Staffordshire side which rolls down towards the outskirts of the potteries.

Mow Cop is just the most recent spelling and pronunciation of this curious name. This latest version is derived from "Moel Coppa" meaning bald crown (the high ridge surmounting the wooded hill).It was on the windswept heights of Mow Cop that the Primitive Methodist Movement began, almost two hundred years ago in 1801. In July of that year,its founder, Hugh Bourne preached a sermon to a great body of followers in a field adjacent to a remote farm house. The house had been used for some time for more modest meetings, but the multitudes who flocked to hear Bourne could only be accommodated in the open air. Six years later, the first camp meeting was held in this same field on Mow Cop.

From the ridge - the parish and county boundary - it is possible to overlook 7 counties, (several of which are Welsh). Leaving bridge No. 86 behind, the canal regains its customary width, but is once more subjected to the narrowing effect of thick belts of sedge growing out from each bank. In the place of the customary pathside hedgerow, the edge of the wide, grassy towpath is marked by a retaining wall of mill grit construction.Beyond this retaining wall, the ground falls away quite acutely. The supporting wall does away with the need for the canal's waterside bank to be reinforced with a sheet metal lining as is usually the case in a half or full embankment. An ornate iron railing fence which is set into the low wall replaces the customary hedgerow beside the towpath. The commencement of this splendid old fence marks the point at which the waterway enters the grounds of Ramsdell Hall.

A pasture rises away from the water's edge toward Old House Green where a substantial range of well built brick shippons and other outbuildings cluster around the huge farmhouse. To the south of the range of outbuildings, the unmistakeable remains of a once substantial kitchen garden wall stretches away into the distance, now in a state of some dereliction. Beyond the retaining wall and the steep embankment, the ground fairly plunges away westwards toward Little Moreton.

The sedge margins disappear and the wide canal and equally wide towpath stretch determinedly on - the whole thing supported or propped up by the massive wall buried in the embankment. Up to the east, tall trees protruding above the old kitchen garden wall from the inside and the decrepit remains of outbuildings or greenhouses leaning to the wall's outer face add to the overall impression of neglect and decay. The pastures which spill away westwards into Odd Rode are not featureless agricultural wastelands but interesting old meadows, full of character: large mature Ash trees, stands or clumps of Hawthorn trees, traces of ancient relic hedgerows and a profusion of flooded pit holes.

The waterway must be curving imperceptibly as bridge No. 86, disappears from view without a great distance being covered. On the far bank, a very large garden reaches down to the canal, partially hidden by a row of Alder and Sycamore trees growing at the waterside.

Fine lawns climb away towards the Coach House but the attention is drawn by a vast rockery of monumental proportions. It is a depression or dell whose steeply sloping sides are completely clad in rough boulders. Steep stone steps lead down into the hole where one assumes a pool must lie for the upper section of an ornate footbridge of rustic timber in elaborate oriental design peeps tantalizingly into view. The bridge is actually a faithful interpretation of the famous 'Willow Pattern' scene, so beautifully depicted on china crockery. Closer inspection reveals that the rockery is actually far more complex that it first appears. In the centre of the boulder strewn incline which faces the canal is an opening or tunnel entrance. This entrance way, situated halfway up the 'rock face' is the cleverly disguised access to Ramsdell Halls ice house. The ice house, (which is now the private property of the Coach House) is surely one of the most cunningly concealed examples of this vital addition to any 'great house'.

The ice house made possible the underground storage of ice for use in just the same ways as we use ice and our electrical refrigerators today. Stored in this manner, underground and in between layers of straw, the ice would keep for up to eighteen months. Another remarkable example of an ice house will be found at Great Moreton Hall where the ice house is concealed by an ornate Gothic tower. The tunnel entrance here at Ramsdell is surmounted by a stone statuette of great antiquity. The whole scene is enhanced by the dark limpid pool which lies at the bottom of the rock face.

Increasingly, the far bank is lined by a belt of mature trees. Beyond the Alders, Sycamores and Hollies, sweeping lawns lead up towards the Coach House, and to Old House Green. This group of properties, i.e. the Coach House, Old House Green and Ramsdell occupy a site of considerable antiquity. When the Moreton family ceased to reside at Little Moreton Hall and the house became a tenanted property, sometime around 1650 - 1660, the family administered their Cheshire holding via a bailiff who resided at and farmed Old House Green Farm. The canal's far bank is temporarily occupied by a dense stand of shrub like Holly trees which abruptly come to an end to reveal a vast lawn 6, 7 or maybe even 8 acres in extent which stretches up to Ramsdell Hall.

Of all of the great houses whose estates were intersected by or merely touched by the coming of the Macclesfield Canal, none was so intimately violated as Ramsdell where the canal cuts directly through the front garden! The owning family, the Chaddock-Lowndes, were cotton and pottery magnates. As a consequence, they were abundantly aware of the advantages of being able to rely upon the canal as a mode of commercial transport and so had little objection to it passing along the bottom of their lawn. On a more general note, the family were skilfully accomplished at influencing the siting of principal trade routes. Their master stroke was in getting Mow Cop station, on the Stoke - Manchester railway sited almost directly opposite the Hall's front gates.

As a station, Mow Cop stood 600 feet below and almost a mile distant from the village of that name yet, just 300 yards from Ramsdell. It opened to passengers and goods traffic on 9 October 1848 and closed on 7 October 1964. The station was originally situated to accommodate the family at Ramsdell just as the halt at Ackers Crossing had been purely for the benefit of the Ackers family. The station eventually went on to serve a much wider cross section of the population. Local farmers ran a horse drawn service to the station for milk which was transported in bulk to dairies in both Manchester and in the Staffordshire Potteries: a special train known as the Milk Train left at 8.35 a.m. each morning. Local children travelling to high schools and grammar schools in Macclesfield boarded the Mow Cop train until this type of education became available in the Congleton area. Mow Cop villagers who worked in shirt and fustian mills in Congleton used the train prior to the introduction of an inexpensive bus service.

From the canal's immaculately manicured far bank this massive lawn sweeps up to the magnificent three storey Queen Anne house. The sudden appearance of this superb brick house amid lush green oceans of rolling turf comes as a delight and an inspiration to those who are familiar with it, but more of shock to the unsuspecting. The three storey main block of the house is flanked on either side by a single storey projecting wing. Each of these is crowned by a glazed, lead roofed cupola which in turn is topped by a tall iron finial. These projecting wings - identical in every way and perfectly symmetrical - were originally coach houses with a hayloft in the roof space. The present house was built in the early seventeenth century but large sections of timber frame and wattle and daub which have survived in some of the courtyard buildings hark back to a much older house on the site. As the canal continues to skirt Ramsdell's lawn, the towpath remains bordered by the iron railings set into the retaining stone wall. The splendid view of Ramsdell is breathtaking. The huge lawn runs so perfectly up to the trim gardens which lie close to the house that the whole vista is unforgettable.

The waterway begins to curve gently to the left. The ground which falls so steeply away to the west from the embankment does so towards a large farmstead. This is Low Farm and, from the elevated position of the canal, it certainly appears to be appropriately named. Low Farm was formerly owned by the Chaddock Lowndes family of Ramsdell but it was subsequently sold to tenant farmers when the family left the area. On the continuing curve, the waterway opens out into a wide bay of considerable area. This extensive reed filled basin was formerly where the family of the Hall built an ornate boathouse. Not only did they tolerate the canal's existence at the bottom of their garden, they even made use of it for their own pleasure. Whereas the majority of wide bays or winding holes along the waterway were specifically designed to facilitate the turning of the working narrow boats, this one was just the opposite, a private boating lake with access to the main waterway. As with so many of the wide areas, the Ramsdell basin is a fine venue from the point of view of the lone, pleasure angler. Being deeper than usual and largely filled with a variety of aquatic vegetation and rarely if ever entered by boats, it represents a wonderful haven for fish and fisherman alike. The angler needs to cast across the normal canal's width and across the boat channel up to the jungle of weed. His efforts will occasionally be rewarded with an encounter with the canal's elusive Tench population.

TENCH

    The Tench is a splendid fish, guaranteed to thrill and excite even the most seasoned of anglers. A strong and sturdy, muscular fish, its fight when hooked is legendary. What sets it apart, visually, from the more common Roach and Bream is that its scales are minute and deeply rooted in the flesh and invariably hidden under a layer of protective mucous. Initially, it appears to be scaleless and very smooth and slippery to the touch. The overall colouration is another factor which sets it apart from its silvery kin. Green is the predominant colour, shading to a brownish hue on the back but lightening to a golden sheen on the sides and the belly is creamy yellow.

    The Tench is a native of shallow lakes, ponds and slow flowing rivers but, like the Bream, has been stocked in large numbers into the canal over many years to improve sport. Whatever type of water it inhabits, the Tench is magnetically attracted to weed beds where it spends its life feeding on or near to the bottom. Consequently, the weedy basin at Ramsdell is an obvious 'holding area' for the canal's Tench. Several thousand Tench formed part of the previously described restocking operation which was carried out in 1989 following the disastrous pollution at Hightown, Congleton two years previously. Apart from the skulking Tench with his tiny blood red eye, the basin fairly teems with small Roach which constantly dimple the normally placid surface.

To the east of this vast sheet of water, Ramsdell Hall is briefly hidden from view by tall Alders which line the edge of the sedge filled bay. The canal gradually narrows back down to its customary width The far bank is now mass planted with Rhododendrons, Birch trees and tall, dark Pines as the great lawn gives way to ornamental woodland and shrubbery. Beyond the Rhododendron shrubbery, the original main driveway serving Ramsdell runs parallel to the waterway, if well below its level. The single carriageway drive sweeps around the edge of the great lawn to deliver the visitor to the Halls private south front. Ramsdell's main entrance, flanked by tall stone gate pillars which are topped by ornately carved stone Griffins and standing almost directly opposite to the now removed Mow Cop station, superceded this original and less than direct route.

To the right of the towpath, mixed woodland of Beech, Lime, Horse Chestnut and Oak stretches away westward concealing the view of Low Farm. Across the canal, Ramsdell Hall's lodge stands beside the former main drive which snakes away eastward towards Station Road, flanked on either side by avenues of Horse Chestnut trees. The lodge is a delightful building. It is separated from the water's edge by the embankment and the modest width of the old drive. Largely rebuilt this century, the house is tightly surrounded by colourful flower borders and the paddock or croft which lies between it and Station Road is bordered by the thick belt of woodland which screens the Hall. To the west, the embanked valley is now at its deepest and the stream which is culverted beneath the canal comes into view. This water course unlike all of its predecessors, is artificial in its origins. The stream is the end product of the various water features in Ramsdell's gardens, the excess water from several pools and ponds. From the canal's embankment, it flows away westwards, picking up tiny natural streams as it goes. It eventually flows into the expansive Rode Pool, a fine sheet of water which is well in excess of thirty acres in area and overlooked by Rode Hall, the ancestral seat of the Rode's and Wilbraham's of Rode.

The canal narrows to one boat's width to pass through the mill grit foundations of the long removed Lowndes swing bridge. On the far bank, an old set of stop planks overlook the point where the canal could be stopped off between the stone foundations of the swing bridge. Beyond the stout pathside hedgerow, Low Farm has disappeared from view and the ground drops away, uninterrupted into Odd Rode. In the most distant east, "The Old Man of Mow" has disappeared from view as the canal has continued to travel alongside the hill. Its place, as a landmark has been taken by Mow Cop's most famous feature - the wrongly named "Mow Cop Castle". Just 240 yards south of The Old Man, the ruinous folly stands on a singularly isolated and rugged outcrop. This is the 'landmark' which will accompany the towpath traveller for the remainder of our journey.

It has been known by generations as Mow Cop Castle but is accepted to have been built as a 'mock ruin'. The favourite theory is that it was built in 1754 by Squire Randel Wilbraham of Rode Hall as an ornamental finial to improve the view of the skyline of Mow Cop as seen from Rode Hall. Conflicting stories tell of the castle being built during the eleventh century by either Godwin (Earl of Wessex) or Godric, Lord of the Manor of Rode at that time. One thing which is certain is that a surviving document dated 1320 grants custom and licence to Thomas de Rode to erect a beacon on Molehill (Mow Cop). From this it is likely that Wilbraham's folly replaced a much earlier beacon tower which had been built and rebuilt over the centuries. The folly as it appears today contains no woodwork at all and has no roof. In consists of a circular tower, a little over 32 feet high and is joined on the south side by a wall which is not unlike a buttress. The circular tower has windows which are no more than holes in the walls. It is likely that the tower was once lived in by a caretaker as there was once a concave lead roof, an upper floor, a staircase and a fireplace serving both floors. Like the nearby "Old Man of Mow", the Castle is now owned by the National Trust. People flock to this unlikely edifice in great numbers to survey the seven surrounding counties from

MOW COP CASTLE

the lofty perch on the rocky outcrop.

Beside the towpath, the next milestone nestles against the hedgerow. The tall original stone reads, "From Hall Green —— Miles". The figure which has been removed should read 1 1/4. The opposite face reads quite clearly, "From Marple 25 Miles". No sooner has the milestone been passed by than the waterway begins to open right out into Kent Green Marina. The marina is small when compared to Poynton, Bollington or Macclesfield but is home to the "Heritage" fleet of hire vessels which are unmistakeable in their smart blue and white livery.

A fairly extensive mooring area lies between the main waterway and Station Road, a proportion of which is under cover. The marina has been much refurbished and revamped in recent years and anything which it may lack in size is more than compensated for in the fact that it is by far the smartest and most 'up-market' of all the marinas. Leaving the actual boatyard areas behind, the long building in modern brick which lies along the canal's far bank is the well equipped shop.

Beyond Kent Green Marina, the towpath is accompanied by an excessively wide sedge margin which has a seriously narrowing effect upon the waterway as a whole. It is in situations such as here where a sedge bed accompanies an unlined bank that the unsuspecting towpath traveller may have a close encounter with one of the canal's less than savoury inhabitants.

In the wake of a prolonged period of heavy summer rain, when the lush towpath side vegetation is sodden and the ground is equally wet, the black or brown slugs which are 'brought out' by the wet and the warmth suddenly seems to appear in profusion. On closer inspection, the multitude of slugs, may in fact, turn out to be leeches. The humble Leech is very common in most freshwater habitats but ranks alongside the snake and the spider in its ability to make the skin crawl. The leech is held in total abhorrence by most people, presumably for the fact that the majority are blood suckers, attacking fish, frogs, snails and insect larvae. Leeches are not normally active creatures, usually being found in the bottom mud or attached to submerged plants. Ordinarily, they move about by means of their suckers, one at either end of the body. First of all, the body is stretched out, often to a great length, and waved around until a suitable point of attachment is found for the front sucker. The rear sucker is then detached and the body is contracted to secure a hold near to the front one and so the process continues. Some leeches can, however swim with graceful undulations of the body. Why then the mass migration out of the canal, by means of the partly submerged sedges, when all of those which are out of the water are bound to perish as they are unable to breath atmospheric air and rapidly dry up?

The author has witnessed several of these mass suicides over the years where the leeches have been so numerous as to cover the towpath. Exactly which type of leech these are is a matter of some debate. There are eleven species of freshwater leech in the British Isles, varying in length, when at rest, from less than half an inch to as much as three or four inches. When extended they may be two or three times these sizes. The colours vary a great deal, not only between the various species but even in the same individual. The only foolproof means of identification is by counting the number and the arrangement of the eyes, but there again, not everyone would wish to get that close!

The canal's far bank is now occupied by a varied selection of private houses which cluster around the junction of Station Road and Spring Bank. Some way prior to the next bridge, No. 87 the houses and bungalows come to an end and are replaced by a long brick building which lies parallel to the waterway. Although considerably extended in recent years, the visually older central section of this building was originally a warehouse which once formed part of a large coal wharf built by the owners of Ramsdell Hall.

This busy wharf was larger than many of its contemporaries along the canal with a full sized crane loading the narrow boats. The original buildings included a goods storage warehouse and a joiners shop which served the estate. This thriving wharf was in operation right through to the late 1880's despite the Macclesfield Canal's general decline as a trade route. The principal cargo to be handled here was coal. The coal was mined at the prolific Tower Hill colliery which lies on the eastern side of Mow Cop over the county border in Staffordshire. This abundant supply of coal competed with the Poynton and Adlington coal in supplying the mills of Congleton, Macclesfield and Bollington. To ensure the speedy delivery of the coal from the colliery to the canal, a tunnel was constructed beneath this southern end of Mow Cop, terminating at Tunnel End Farm. Between Tunnel End and the wharf, a 'brake' was constructed. This consisted of a double or twin track whereby the downhill track carried the loaded carts to the wharf while the uphill track returned the empty ones. Situated at the top of the brake was a large wheel which was, in itself, controlled by a brake to which the waggons were attached. This ingenious method meant that the weight of the laden waggons travelling downhill pulled the empty ones back up the steep incline to the colliery.

Beyond the pathside hedgerow, an unsurfaced roadway serves a group of detached properties which lie down to the west. An indication as to how industrious the wharf originally was can be gauged by the fact that immediately prior to the bridge, both the towpath bank and the far bank are lined by stones and become a loading jetty or quay. On the final approach, Station Road Bridge proves to be a very fine skew bridge in its design. Station Road crosses the canal at a bizarre angle and consequently the bridge is twisted and contorted at a fantastic angle. It is built from big, roughly finished blocks unlike the precision finished stones of Bollington, Hurdsfield and Macclesfield. The fact that the stone of its inner arch has not weathered as well as usual makes the bridge all the more dramatic. Emerging from bridge No. 87, the scene is rather more 'quiet' and tranquil after the grandeur of Ramsdell Hall, the bustle of the marina and the industry of the old wharf which is now a thriving plumbers yard.

During a summers journey along the canal, several species of large Hawker Dragonflys will be encountered. The Hawker Dragonfly is the ultimate insect predator. Apart from their sheer size, the likes of the Emperor, the Blue Hawker and the Common Hawker Dragonfly are unmistakable for their habit of perpetually patrolling or "hawking" a fairly compact and well defined length of canal or "beat". This beat need not necessarily be a length of canal, it may be a section of towpath for this great insect is actually combing a predetermined area in a totally methodical fashion. It will intercept and devour any winged insect which is luckless enough to stray into its airspace. With the precision of a military aircraft, the Emperor Dragonfly quarters its beat on transparent wings which can span 4 1/2 inches. When this wing span is considered along with the overall body length (which may exceed 5 1/4 inches) a picture emerges of an insect which is considerably larger than many of our smallest birds. Unlike the hesitant, butterfly like flight of the Damselfly, the Hawker can achieve speeds of 18 miles per hour on wings that can actually be heard before the insect is seen. The whirring of the wings, the huge compound eyes and the vivid body colours of brilliant metallic greens and blues combine to make the dragonfly a spectacular and awesome flying machine.

To the east, a pasture field rises directly from the water's edge and slopes gently up to the mainline railway which has never been too far distant since leaving Macclesfield. The track runs directly parallel to the canal and beyond the village of Mount Pleasant seems to cling to the end of Mow Cop. Mount Pleasant is just one of four or five villages or separate areas of settlement on Mow Cop. Mount Pleasant, Rookery and Mow Cop are sizeable settlements in their own right while Bank, Dales Green and the larger Harrishead are all individual entities which together represent the colonization of Mow Cop. From this particular angle, it is Mount Pleasant and The Bank which dominate the view. Mow Cop castle can now be seen in all its glory . There can be no finer view of the folly than from right here. From Kent Green, the view is absolutely square on accentuating the isolated position and revealing the tower and the adjoining buttress wall to perfection.

Beyond a neat pathside hedgerow, a small paddock of almost perfect triangular shape provides seasonal grazing for several ponies. The triangle is formed by the canal hedgerow, Station Road hedgerow and by an extensive old orchard which runs between two public houses. Incredible as it may seem, the two inns are actually next door to one another. Just as Mount Pleasant is but one small part of Mow Cop, Kent Green is one component part of the much larger Scholar Green. For the record, there are as many if not more component parts to Scholar Green than to Mow Cop. Amazingly, the tiny Kent Green alone has three pubs! The one which flanks Station Road and is clearly visible across the paddock is the Rising Sun; a fairly typical village pub offering good ale and excellent bar food. The long overgrown orchard belongs to its neighbour, the canal-side Bird in Hand.

As Station Road begins to disappear from view behind, the wide towpath is, during May, June and July, enriched by the presence of one of the Macclesfield Canal's commonest of flowers. Like the Lady's Smock of spring and the Dandelion of early summer, the Bugle is so prolific among the summer grasses to rarely warrant a second glance. Unlike the Dandelion however, the Bugle is not one of the instantly recognizable plants. One of the many blue flowers of summer grassland, Bugle bears its small spikes of flowers on short, stiff stems with great dignity. Because it spreads easily by means of long runners, it often forms large patches.

Up ahead, the waterway narrows drastically to pass through bridge No. 88, the Bird in Hand swing bridge. The paddock comes to an end beyond the pathside Hawthorn and is replaced by the long overgrown orchard. Arriving at the Bird in Hand swing bridge, it is found to be permanently swung open and in a state of considerable dilapidation. The old bridge lies upon its gritstone foundations on the far bank looking very sad and forlorn. Equally sad and forlorn is the canal-side inn which was once an integral part of the waterway. The canal-side pubs which were adopted by the working bargee families as social centres where they were able to meet with their own kind to swap gossip and news. The men folk could be forgiven for wishing to spend a few precious hours in the company of other men as a temporary escape from the claustrophobic nine foot by seven foot living quarters in which the entire family ate, slept and lived. The Bird in Hand represented a complete canal pub, providing not only an ale house but also an on-site smithy and stables. In fact, the pub was even called 'The Navigation Arms' prior to acquiring the Bird in Hand name.

The new name was the only modern attribute which it did acquire. The inn became a victim of its own circumstances - a hostelry in a time warp. It had remained in the same family ownership right through from the heady day of the canal's industrial life, through the onset of the decline in the 1920's when the canal passed into the hands of the London and North Eastern Railway and to the British Transport Commission in 1948. All of this without any modernisation or improvement to help carry it forward into the new era of canal use. The Bird in Hand became a novelty or even an oddity. The ale was transported up a steep flight of cellar steps in an enameled jug right up to the eventual closure in 1990. The inn stubbornly continued to survive by catering almost exclusively for business which arrived via the canal - just as it always had. It was never licensed to sell spirits so, as there was no bar as such, wines, sherries, ports and cordials were dispensed from a sideboard in the licensees living room. To state that the furnishings were sparse would be a massive overstatement, the only comfort available in the one room which was normally in use was a small open fire.

Any customer enquiring about the possibility of acquiring food was directed to the nearby fish and chip shop. These facts need recording as so few places as unique as this have survived into the twentieth century. With the passing of the landlady in 1990, this most atmospheric of canal side hostelries closed its doors for all time. It had shunned the twentieth century but, in the end, the twentieth century had the upper hand. It now stands beside the neglected swing bridge, boarded up and waiting. Its structural decline in the twelve or so months which have elapsed so far since its closure has been rapid and total. It is dying.

Beside the Bird In Hand, the uneven and unsurfaced Foundry Lane runs directly from the towpath, at the site of the swing bridge down, to Cinderhill Lane. Beyond the swing bridge, modern housing crowds up to the pathside Hawthorn hedgerow as the tiny Kent Green has expanded within the last two years. The canal and wide grassy towpath begin to curve quite sharply to the right, the latter needing to be sheet metal lined as the petite dwellings to the west lie noticeably below canal level. The modern houses are replaced by more mature properties which lie even further below the level of the water. As if to compensate for its momentary deviation, the waterway now begins to curve to the left and, as it does, the next bridge, No. 89 comes into view ahead.

A sedge bed of considerable width accompanies the towpath towards Kent Green Wharf or Cinderhill Lane Bridge. The neat pathside Hawthorn is replaced by a solid fence of rugged concrete construction which screens a busy plant hire yard from view along with the general view to the west. Upon entering Kent Green, the rolling, panoramic views down to the west which have typified the twenty five and a half miles or so of our journey from Marple junction thus far are a thing of the past. The majority of the closing stages pass through a suburban situation where a distant view plays no part. A jungle of raspberry canes inhabit the area between the towpath and the solid fence which tends to soften and, in places, almost hide the prefabricated boundary. The raspberries are replaced by an equally thick belt of Blackcurrant bushes which, along with untidy Elder scrub forms a considerable thicket between the towpath and the fence.

The plant hire yard with its screening fence come to an end providing a view of the cottages which lie alongside Cinderhill Lane. Centuries ago, when Scholar Green was a small community surrounded by outlying settlements or hamlets, Cinderhill ranked alongside Old House Green and Kent Green as an individual settlement before being engulfed by Kent Green. Cinderhill Lane can be seen running parallel to the canal but inching nearer and nearer to it all the time. As bridge No. 89 draws nearer, the lane arrives directly alongside the towpath. Before the canal begins to narrow to pass beneath the bridge, the waterway briefly opens out at the site of another wharf.. The far bank becomes lined by huge blocks of gritstone. Whereas the previous wharf was the eventual destination for coal from the Tower Hill Colliery, Cinderhill wharf was the ultimate destination for coal from the Hall O'Lea colliery which lay up to the east between The Rookery and Little Moss.

Prior to the advent of coal mining on the site, Hall O' Lea was the site of an ancient moated manor house. The moat at Hall O' Lea survived until quite recently despite the manor house itself being long demolished. Hall O' Lea Colliery represents just one of nearly ten disused shafts which riddle the small area between Scholar Green and The Bank. The majority of this coal was loaded here at Cinderhill Wharf. Looking to the distant east, Mow Cop's folly towers above

Mount Pleasant village on its rocky bluff. Slightly north of "The Castle", the "Old Man" comes back into view, peering over the upper edge of Quarry Wood. Beyond the stone lining of the bank, the ground is of an extremely undulating and impoverished nature. In places, the thin turf has broken through to reveal not soil but coal dust.

Although it formerly served as a busy wharf, Cinderhill or Kent Green Wharf bridge carries no road or trackway, simply a footpath which leads up through Sludge Wood to Mount Pleasant. The bridge has been partially rebuilt at some point. The arch itself, beyond the keystone and up to the string course is the original gritstone. The courses above the string course are of more recent date and are built from sandstone. The more recent top is surmounted by the original mill grit coping.

Passing through bridge No. 89, the canal widens out to proceed via a shallow cutting. A rough bank which is covered by brambles and squat Oak trees has risen up beside the towpath to obscure the view to the west. Across the canal, a tall tree-lined bank rises away from the unlined margin, completing the effect of the cutting. The ground which falls westwards from the towpath does so into a grassy valley which, in turn, rises up to the back gardens of houses which stand beside Cinderhill Lane. The waterway which is culverted beneath the canal rises in Sludge Wood, up to the east and runs through Scholar Green to join the flow of water towards Rode Pool.

Beyond the high, if brief embankment, the waterway begins to curve slightly to the left. No sooner is the embankment crossed than the waterway narrows right down to a single boat's width to pass through bridge No. 90, the removed Cinderhill swing bridge. The mill grit foundations relentlessly squeeze the canal down to a sliver of its former width. Cinderhill swing bridge is overlooked by a short terrace of three delightful whitewashed canal-side cottages. The tiny front gardens reach the towpath at neat wooden fences. Totally cut off from any roadway, the three dwellings are served by a narrow footpath which plunges steeply down the embankment, crosses the stream and climbs equally steeply up to Cinderhill Lane.. The ' traffic 'which passes almost within touching distance of the living room windows of these cottages is virtually silent in passage and leisurely in pace. The ground which surrounds the mill stone foundations on either bank is kept immaculately tidy and is owned by the cottages. The strip of ground on the far bank between the canal and hedgerow is kept beautifully mowed and is occupied by several sheds and stacks of logs for winter fuel. An improvised swing bridge facilitates access to either bank - a stout plank fixed to the 'swivel' or swing mechanism of the original structure.

The canal rapidly attains its normal width beyond the swing bridge site. The far bank sports poultry sheds and a magnificent clump of ornamental pampas grass which towers above the waterway, its flamboyant ostrich-plume flower heads upstaging the natural heads of the waterside Rushes and Sedges. The modern building which lies down to the west beyond the croft is Scholar Green primary school. Across to the east, the scene is dominated by a magnificent view of "Mow Cop Castle" silhouetted against the sky. Beyond the brief embankment of the stream valley, the canal visibly enters a cutting. The dilapidated remains of a drain-off paddle is situated in the pathside hedgerow as the cutting is entered. The paddle formerly discharged its water into a typical stone built channel which eventually unites with the natural watercourse nearby.

Across to the east, the main line railway is still clearly visible just one field away. A towering hedgerow of Hawthorn and Elder partly conceals the view to the west of extensive playing fields which serve Scholar Green School. With a total lack of view to either side, the next bridge, which lies directly ahead, completely monopolizes the attention and initially, appears to be quite out of context. It is a huge affair, a towering arch, not unlike No. 74 which carried Morley Drive across the canal at Hightown, Congleton. On closer inspection, bridge No. 91, Fall Bridge proves to be a virtual carbon copy of the Morley Drive bridge. The wide, shady waterway is heavily overhung from the far bank by Hawthorn and Ash trees which stoop to touch the water. The towering bank beside the towpath which is surmounted by the mountainous hedgerow is an impenetrable jungle of brambles.

Thirty dangerously uneven stone steps climb steeply up the side of the bridge, linking the towpath with the bridge top. Like Morley Drive Bridge, the centre of the arch of Fall Bridge, marked by the keystone is some twenty feet above the water. When the steep steps are climbed, it comes as some surprise to discover that the bridge carries nothing of any consequence, simply an unmade track, a public footpath which runs from Scholar Green across the canal and railway and up to either Sludge Wood or Hall O' Lea. To add to the excessive height of the bridge, its overall width is more than generous. The turf-covered track which passes over is in excess of 24 feet in width. Leaving the more than substantial bridge No. 91 behind, an exceptionally straight length of canal stretches away towards the next bridge which also lies within the same deep cutting. It is only upon gazing up at the height of the banks which tower to the left and right of the canal that some hint is gained as to why the bridge was built to such a height. In a cutting as deep as this, a bridge of normal proportions would be lost without trace. The canal is now passing through Little Moss, one more component part of the larger Scholar Green.

The cottages and smallholdings which lie beyond the canal's high bank are situated along side a lane which shares the name Little Moss with the isolated community that depends upon it as a link with the outside world. The cutting becomes somewhat shallower as bridge No. 92 is approached but never sufficiently to provide an unimpeded view to either east or west. Due to the shallowing of the cutting, the cottages on the far bank seem to reach closer to the canal-side and their gardens begin to extend down to the water's edge. In time honoured tradition, terraced gardens begin to arrive at improvised landing stages and mooring jetties.

As the waterway begins to narrow to arrive at bridge No. 92, the wide and beautifully surfaced towpath splits. One half becomes a long, shallow ramp of uneven stone cobbled setts which leads up to the bridge top. The other half continues graveled to arrive at the bridge which, like the hamlet and the lane, is also known as Little Moss. Compared to the preceding bridge, No. 92 seems squat and diminutive. In actual fact, No. 92 - Little Moss is a reasonably sturdy bridge which happens to have a rather low arch. It is another example, like No. 89 at Cinderhill Lane, which has obviously been altered over the years. Above the keystone of the low arch, three or four courses of masonry extend up to the string course. Above that, a further nine courses have been added in new stone and the whole thing is topped off by what is obviously the original coping. The single carriageway Little Moss (the lane) is transported over Little Moss (the bridge) to link the two halves of Little Moss (the hamlet) which is dissected by the canal!

For those of us who have spent the last 26 or so miles travelling determinedly southwards from Marple, Little Moss Bridge is the last stone bridge to span the Macclesfield Canal proper. If the cobbled ramp is climbed from the towpath, a wooden gatepost will be encountered at the bridge top from which an iron gate was originally hung. It is on this post that a fragment of history has survived, more by sheer good luck than by any act of intentional conservation. An inconspicuous metal plate is fixed to the post and it was the wording on this plate which was supposed to be read and heeded by anyone wishing to gain access to the towpath from Little Moss. The wording, almost unreadable due to corrosion, says "right of way act 1832, private property". This would indicate that at the time, the towpath which today we take so much for granted was actually private property.

The canal begins to curve quite sharply to the right ahead. The unlined margins are colonised by well established clumps of Great Water Dock. As a native semi-aquatic plant, the Great Water Dock must surely take the prize for having the largest leaves in terms of surface area. Each of the elongated dock shaped leaves are well in excess of 2 feet in length. It would be grossly inaccurate to classify Great Water Dock as common but it will certainly be encountered all along the Macclesfield Canal. Its massive leaves are unmistakeable during spring, summer and autumn but its position can be pin-pointed even in the depths of winter as its long seeding flower spike tends to survive the winter in a dried out, almost petrified form.

Goat or Pussy Willows (Salix Caprea) and Grey Willows or Grey Sallows (Salix Cinerea) overhang the water from the far bank on the continuing curve. The next milestone appears at the foot of the grass bank beside the towpath. Not only is this the next - it is also the last of the stones. Whereas the first to be encountered at bridge No. 1 at Marple was a new stone, it is somehow fitting to find that this is a tall original stone which reads "From Marple 26 Miles". The reverse side however has been defaced and has never been restored, which is a pity as it now reads "From Hall Green ------- Miles". The foregoing information is somewhat disturbing as the view ahead is that of Hall Green itself.! The deleted numeral can only have been the odd 1/4 mile which has been in evidence all along the journey. Looking ahead, with what is technically the end of the Macclesfield Canal firmley in sight, it must be said that the terminus hardly seems to be 1/4 mile distant.

The straight length of waterway which lies ahead is overlooked from the far bank by a pretty, whitewashed cottage. The cottage faces the canal instead of backing onto it as is normally the case with dwellings which are not situated on the towpath bank. The cottage stands alongside bridge No. 93, a fine, metal footbridge which carries a public footpath and represents the only link with the outside world for the house which would otherwise be marooned on the far bank. . The pedestrian bridge consists of a sturdy support of mill grit on either bank between which an all metal bridge of girder construction is slung. The 'lattice' style panels which form a safety enclosure between the footway and the handrail gives the bridge as a whole, a somewhat ornate and highly pleasing appearance.

As the wide gravel towpath draws near to the bridge, mooring rings are spaced at regular intervals. Garden shrubs overhang the water from the cultivated plot which separates the canal side cottage from the water's edge. During April, masses of golden Forsythia spills outwards over the water followed by the antler-like branches of the exotic Stag's Horn Sumach. A concrete ramp leads from the towpath up to the narrow footpath which leads to Little Moss Lane. The towpath bank becomes stone lined as it passes beneath the 93rd and last bridge to have been built by the Macclesfield Canal Company to span their waterway.

Beyond the bridge, the canal's far bank becomes an overflow sill which extends for 65 feet from bridge No. 93 to the top gate of the Stop Lock. The excess water from the Macclesfield Canal spills over the sill and enters a culverted tunnel which runs underground alongside the stone lined chamber of the Stop Lock. The canal narrows right down between the banks which are formed from huge blocks of mill grit to arrive at the top gates of the Hall Green Stop Lock ,marking the official terminus of the waterway which has covered 26 1/4 miles to arrive at this less than spectacular destination.

CHAPTER ELEVEN

HALL GREEN TO KIDSGROVE

In 1827, the Trent and Mersey Amendment Act empowered the Trent and Mersey Canal Company to construct and maintain a length of canal running from a junction with the Trent and Mersey Canal at Hardingswood to Hall Green. As a waterway, the Trent and Mersey's only shortcoming was that it failed to reach Manchester. The Macclesfield Canal achieved the Manchester connection - if by a somewhat indirect means, but was denied the final glory (by a little over a mile) of forming the complete link at Kidsgrove. The bitter rivalry which existed between the canal companies was taken to such extreme lengths that today they seem ludicrous.

It almost seems sad and anticlimatic that the wonderfully engineered waterway which we have followed diligently for 26 1/4 miles should have to end here, having fallen short of its objective by so trifling a distance. The greater pity (and inconvenience) was that its boat traffic was forced to negotiate this tedious stop lock.

The Hall Green Lock was specifically constructed to prevent any water from the Trent and Mersey being stolen by the Macclesfield. The lock adjusts the water level by just one foot and still performs its original task in preventing any of the Trent and Mersey summit water from entering the Macclesfield Canal. In complete contrast, the overflow weir which comprised the Macclesfield's far bank between the foot bridge and the lock, delivers copious quantities of water, gathered from Sutton and Bosley directly into the Trent and Mersey. The previously mentioned 1827 amendment act ensured that the Trent and Mersey Company had secured the right to receive all of this water which flowed down the Macclesfield Canal.

The drama continued with each canal company installing a lock within the confines of the unusually lengthy chamber, thus enabling both companies to collect a toll fee - to the doubtless annoyance of the working barges. The top lock which survives today to enable the twelve inch adjustment in level to be made is the Macclesfield one. Recesses further down the one hundred or so yards of chamber clearly demonstrate where the second of the two locks was originally situated. Along with the two locks, one owned by each company, two cottages overlook the lock chamber, one built by each rival.

The first of the two was stone built by the Macclesfield Canal Company and originally incorporated stables and represented the toll office for this extreme southern end of the waterway. The brick built cottage directly alongside it fulfilled exactly the same role for the Trent and Mersey Canal Company. Today, the cottages face directly onto the towpath which, alongside the lock, is stone cobbled. The total lack of any front garden means that the front doors almost open into the lock chamber and it is necessary to dodge around the balance beams of the lock gates to walk the length of the cobbled towpath. The length of water which lies within the chamber beyond the double top gates is technically part of the Macclesfield Canal but, beyond the single bottom gate, and one foot lower, is the onset of the Trent and Mersey branch canal.

Having passed through the 100 yards of stone lined chamber, the waterway opens out in width and the stone sett towpath becomes a more conventional gravel surface. The next bridge, which is No. 94 and not No. 1, is clearly visible ahead along a continuing cutting. The housing which lies just out of sight above the high pathside bank faces out onto the incredibly busy A34 which transports a colossal volume of traffic between Birmingham and Manchester or, on a more local level, Newcastle Under Lyne in Staffordshire and Congleton.

The drone of the traffic which invades the air betrays the presence of this major arterial trunk route. The A34 cuts relentlessly through Scholar Green, serving, in a small way to isolate Hall Green and Little Moss. At the point where Little Moss, (the lane) joins the A34, just out of sight to the east, stands "the Bleeding Wolf" public house. This large building is of great interest, not only for its extraordinary size, unusual architecture and the fact that it is thatched (definitely not a roofing material which is representative of Cheshire) but also in the way that its odd name recalls a local legend. The curious name is supposedly medieval in origin.

The legend tells that King John was hunting in this vicinity when much of medieval Cheshire was covered by the great forest of Macclesfield. He somehow became separated from his party and was attacked and wounded by a wolf. A passing peasant was alerted by the commotion and was able to drive the wolf away by wounding it. The bleeding wolf limped away into the forest and the grateful monarch showed his appreciation by granting the peasant as much land as he was capable of walking around in a stipulated time. The peasant and his family established their home just over the modern day parochial boundary in the parish of Church Lawton and assumed the family name of Lawton.

The original manor house at Lawton amid an extensive holding of ground has been the subject of much rebuilding over the centuries. In years gone by, the main entrance to Lawton Hall was in the vicinity of the Bleeding Wolf Inn so it would be logical to assume that Hall Green could originally have been a settlement which sprang up around the manor house. Like Great Moreton Hall and Buglawton Hall, the present Lawton Hall has operated as an educational establishment for many decades but currently stands empty and in a state of dilapidation after unsuccessfully attempting to follow Great Moreton Hall and Sutton Hall into the realms of prestigious country house hotel. The grounds at Lawton contain what must rank as the most curious of inscriptions to be found on a headstone, - "On the death of Bull Finch that sang God Save the Queen when bidden to do so"!

As the canal continues along its deep cutting, the approaching bridge, No. 94 can be seen to be completely different in architectural style to the typical Macclesfield Canal bridge. Looking ahead, the waterway hardly narrows to pass beneath the yawning arch. Not only does the towpath enjoy a greatly improved surface since leaving Hall Green stop lock but it is also noticeably higher in relation to the surface of the water. The high bank to the east of the canal is clothed with mature Birch and Alder which are, in early spring, underplanted with dense blankets of Lesser Celandine. One of the first wild flowers to appear in a mild spring, each of the solitary yellow flowers has up to twelve petals. William Wordsworth wrote a poem which paid tribute to the beautiful buttercup yellow flowers which "shine bright as the sun himself."

Drawing nearer to bridge No. 94, it becomes clear that it is not just the style which has altered but the fabric is constructed from a completely different material. The Trent and Mersey Canal Company chose blue brick as their basic bridge building material. Compared with the Macclesfield's tasteful use of mill stone, brick falls well short of being the ideal commodity from the aesthetic point of view. The bridge wears its British Waterways blue and yellow number plate, No. 94, with pride, above its exceptionally high arch. No. 94 or Moss Lane Bridge carries the lane of that name from its junction with the A34, immediately to the east, high over the canal and eastwards to Hall O'Lea and eventually up to The Rookery and Dales Green via "The Hollows". Beyond the spacious arch, a steep flight of concrete steps lead up from the towpath to Moss Lane.

Looking back through the huge arch of the bridge, the stop lock and the attendant cottages are still clearly visible as is the preceding foot bridge. The wide, placid waterway, overhung by large trees from the far bank would seem to be a million miles away from the buzzing highway which fills the air with the roar of traffic. Thick beds of Stinging Nettles, Garlic Mustard and Dogs Mercury throng with insects whose droning competes with that of the relentless traffic. Spirea and Damson bushes have made good their escape from the restrictions of the gardens above and grow rampant beside the towpath.

An area is reached where the householders have brought the pathside bank and also the towpath itself into the realms of the garden landscape. From the backs of the gardens the ground right up to the water's edge is kept immaculately mowed to the extent that it resembles a sweeping green baize. As the continuing cutting begins to shallow out, the woodland drops away from the far bank and is replaced by a lush grass field which stretches away eastwards. The luxurious turf towpath rivals the centre court at Wimbledon when compared with the usual unkempt jungle of herbage.

As the wide waterway sweeps around its curve, the next bridge comes into view. Even from this distance, it is clear that the bridges which span the branch canal not only lack the style of Macclesfield Canal but also its wonderful continuity. Bridge No. 95 bares not the slightest resemblance to the preceding No. 94 in either architectural style or in size.

The immaculately mown towpath comes to an end and as if by complete contrast the pathside bank is now colonized by masses of Ground Elder - the gardeners nightmare. Ground Elder has long, white, underground runners which enable it to spread, safely, secretly, rapidly and totally, forming huge colonies. The large leaves, which bear a striking resemblance to those of the Elder tree, form a canopy which excludes all available light from anything attempting to grow beneath. The rather inconspicuous white heads of flowers are not unlike a minute version of the Elder's distinctive flower clusters.

GROUND ELDER

As the wide waterway straightens out on its final approach to Knowsley Lane, bridge No. 95, the canal is overhung from the far bank by an almost unbroken line of bushy Willow trees whose fine foliage reaches out to touch the water. Although the approaching bridge is a road bridge, carrying a lane which is virtually identical in proportions to the preceding Moss Lane, it is not even a complete arch. In fact, it is reminiscent of the adjustable bridges of Poynton and Adlington on the Macclesfield Canal. It comprises a support on either bank built from the blue brick and a girder bridge slung across with a tarmac roadway built across it in the normal manner.

Like Moss Lane before it, Knowsley Lane begins in a junction with the A34 just to the west but is actually joined by Moss Lane up to the east on its way to Hall O'Lea and Mount Pleasant. Immediately prior to arriving at Knowsley Lane Bridge, the view to the east opens right out. Across rolling acres of lush seed grass, Mow Cop castle towers above the upper village of Mow Cop which, in turn, appears distinct from Dales Green, occupying the lower slopes of the hill. Again, the waterway makes little effort to narrow to pass beneath bridge No. 95. Another interesting departure from the Macclesfield Canal's architectural style is evident beneath the bridge. The waterway can be 'stopped off' at bridge No. 95 by the use of stop planks , but ,instead of the frequently encountered stop plank grooves cut into the stonework of the banks beneath the arch of the bridge, the Trent and Mersey Canal Company employed stop plank sleeves, metal slots or sleeves bolted onto the stonework to take the planks. Correspondingly, just beyond the bridge, a set of stop planks is situated beside the towpath. Unlike the familiar eight or nine feet long planks of the Macclesfield, these are sixteen feet in length which illustrates perfectly the greater overall width of this linking waterway.

The canal's margins are formed by extensive sedge beds and colonies of Great Water Dock. Beyond the pathside Hawthorn, a small pasture or croft occupies the western bank. The croft is, in turn, bordered on all sides by housing, reminding us that habitation and the busy highway are never far away. It is sad to note that, as far as the western aspect is concerned, this will prove to be the last area of grassland, or for that matter, open space to accompany our waterway journey. Up to the distant east, a fine view is available of the outskirts of Kidsgrove.

All too soon, the croft which lay beyond the pathside hedgerow is replaced by houses and gardens once more. Across the water, it is almost back to old times once more as a pasture field rises away from the canal's unlined far bank where fat, young beef cattle churn the margin into a quagmire in their eagerness to drink. Large gardens reach up to the canal's towpath bank where the hawthorn hedgerow has been replaced by a pathside fence. Ahead, the waterway narrows drastically down to the degree that the seasoned towpath traveller would expect to find the visible remains of a dismantled and removed swing bridge. Instead of the foundations of a swing bridge, however, 'folded back' wooden gates are found to be recessed into the concrete lined banks at this greatly narrowed point.

The wooden gates are actually flood gates which are designed to close automatically in the event of the canal breaching its banks ahead. The violent rush of water through this narrow bottle neck would have the effect of pulling the gates firmly shut together. This general principle was found to have been employed once before, on the main Macclesfield Canal (although the actual gates were missing) immediately prior to the major embankment at Dane-in-Shaw. At the flood gate site, the pasture comes to an end on the far bank and is replaced by a narrow strip of waste ground. This insignificant strip of nondescript land is actually of paramount importance in that it is the onset of the county of Staffordshire. Although the towpath bank is still within Cheshire, the far bank is now firmly within Staffordshire!

On a hot August afternoon, each footfall brings billowing clouds of small moths streaming from the pathside grasses. It is reminicent of wading ankle deep through a living confetti. The multitude is made up of creatures which when observed individually appear insignificant yet, when encountered in such profusion, invite closer inspection.

The majority of the flittering confetti are moths in nondescript shades of buff, grey, brown and fawn which, despite their vast numbers have failed to arouse sufficient interest to be awarded a common name. Collectively they are grouped together and classified under the general name of 'Grass Moths'. They are all typical species of grassy places which find the pathside grasses and sedges to be the ideal habitat. With names as unlikely as Crambus Pratellus and Eurrhypara

Coronata it is little wonder that a simple term such as grass moth is preferable.

Nymphula Nymphaeaeta will be encountered in hundreds of thousands along the canal around dusk during the summer months and will almost certainly be passed by completely unnoticed, but it is in fact quite an exceptional insect. This somewhat variable species is one of the China Mark Moths which get their name from the fact that the distinctive markings on their wings are said to resemble the marks potters use on the underside of crockery and other ceramic items. What sets the China Mark Moth aside from all other Lepidoptera (Butterflies and Moths) is that they pass their laval stage under water. The adult insect hides in the canals marginal vegetation by day but has spent its infancy as a totally aquatic creature. The larva feeds on various aquatic plants and lives,in its early stages,inside floating leaves. It goes on to make a case out of leaf fragments and adopts a more active existance on the underside of the leaves before joining the multitude which throng the summer air.

As the waterway curves determinedly to the right, the view down to the east becomes a view into a densely built up environment and the loud droning of incessant traffic becomes ever more apparent. Having rounded the sharp curve, the waterway briefly straightens out and the ground to the west plummets away down a lofty embankment. This is the massive embankment which straddles the county boundary and the busy A50 which runs between Lawton in Cheshire and the five towns of the Staffordshire Potteries.

As the waterway once again begins to narrow the bridge walls of the massive Red Bull Aqueduct appear on either bank. This towering blue brick aqueduct transports the branch canal high above the buzzing A50 and actually forms the county boundary between the parish of Church Lawton in the county of Cheshire and the township of Kidsgrove in the district of Newcastle Under Lyme. Visible only from the busy roadway below, the towering brick aqueduct has as its centrepice, a commemorative stone plaque, set above the apex of its lofty arch. Considering that the bridge actually carries a branch canal which was cut by the Trent and Mersey Canal Company, the wording on the stone seems somewhat contradictory, "Red Bull Aqueduct Macclesfield Canal - MDCCCXXVIII".

Beyond Red Bull Aqueduct, the waterway opens out once more to its customary width and it is accompanied by an ambitious towpath which is almost twenty feet wide. It is only now, leaving the aqueduct behind that it becomes clear that the canal is being embanked at a tremendous height across the surrounding landscape. Far below the canal's level to the west, the extensive Lawton sewage treatment plant stretches away in all directions. Lawton is one of the largest sewage treatment works in the area and, although it could hardly be described as aesthetically beautiful, it is by no means offensive and surprisingly, contributes very little in the way of aroma!

By comparison, the large vehicle breaking yard which lurks beneath the embankment to the east leaves rather more to be desired from the aesthetic point of view. The housing and industry which presses in from all sides is a far cry from the intense beauty and blissful, sometimes remote serenity which epitomized a high proportion of the journey along the Macclesfield Canal. The overriding fact, however, is that the waterway came into existence purely to serve the industrial centres such as here.

Ahead, the waterway can be seen to narrow once more as it prepares to be carried aloft by a second aqueduct. Even from some distance away, this second aqueduct can be seen to be every bit as ambitious in its scale as the preceding one at Red Bull. In fact, Pool Lock Aqueduct is actually considerably larger overall, particularly in its span. Unlike Red Bull however, Pool Lock is actually a rare and curious feature as the Macclesfield Branch Canal is transported high above the Trent and Mersey Canal which is running east to west. A dizzy flight of steps connect the branch canal towpath with that of the Trent and Mersey. From the high vantage point on top of Pool Lock Aqueduct, the towpath traveller can contemplate the operation of locks on the Trent and Mersey far below.

The canal continues to represent the county boundary as it dissects the area which is known as Red Bull Basin. The section of the Trent and Mersey which stretches away from Pool Lock Aqueduct westward into Lawton is in Cheshire whereas everything which lies to the east is in Staffordshire. This huge bridge is built from a mixture of blue and red brick with the exception of the copeing which is of stone.

The Trent and Mersey section which lies to the west tends to be solidly moored with boats up to the lock which is visible in the distance. The view eastward is of the Trent and Mersey climbing away into Staffordshire via several more sets of locks. Directly beyond Pool Lock Aqueduct, the branch canal passes beneath the next bridge, No. 96. Since leaving Hall Green stop lock and the Macclesfield Canal behind, the two bridges which have already been encountered have been, not only very different from those of the Macclesfield Canal but also very different from each other - the third continues this trend.

Bridge No. 96, Pool Lock Bridge, is a pedestrian footway but not only a footbridge, it is technically a roving or turnover bridge. It consists of a substantial pillar of blue brick on either bank between which a metal girder bridge is slung. The towpath, upon leaving Pool Aqueduct, passes beneath the foot bridge to arrive at what would, at first glace, appear to be the end or terminus of the waterway as it seems to reach a dead end. Having passed beneath the foot bridge, the towpath opens out into a wide area of neatly kept grass. The broad grassy area complete with seats and lavish drifts of naturalized daffodils is the access to a major boat builders yard.

The main body of the Red Bull Basin boat yard lies off to the right within a short canal arm of its own creation. The David Piper Red Bull Yard covers the whole spectrum of narrow canal boating, from pump out, fuel and gas supply through to boat and engine sales, winter storage ,boat building and fitting out from new. The undercover workshops which lie within the canal arm invariably buzz with activity and every available inch of mooring is usually spoken for. At the point which, initially, appears to be the end of the waterway, it widens and opens out to provide a manoeuvreing and turning area for craft entering and leaving the boatyard.

Instead of coming to an end, the canal now veers off in a most acute manner to the left - literally at forty five degrees. If the position of the boatyard is taken into consideration, the original waterway has almost arrived at a 'T' junction. To gain access to the continuation of the waterway and to deviate away from the boatyard and its dead end or 'no through route' it is now necessary to climb the incredibly steep **tarmacced** ramp which leads up to the top of bridge No. 96. The footway across the top of the bridge itself is similarly of tarmac and it is from this vantage point that one can contemplate the wonders of canal architecture and engineering while gazing back in a northerly direction. Within the relatively short length of waterway which is visible from here, the canal has been transported over the Trent and Mersey by what amounts to a canal flyover. It has been similarly transported over the busy A50 road by means of the ambitious aqueduct and, in the distance, it narrows to pass through the flood gate safety provision, installed in the unlikely eventuality of the canal breachings its banks while negotiating these various obstacles.

A correspondingly steep ramp deposits the traveller down on the eastern bank beside the widened section. Trent and Mersey Lock No. 42 lies far below to the east as the pathway swings sharply left to accompany the continuing waterway. This single move represents the most radical alteration in perspective since leaving Marple some 27 1/4 miles back as now, the direction of travel is due east.

Proceeding along the left or northern bank, the waterway is effectively narrowed as the far bank is solidly moored with craft as far as the eye can see. The forty five degrees turn marked the point where the waterway moved wholly into Staffordshire at last, having marked the county boundary for some considerable distance. An extensive area of ground which is covered by a rampant growth of vegetation lies to the north, forming a physical boundary between the branch canal and the Trent and Mersey. The far bank or southern bank is neatly mown as it forms the long term mooring which accompanies Red Bull Boatyard. An additional sign board on the southern bank advertises hand painted canal ware, postcards, maps, chandlery and canal guides.

Beyond the Hawthorn hedgerow which borders the far bank, a working railway line uns directly parallel to the branch canal. The waterway is effectively sandwiched between the Trent and Mersey which lies far below and to the north and the railway to the south. The high bank beside the towpath totally hides from view the fact that, over the next quarter mile or so, the Trent and Mersey will be lifted by at least three locks to arrive at the height of the branch canal. In places, the solid line of boats along the far bank are actually moored two abreast, drastically narrowing the available through channel.

As the high bank beside the towpath begins to finally lower, extensive factories and works come into view to the north which lie beyond the Trent and Mersey. The railway line which faithfully maintains an accompanying course to the south is heading determinedly towards a junction with the Manchester - Stoke line which accompanied the Macclesfield Canal for so many miles from Macclesfield. The area beyond the rail line is Hardings Wood, a place name which echoes back to a time before the coming of the Trent and Mersey Canal when Kidsgrove was little more than a deep, wooded valley - almost impossible to imagine when surveying the area today.

Despite Kidsgrove's position - sitting fairly and squarely upon the great North Staffordshire coal field, and also having access to quantities of ironstone, the hamlet enjoyed so isolated a situation that its industrial development remained negligible until the canal arrived. Historically Kidsgrove was described as "a deep, dark wood" which goes some way to explaining the presence of places such as Hardings Wood and Woodshutts, both of which lie to the immediate south. Eventually, the next bridge comes into view ahead, a real architectural hotchpotch!

No. 97. Hardings Wood Bridge carries a roadway which runs, from Woodshutts in the south to the higher Dove Bank area of Kidsgrove to the north. The bridge comprises a support of blue brick on either bank and a concrete and metal girder bridge which carries the roadway between the two. The canal bridge abuts to a stone railway bridge immediately to the south which is totally dissimilar in style. Passing beneath Bridge No. 97, the waterway takes on a somewhat softer, more sheltered appearance than of late. A high bank of rampant vegetation soars upward from the towpath to unseen gardens which lie above. The waterway begins to sweep sharply to the left which means that, in effect, it now completes its journey around the compass to progress due north.

The moored boats have come to an end now that the penultimate bridge, No. 97 has been negotiated. From the far bank, tall Willows overhang the water from a rough bank which has sprung up from nowhere. The waterway continues to curve very sharply as an area of paddock land, grazed by ponies, briefly occupies the far bank. The paddock is replaced by the outbuildings relating to a boarding kennels and cattery as the final bridge, No. 98 - standing 27 3/4 miles from No. 1, comes into view ahead. The waterway briefly straightens out to approach the squat arch of blue brick which marks journeys end. The graveled towpath swings round to arrive at and pass beneath bridge No. 98, Plants Lock Bridge.

No. 98 wears it blue and yellow British Waterways Board number plate above a stone plaque which is set into the blue brick of the bridge which reads, "Macclesfield Canal MDCCCXXVIII". Beyond Plants Lock Bridge at Hardings Wood junction lies the Trent and Mersey Canal. Standing at the junction of the two waterways, it is noticeable that the Trent and Mersey is strongly discoloured. The water is permanently stained by a pigmentation of ochre.

This quite vivid colouration was first seen as the Trent and Mersey passed beneath the branch canal at Pool Lock. The strange thing is that the discolouration fails to leach into the branch canal although the two waterways are at precisely the same level. Although it initially resembles a pollution of catastrophic proportions, the pigment is actually a result of a natural oxidization process.

A little less than half a mile along the Trent and Mersey to the right are the famous Harecastle Tunnels. The original was built in the late 1760's by James Brindley and was heralded as the eighth wonder of the world as he ran his 'subterranean navigations' through the solid rock of the hillside. Seventy years later, the second tunnel had to be built and the original was abandoned due to to subsidence. The hill through which both tunnels pass is absolutely riddled with mine workings and tunneling. Thomas Telford was responsible for the design and building of the second tunnel which has been repaired and altered on numerous occasions because of the subsidence problems. It is from the walls of Telford's tunnel that the oxidization leaches into the Trent and Mersey from the labyrinth of mine workings. The fact that the pigment fails to leach into the branch canal can only be due to the imperceptible downward flow from the Macclesfield - generated by the fall at Bosley and the drop of one foot at Hall Green.

Opposite to the bridge and the canal junction, a sign post stands on the bank of the Trent and Mersey. It is situated for the benefit of craft entering the Trent and Mersey from the branch canal. Its arms point to left and right and read the distances to Middlewich and Stoke respectively. It would be most fitting if there had been a third arm to point back up through the arch of Plants Lock Bridge which could have proclaimed to those using the Trent and Mersey......Marple 27 3/4 miles.

NORTH-SOUTH PLACE NAME INDEX.

The following index plots the canals route following the north-south direction adopted by the manuscript. This enables anyone joining the waterway, anywhere along the route, to pick up the relevant point in the text.

Marple	1	Oakgrove	112
Hawk Green	5	Gawsworth	113
Doodfield	8	Cowley	120
High Lane	12	Bosley	125
Middlewood	19	North Rode	135
Poynton	26	Crossley	154
Higher Poynton	33	Buglawton	161
Mitchell Fold	36	Bath Vale	169
Wood Lanes	40	Timbersbrook	170
Booth Green	48	Dane-In-Shaw	175
Adlington	50	Hightown	179
Pott Shrigley	48	Congleton	185
Styperson	52	Astbury Lane Ends	189
Clark Green	54	Astbury	195
Whiteley Green	55	Newbold	200
Bollington	57	Ciss Green	201
Kerridge	70	Moreton	206
Higher Hurdsfield	80	Ackers Crossing	211
Hurdsfield	81	Old House Green	214
Macclesfield	83	Kent Green	222
Gurnett	97	Scholar Green	225
Sutton	98	Little Moss	228
Lyme Green	102	Hall Green	229
Danes Moss	105	Red Bull	235
Sutton Oaks	111	Hardings Wood	238

BRIDGE NAME INDEX

The following list of bridges gives the original name and also the modern name, (where applicable), of the bridge, along with its official number.

The list is as concise as possible but remains far from complete. Alongside each bridge, the page number is given where the particular bridge first appears or is described in the text.

Bridge No. 1		1
Bridge No. 2		3
Bridge No. 3	Eccles Bridge	5
Bridge No. 4		5
Bridge No 5	Barns Fold Bridge	6
Bridge No. 6		8
Bridge No. 7		8
Bridge No. 8	Bancroft Bridge	10
Bridge No. 9	Windlhurst or Back Lane Bridge	12
Bridge No. 10	Mariotts Bridge	13
Bridge No 11	A6 Road Bridge	14
Bridge No. 12	High Lane Arm Bridge	16
Bridge No. 13	Bullocks Girder Bridge	23
Bridge No. 14	Smiths Bridge	27
Bridge No. 15	Brownhills, Lyme Road or Mount Vernon Bridge	28
Bridge No. 16	Hags Foot Swing and Foot Bridge	33
Bridge No. 17	Mitchells or Mitchell Fold Bridge	36
Bridge No. 18	Grimshaws Bridge	41
Bridge No. 19	Braddocks Bridge	45
Bridge No. 20	Ryles Bridge	49
Bridge No. 21	Hibberts Brow or Brookledge Lane Bridge	50
Bridge No. 22	Bartons or Bartons Clough Bridge	52
Bridge No. 23	Wilds Bridge	53
Bridge No. 24	Snapes Bridge	54
Bridge No. 25	Whitely Green or Holehouse Lane Bridge	55
Bridge No. 26	Sugar Lane Bridge	57
Bridge No. 27		62
Bridge No. 28	Greens or Tinkers Clough Bridge	67
Bridge No 29	Clarkes Change Bridge	71

Bridge No. 30	Woods Bridge	76
Bridge No. 31	Missing	77
Bridge No. 32	Missing	79
Bridge No. 33	Higherfold Bridge	80
Bridge No. 34	Chapel en le Frith Road Bridge	81
Bridge No. 35	Barrack Road Bridge	82
Bridge No. 36	Smyths Bridge	83
Bridge No. 37	Buxton Road Bridge	85
Bridge No. 38		90
Bridge No. 39	Hollands Bridge	91
Bridge No. 40	Windmill Street Bridge	91
Bridge No. 41	Verdons Bridge	
Bridge No. 42	Missing	92
Bridge No. 43	Foden Bank Bridge	96
Bridge No. 44	Leek Old Road Bridge or Bullocks Lane Bridge	101
Bridge No. 45	Leek New Road Bridge	103
Bridge No. 46	Danes Moss Bridge	105
Bridge No. 47	Broadhurst Swing Bridge	107
Bridge No. 48	Missing	109
Bridge No. 49	Fool's Nook or Oakgrove Swing Bridge	112
Bridge No. 50	Mottersheads Bridge	118
Bridge No. 51	Cowley Farm Bridge	120
Bridge No. 52	Crowholt Bridge	122
Bridge No. 53	Lockets Bridge	125
Bridge No. 54	Daintry Road Bridge	131
Bridge No. 55	Congleton and Buxton Road Bridge or Peckerpool Wood Bridge	134
Bridge No. 56	Swindells Bridge	139
Bridge No. 57	Old Driving Lane Bridge	148
Bridge No. 58	Wallworths Bridge	150
Bridge No. 59	Lomas Bridge	151
Bridge No. 60	Stringers Bridge	154
Bridge No. 61	Congleton and Buxton Road Bridge or Crossley Hall Bridge	156
Bridge No. 62	Stanier's No. 1 Bridge	157
Bridge No. 63	Stanier's No. 2 Bridge	158
Bridge No. 64	Pearsons Bridge	159
Bridge No. 65	Pointons or Stanleys Bridge	163
Bridge No. 66	Town Field	165
Bridge No. 67	Fodens Bridge	165

Bridge No. 68	Congleton and Buxton Road at Tall Ash	166
Bridge No. 69	Wallworths Bridge	167
Bridge No. 70	Jollys Bridge or Galleys Bridge	169
Bridge No. 71	Foot Bridge	172
Bridge No. 72	Porters Farm Bridge or Brookhouse Lane Bridge	172
Bridge No. 73	Galleys or Henshall Hall Bridge	178
Bridge No. 74	Locketts, Nestles or Morley Drive Bridge	180
Bridge No. 75	Park Lane Station Bridge	182
Bridge No. 76	Morris Change Bridge	184
Bridge No. 77	Lamberts Lane Bridge	189
Bridge No. 78	Billy Tights Swing Bridge (removed) now Foot Bridge	192
Bridge No. 79	Peel Lane Bridge	194
Bridge No. 80	Dodds Lane or Thornhills or Henshalls Bridge	197
Bridge No. 81	Oak Farm or Oak Lane Bridge	205
Bridge No. 82	Hockenhalls Bridge	206
Bridge No. 83	Gravel Pit or Wharf Lane Bridge	208
Bridge No. 84	Deakins Bridge	210
Bridge No. 85	Simpsons or Ackers Crossing Bridge	211
Bridge No. 86	Lowndes or Lowndes No. 2 Bridge	214
Bridge No. 87	Lowndes, Station Road or Kent Green Bridge	222
Bridge No. 88	Bird in Hand Swing Bridge	224
Bridge No. 89	Cinderhill Lane or Kent Green Wharf Bridge	226
Bridge No. 90	Cinderhill Swing Bridge	226
Bridge No. 91	Tramroad or Fall Bridge	227
Bridge No. 92	Little Moss Bridge	228
Bridge No. 93	Foot Bridge Lock or Hall Green Foot Bridge	229
Bridge No. 94	Moss Lane Bridge	232
Bridge No. 95	Knowsley Lane Bridge	233
Bridge No. 96	Pool Lock Bridge	236
Bridge No. 97	Hardings Wood Bridge	238
Bridge No. 98	Plants Lock Bridge	238

PUB LIST

During the latter stages of the preparation of this manuscript, it was felt that it would be a good idea to include a list of canal side hostelries which provide refreshment (both liquid and solid) for the footsore traveller or the cruising holidaymaker. In common with the main text, this index is arranged on a north-south basis, i.e. beginning at Marple.

"Ring O Bells"
The "Ring O Bells" is situated directly upon Bridge No. 2 at Marple and displays much canal memorabillia. The old "Commerial Room" (tap-room) now re-christened "Waterways" contains a considerable quantity of good canal artwork. The liquid refreshment is provided by Robinsons, the Stockport brewers, and the catering facilities are on a bar meal basis.

"Dog and Partridge"
The "Dog and Partridge" is situated some 200 yards east of Bridge No.11 at High Lane. Situated along the busy A6 road, this is a former coaching house which now incorporates a roadside well into its patio bar. The "Dog and Partridge" provides a good range of hot and cold bar snacks and is served by Grand Met-Websters and Yorkshire breweries.

"The Bulls Head"
The "Bulls Head" overshadows the canal at Bridge No. 11 at High Lane and sports a beer garden which directly overlooks the towpath. Snacks, lunches and a children's menu are all available. Dating from circa 1714, this historic hostelry was once patronized by colliers who were employed by High Lanes intense mining industry and later, became a favourite haunt of bargees waiting to negotiate the busy High Lane canal arm. The "Bulls Head" is served by Boddington brewery.

"The Boars Head"
The "Boars Head" is at Poynton, some 150 yards west of Mount Vernon. This exceedingly handsome building stands directly alongside the Middlewood Way. It was built in 1904 to replace a much older "Boars Head" which had long been frequented by local miners, Mount Vernon being the very heart of the Poynton coal field. The new "Boars Head" was built in classic railway style, directly alongside a halt on the railway. Lunchtime food is served 12.00-2.00 p.m. on a seven day basis. The summer period sees evening food being available from Monday to Saturday 6.00-9.00 p.m. During the summer months, a specially

converted narrowboat which caters for the needs of the physically handicapped." The New Horizon", travels between its base at Marple and Mount Vernon, using the "Boars Head" as its destination. This Boddington house is in the "Good Beer Guide"

"Miners Arms"
The 'Miners Arms", another Boddingtons house is situated within the hamlet of Woods Lanes, west of Bridge No. 18. The original 16th century building served as both a farm and an inn. Lunch time and evening food is served from Tuesday through to Saturday.

"Kens Canalside Cafe"
This is a purpose built cafe which is delightfully situated beside the towpath at Woods Lanes, alongside Lyme View Marina at Bridge No. 18. The cafe is licensed and is open until dusk for six days, being closed on Mondays. Very pleasant surroundings are complimented by a varied menu and incorporates disabled access and toilet facilities.

"The Windmill Inn"
If towpath wandering has stimulated the appetite, "The Windmill" is the place to satisfy it! This spacious and comfortable Inn is situated some 150 yards west of Bridge No. 25 at Whitely Green. The catering facilities are extensive, ranging from a full scale carvery restaurant to basic bar food. If the satisfying menus were not comprehensive enough, bar-ba-ques are often held during the summer months in what must qualify as Cheshires largest beer garden at 2 1/2 acres in extent! This extensive recreation area often provides 'special' children's entertainment in the shape of 'bouncy castles' etc. There is also an emphasis on 'good quality' beers including a weekly 'guest beer'!

"The Vale Inn"
"The Vale Inn" at Bollington (near the Clanrence Mill), is reached by means of a delightful 250 yard woodland walk from the towpath. Just before the inn is reached, the children's play area is encountered in an idyllic situation among the trees. The delightful stone built inn is an absolute gem, both from the view of architecture and situation. The Vale has constantly featured in the Good Pub Guide for more than a decade. The fine and varied lunchtime menu is available from Tuesday to Saturday 11.30-2.15 p.m. and Sunday 12.00-3.00 p.m. The equivalent evening menu is available from Tuesday to Saturday 7.00-9.00 p.m..In 1988, The Vale was described as "one of Cheshires top 10 Inns "by Sunday Magazine. Free House.

"The Brittania"
"The Brittania" is west of Bridge No.34 at Hurdsfield. A traditional stone building, it offers 'hand pulled cask beers ' and traditional pub games. Greenhalls.

"The Three Crowns"
At the time of writing "The Three Crowns" which is 150-200 yards east of Bridge No.34 at Higher Hurdsfield is undergoing a total refurbishment and hopes to offer 'bar snack' food both at lunchtime and in the evening.

"The Puss in Boots"
The "Puss" is ideally situated directly alongside the towpath at Macclesfield/ Buxton Road Marina. This busy hostelry was orginally a coaching Inn on the Macclesfield/Buxton highway. With the arrival of the canal in the 1830's, the "Puss" adapted itself to cater for the new travellers along the waterway. Where the towpath -side beer garden is now, the sealed up archways in the gable wall were formerly access to stabling for the canals draught horses. "The Puss" offers extensive restaurant facilities with families being welcomed for both full meals or bar snacks. Boddingtons brewery are planning to open up the old stable area and convert it to family dining facilities aimed specifically at the canal bourne trade in 1992.

"Bridgewater Arms"
The "Bridgewater" is situated directly to the west of Buxton Road Marina , Macclesfield It is a traditional town pub and serves no food. Wilson beers.

"Navigation Inn"
The "Navigation " lies some 300 yards west of Bridge No.38 in Macclesfield. Traditional ales and pub games are on offer at this Tetley house with a serious canal influence.

"Beehive Inn"
The "Beehive" lies to the west of Bridge No. 41 in Black Road, Macclesfield. This Boddingtons house serves lunchtime food on a seven day basis. For the family, a children's room and a beer garden are available

"The Olde Kings Head"
As described in the text, this very fine old building lies directly along-side the aqueduct at Sutton. The building has served its community as a coaching Inn and smithy since 1695. Today, this free house serves both lunch time and evening food on a seven day basis. In addition to the fine food and luxurious decor, accommodation

is available in the form of three en-suite double rooms. With all day opening, a visit to this delightful Inn is never poorly timed.

"The Star"
Lying alongside the busy A523, Leek/Maclesfield road, west of Bridge No.45, "The Star" provides lunchtime food on a six daily basis, no Sunday. Evening food is available on request. Children are welcome in both the beer garden and the T.V. room A game of pool, darts or dominoes can be enjoyed at this Marstons house.

"The Fools Nook Inn"
As described at length in the text, "The Fools Nook" is delightfully and strategically situated at one of the Maclesfield canals stops, Oakgrove (or should it be Sutton oaks, Fools Nook or Sutton?) An excellent choice of quality food is available 12.00-2.00 p.m Sunday - Saturday and 6.30-9.00p.m. for six evenings and 7.15-9.00p.m. Sunday. The beer garden at the Fools Nook is a delight in itself, with cascading waterfall and stocked fish pond. Children are enthusiastically welcomed at this Boddingtons house.

"The Robin Hood"
Although not actually in direct view from the towpath, the "Robin Hood" lies some 300-350 yards west of Bridge No.61 at Buglawton. It is the first hostelry to be encountered for several miles so, consequently, may represent a very welcome stop. A varied menu is available both lunchtime and in the evenings with the exception of Monday evening. This pleasantly situated old inn boasts a beer garden which compliments the rural location. "The Robin Inn" is a Marstons house specializing in 'real ale'.

"The Railway"
This finely proportioned building served as a coaching inn for several centuries before being enlarged and 'improved' with the coming of the railway to become Congleton's Railway Hotel. It is situated directly alongside the canal and beside Congleton railway station at Bridge No.75. The railway serves hot and cold lunches from Monday to Sunday, 12.00-2.00p.m. Food is also available during the evenings at this Bass House.

"The Queens Head"
The "Queens" is situated directly across the canal and the railway line from "The Railway", in fact, it is actually next door but one. Lunchtime food is available 12.00-2.p.m. at this Ansells House. Food in the evening is available 7.00-10.00p.m. on a seven day basis. "The Queens" has a substantial beer garden with actual seating for 66 people which may be invaluable for summer parties or maybe

the disabled. Children are welcome at this friendly inn,which for adults has a games room and specializes in real ales.

"The Wharf"
"The Wharf" at Congleton stands in the shadow of Canal Road Aqueduct,which, in turn,lies half way between Bridges 76 and 77. The wharf is a canal pub in the purest sense of the word. It has recently benefited from a total and lavish refurbishment. This Greenalls house welcomes children in the family room.The lunchtime menu is served from 12.00 noon to 3.p.m and includes almost 20 main course choices not counting jacket potato dishes and no less than six salads! The evening menu which is served from 7.00-10.00 pm every day except Tuesday is equally varied. A beer garden compliments this splendidly restored Inn.

"The Rising Sun"
The "Sun" is situated at Kent Green some 200 yards from bridge No.87 and is another example of being the first convenient hostelry to be encountered for many miles.This free house is open every day from 12.00 noon and from 7.00-11.p.m but is closed for Tuesday lunchtimes. Food is available every lunchtime and Monday, Wednesday and Saturday evenings.

"The Bleeding Wolf"
"The Bleeding Wolf" at Scholar Green is situated near to the terminus of the main Macclesfield Canal close to Bridge No.93. This Robinsons house serves a wide selection of bar food from simple bar snacks through to the special carvery style Sunday lunch in the delightfully appointed restaurant. The lunchtime menu is operative from 12.00 to 3.30 pm every day and the evening menu runs from 7.00-10.00 pm(excluding Mondays.)

"The Tavern"
Although "The Tavern" actually stands alongside the Trent and Mersey canal, it is within sight of the Hardings Wood Junction and Bridge No.98. This Ansells house is sandwiched between Hardings Wood Road and the Trent and Mersey lock flight. "The Tavern is both a true canal pub and a real 'community' pub,offering facilities as diverse as darts and pool, piano sing-along entertainment and a twice weekly disco! Lunchtime food and evening food is available and the access is on flexible timing,i.e ,a late or an early order will be catered for (within reason).Similarly, a breakfast service is available on request. Full family facilities are currently in preparation although children are always catered for. With a beer garden and good tradional beers on offer,"The Tavern" is always worth a visit before launching off onto the Trent and Mersey.

BIBLIOGRAPHY - FURTHER READING.

The Macclesfield Canal features in numerous works dealing with the national canal system and almost every book which features 'Cheshire' in its title. Of specific interest is a series of 11 booklets produced by the Countryside and Recreation Department of Cheshire County Council. Numbers 1, 2 and 3 describe the full length of the Macclesfield Canal from Marple to Kidsgrove. The 11 booklets cover the whole 97 miles of the Cheshire Ring of canals and is entitled The Cheshire Ring Canal Walk. Also produced by the Cheshire County Council but dealing with a more specific section of the Macclesfield Canal is a booklet entitled "Rail, Water and Tramways, Three Walks in North East Cheshire" This describes walks in the Middlewood, Poynton and Bollington areas on both the canal and the Middlewood Way.

I have lifted quotes directly from two general works i.e.
"Newbold Astbury and its History" The Rev. J.E. Gordon Cartlidge.
Published by Old Vicarage Publications

"Antiquities of Macclesfield" I.A. Finney
Produced by I.A. Finney, Chestergate, Macclesfield cicra. 1871
(out of print for over a century,)